PHILOSOPHY AND TECHNOLOGY
Toward a New Orientation in Modern Thinking

Philosophy and Technology

Toward a New Orientation in Modern Thinking

ALEXANDER S. KOHANSKI

PHILOSOPHICAL LIBRARY
New York

DEDICATED

*to my students at Kean College of New Jersey,
whose genuine search for a knowledge of themselves and of the world around them has been
to me a source of inspiration.*

Contents

Preface

The problem of modern man may be characterized as a conflict between thinking and doing not in the moral but rather in the technological sense. This problem had its inception in the early stages of the Era of Enlightenment and has been propelling itself for the past three centuries along the same path of scientific-technological advancement that we witness in our own time. I view these centuries of development as a single era dominated by the spirit of Enlightenment, by its concepts, aspirations, successes, and failures. Its foundations are now crumbling, and its world outlook no longer serves as a guideline toward finding ourselves in reality. The crisis is a crisis in orientation—intellectually, emotionally, spiritually—inasmuch as we do not know where to turn.

I have treated this problem on the philosophical level, because I maintain that that is where the breakdown has done most of the damage. Whatever view one may take of philosophy, if one does not discredit it, one must see it as the conscious human endeavor to form a comprehensive orientation in living reality. Philosophy deals with the same phenomena that come within the purview of science, technology, and theology, but its center of attention is man—the human being as a whole, not as a scientific concept but as an acting real entity. While there may be scientific, technological, and theological data without man, there can be no philosophical datum without him. The other data may eliminate man as material content, allowing him only a formal entry into their schemata. Although they promise him freedom or salvation, they actually contribute in no small measure to his dehumanization; for what they often try to save is not living man but a concept of him. In order to resolve this crisis, modern man needs a new philosophical orientation with regard to his ever-expanding technological advancement.

A prevailing view in modern thought is that man is an incomplete being who strives toward self-completion or self-fulfillment in a world of endless possibilities. Yet each time he tries to soar toward the infinite, he finds that his wingspread can raise him only a short distance from the ground. And when he is forced down again, he continues to gaze at the heavens and loses his bearings on earth. Each time he comes down he faces the problem of correlating his limitations with his new vistas, of finding the bounds of his new horizons. The greatest promise for endless possibilities in human history has come with the advent of the age of technology. It has advanced with such breathtaking speed that man has not yet realized that here too it is he who must set the limits lest he be crushed by his own technical devices.

In this book I analyze man's efforts to establish his physical, intellectual, and spiritual boundaries in an ever-growing scientific-technological proliferation which he himself has created. Now that he has arrived at a critical stage, he must reach out for a new orientation in the realities of his extended technical skills. He must temper his technology with a new outlook in philosophy.

My topics are grouped in five parts, each dealing with a specific aspect of the problem. The thinkers and subjects selected for discussion may be regarded as representative of trends of thought which characterize our era, but are not meant to be exhaustive of the entire range of ideas which have prevailed throughout this era. The concluding part charts a new orientation not as a blueprint for quick action, but rather as a direction which may lead man out of his predicament.

ALEXANDER S. KOHANSKI

Passaic, N. J.
December 1976.

Introduction

1. THE ERA OF ENLIGHTENMENT, 1689-1989

The Age of Enlightenment, we are told, was inaugurated by John Locke with his first "Letter Concerning Toleration" in 1689. In histories of philosophy this period is usually confined to the eighteenth century, ending with Kant. Yet the forces released by it have been operative continually to our own day and may extend to 1989, to mark the end of an era of three centuries of the most turbulent happenings in human destiny. Its earmarks in terms of man's strivings are individualism and scepticism, his enthronement as conqueror of nature through science and technology, and his wrestling with God to arrogate unto himself the powers of creation and providence.

Individualism and Scepticism

The eighteenth century has been designated as the age of reason, and those who limit the Enlightenment to that century alone are prone to characterize it as one that set the supremacy of reason above all. However, this is not its chief characteristic. The golden thread which runs through this entire era and which is still woven into the fabric of our time is the idea of man becoming of age, or as Kant formulated it: "Enlightenment is man's emergence out of his self-encumbered immaturity." To be sure, Kant put the emphasis on the understanding. "Immaturity," he said, "is the incapacity to make use of one's own understanding without direction from another. This immaturity is self-encumbered when its cause is not a lack of understanding but of decision and courage to make use of one's understanding without direction from another." And he admonished man: *"Sapere aude* (Dare to think)!

1

Have courage to use your own understanding! This, then, is the motto of Enlightenment." [1] Its broader meaning, even in Kant's critical philosophy, is that every man must be free to avail himself of all his faculties without outside restriction or interference. Kant considered the faculty of understanding as "the most harmless of all" that might exercise this kind of freedom in public. But he pleaded even more emphatically for freedom of will in the moral order and for freedom of self-expression in the realm of esthetics. Taking a leap from Kant to Freud, we find that the latter, too, was concerned with helping man to attain maturity, in this case, of the emotions but not without the understanding.

The meaning of reason and thinking, which dominated the early stages of Enlightenment, was best described by Descartes (an influential forerunner) in his Third Meditation. Man, he said, is "a thing that thinks, that is to say, that doubts, affirms, denies, that knows a few things, that is ignorant of many, that wills, that desires, that also imagines and perceives." Descartes' aim was to know man and through him the world. "I entirely abandoned the study of letters," he wrote in his *Discourse on Method* (I), "and resolved no longer to seek any other science than the knowledge of myself, or of the great book of the world." Self-knowledge, self-awareness, exploration of man's own capacities, whether intellectual or instinctive, and of their powers to free him from dependence on other powers, whether natural or supernatural, became the goal of Enlightenment. Pope expressed it in his well-known couplet:

> Know then thyself, presume not God to scan,
> The proper study of mankind is Man. [2]

And through his self-study the man of Enlightenment sought to attain his maturity. As Wilhelm Windelband sums up the spirit of that age: "Having been awakened to the consciousness of its

---

1. Immanuel Kant, *Beantwortung der Frage: Was ist Aufklärung?* Opening statement.

2. Alexander Pope, *An Essay on Man*. Epistle II, lines 1-2. Cf. Ernst Cassirer, *Die Philosophie der Aufklärung* (Tübingen: Verlag von J.C.B. Mohr, 1923), p. 2, on the sense of the Age of Enlightenment which found expression in Pope's epigram.

own maturity, modern thought wished in every respect to set its own laws, to find the principles of action and inaction through rational deliberation, and to recognize no other judge over itself." [3]

It has been said of the Age of Enlightenment that it was not conscious of historical processes. Quite so, because it was concerned not with the development of mankind but with the essence of man. If we read Pope's dictum correctly, the center of attention was individual man and his specific abilities to direct his life and surroundings for his own well-being and happiness. This may assume a universal character only insofar as the human faculties are in essence the possession of all men alike, even though varying in degree. Thus the Era of Enlightenment essentially expresses the spirit of individualism which is still dominant in our time. From Pope's *Essay on Man* in the eighteenth century to Cassirer's *Essay on Man* in the twentieth, the quest is the same: for man to find himself as an individual and to establish his freedom through his own powers. This centuries-long quest has now reached a crisis. It is "the crisis of man's knowledge of himself," as Cassirer phrases it, or the crisis of science, technology, and religion, as others see it. Just the same, modern man's problem is that in his search for a knowledge of himself as individual he has lost the frames of reference which he has devised along his road to freedom. None of the metaphysical, scientific, social, and theological structures which he has erected can offer him now a home to live in securely. In Buber's words, man now lives "as in an open field and at times does not even have four pegs with which to set up a tent." [4]

The crisis in man's knowledge is most pronounced in the new doubts that have been engendered as a result of his scientific in-

---

3. Wilhelm Windelband, *Die Geschichte der neueren Philosophie.* Erster Band (Leipzig: Verlag von Breitkopf und Härtel, 1899), p. 245. To this day, maturity of thought is identified with scientific explanation; immaturity, with theology and metaphysics. Cf. Herbert Feigl, "Logical Empiricism," *Twentieth Century Philosophy.* Edited by Dagobert D. Runes (New York: Philosophical Library, 1947), p. 376. "Immature attitudes are associated with attempts to explain experience in ways which lack the distinguishing marks of science. Certain of these pre-scientific modes of explanation, . . . like the theological and metaphysical, still prevail."
4. Martin Buber, *Between Man and Man* (New York: Macmillan Company, 1965), p. 126.

vestigations. Are his perceptual, instinctive, emotional, or intellectual faculties, which he has discovered in himself as an individual, actually capable of directing him toward the kind of happiness he has dreamed of? Can he really know the world through a knowledge of himself? And yet, his scepticism is not so much about his knowledge of the world of things as about his knowledge of himself as a human being, and about his ability to master the world.

Conquest of Nature

Another main characteristic of the Age of Enlightenment is its scientific approach to the realities of nature. Methodologically, its chief instruments are measurement and calculation of decomposed elements; metaphysically, its goal is a comprehensive system of those elements in a closed-in world. These factors do not always tolerate each other; their ways separate when measured phenomena of physical reality do not fit into the universal system. The system-builders then introduce non-physical principles in one form or another, in order to hold the phenomena together within a universe-as-a-whole. This is as true of Newton's theory of gravitation as of Einstein's unified field. The natural sciences cannot pull themselves together without the aid of first principles which lie beyond their ken, but which they must employ for their universal frame of reference. Therein lies the so-called conflict between science and metaphysics, which had its origin yet in the days of Plato and Aristotle and, after lying dormant through the "Dark Ages," erupted again with increased intensity in the modern world. The struggle is for the control of nature through the human understanding. Can the scientists do it without the metaphysicians?

Strange as it may seem, this conflict is inherent in the scientific world outlook, as such. That is, while it appears as a controversy between scientists and metaphysicians, as, for example, the empiricists have portrayed it, it is really a battle between researchers in the field of science itself, which in no small measure has contributed to its present-day crisis. For the thing to bear in mind is that metaphysics is not just a speculative doctrine completely detached from physical reality. Quite the contrary, it is an outgrowth or extension of that reality insofar as the latter aims at a closed, sys-

4

tematically unified world-order. We may say that science of metaphysics complements the science of physics when each recognizes its limits within the same logico-scientific world-view.

Now the physicist may hold himself back from taking a leap beyond the confines of natural causes and try to sharpen his scientific tools for further analysis in the hope of discovering the final causes within the bounds of his own domain. Both Newton and Einstein struggled to maintain such a position within their respective theories, but in the final analysis (as far as they went), neither of them succeeded in avoiding a leap beyond, the one into metaphysics and the other into metamathematics. Be this as it may, the physicist can stop short on the edge of nature's ridge and go around it in pursuit of ever-refined connections within his circle of scientific analysis, so long as he does not touch the infinite that lies over the ridge. But man, as Voltaire noted, is a metaphysical animal. He feels he can best control nature if he has it completely within his intellectual grip—if he can "see it whole and see it steady," grasp it theoretically and use it practically. He therefore envisions a world-order composed of elements which he is certain of as to their potencies and laws of operation, and which he may turn into reliable instruments for the mastery of that order at will. This is man's striving for certainty, and his hope for overcoming scepticism about himself and the world, as conceived by Descartes on the threshold of the modern age; or, as we see it today, man's search for security against the exigencies of nature. It is, in essence, the freedom held out to man by modern science, and his fulfillment promised by modern technology, the ultimate goal of the Era of Enlightenment.

The Promise of Science and Technology

While theoretical or pure science has given great stimulus to modern technological advancement, technology as such is not necessarily bounded by it and has often struck an independent path of invention, especially in the industrial field.[5] Furthermore, even

---

5. Cf. A. Wolf, *A History of Science, Technology and Philosophy in the 16th and 17th Centuries* (New York: Harper Torchbooks, 1959), Vol. I, pp. 72ff. Cf. Eric Ashby, *Technology and the Academics* (New York: St. Martin's Press, 1963), pp. 50-51. "Britain's industrial

though all technological instruments may be reduced to their basic natural laws, there is a fundamental difference between the scientific and technological grasp of nature. Science comprehends the world and man in terms of concepts organized into a rational theory which explains phenomena. Technology gets hold of the world and man in terms of sense-perceptual data augmented by external physical devices. Science is an extension of the intellect or reason; technology is an extension of the senses and muscular motor apparatus. When man relates himself to the world and fellowman by means of technological tools, he is under the illusion that he communicates with reality as is, directly through his senses. But in truth, what he perceives is a conglomerate of spatiotemporal elements, or "bits of information," as the computer analyst calls them, filtered through automated machines. Out of these he is expected, again with the aid of automata, to compose his real world. Since content is excluded from this process, man cannot find himself, his fellow man, or things in nature in reality. This is the source of his alienation from the world.

Beginnings in the Seventeenth Century

The underlying principles of technology may be traced to the period of English Enlightenment in the seventeenth century. John Locke, who is reputed to have fathered modern psychology and many ideas of present-day government, may be said also to have been the father of modern technology. His original notion on this subject appeared to him so revolutionary that he dismissed it as impossible and even undesirable of attainment. Thus we read in his *Essay Concerning Human Understanding* (Book II, Ch. XXIII, 11-12):

> Had we sense acute enough to discern the minute particles of bodies, and the real constitution on which their sensible qualities depend, I doubt not but they would produce quite dif-

---

strength lay in its amateurs and self-made men. . . . In this rise of British industry the English universities played no part whatever, and the Scottish universities only a very small part; indeed formal education of any sort was a negligible factor in its success. . . . There was practically no exchange of ideas between the scientists and the designers of industrial processes."

ferent ideas in us, and that which is now the yellow color of gold, would then disappear, and instead of it we should see an admirable texture of parts of a certain size and figure. . . . Nay, if that most instructive of our senses, seeing, were in any man a thousand or a hundred thousand times more acute than it is by the best microscope, things several million of times less than the smallest object of his sight now would then be visible to his naked eyes, and so he would come nearer the discovery of the texture and motion of the minute parts of corporeal things, and in many of them probably get ideas of their internal constitutions; . . . But it appears not that God intended we should have a perfect, clear, and adequate knowledge of them; that perhaps is not in the comprehension of any finite being.

Nor, said he, would such extreme visual acuity be desirable, as we could then see the minutest spatial parts of a thing but not the the thing as a whole, and we would therefore not be able to see it as intended for us in our earthly habit. What is important in this conjecture is that Locke, in a flash of genius, anticipated the kind of sensible experience which our modern technical media— the radio, TV, and the automaton—have made possible. Through these media Locke's secondary qualities of color, sound, and touch have been decomposed into primary qualities of space and number,[6] and transmitted to the sense organs back again in their original perceptual forms.

The moderns and Locke hold in common that the ultimate perceivable reality of things is their quality of space, which could be apprehended by the senses, if not for the fact that it is intermingled with the secondary qualities. But Locke and the moderns differ on how to overcome this admixture. The former assumes that *"The now secondary qualities of bodies would disappear, if we could discover the primary ones of their minute parts"* (*ibid.*, 11). But he realizes that in that case a thing would appear disconnected through spatial separateness and thus cease to be a thing-as-a-whole. The moderns take the opposite view. The sec-

---

6. Locke's primary qualities which, according to him, make up the things as they are, include solidity, extension, figure, and mobility, to which he added number. These are all spatial modes which may be expressed through number as their mathematical form. Locke asserted "the reality of mathematical knowledge."

ondary qualities, they maintain, will become the dominant reality of their perception, and the spatial separateness, which hinders their unification, will be overcome through the senses themselves. The difference in the two positions is their choice of a particular sense organ that may serve this purpose. Locke conceives of the possibility of perceiving the ultimate spatial configuration of a thing through the sense of sight (vision being "the most instructive of our senses"), and he therefore cannot imagine how vision may also unify these parts into a whole. The moderns, on the other hand, project the sense of touch as the only one which can apprehend spatial quality directly. Through its tactility, they maintain, this sense can at the same time unify the other senses, so that the thing is perceived in its spatial qualities and also as a unity. Spatial separateness is thus overcome through the extremely heightened acuity of tactility by means of electric media, as is claimed, for example, by Marshall McLuhan's *Understanding Media*. It would seem that the dream of seeing the world as things in themselves and as a unified whole, which philosophers had dreamed but could not materialize, has now become a reality through the modern media of communication.

In its broadest outlook, technology covers all areas of human communication through physical, social, psychical, even spiritual instrumentalities. To this extent, the technological issue resolves itself into a problem of man facing the machine as the instrument which endangers his very existence. Man thinks he can handle this instrument to control nature at his own will, but does not realize that nature itself, insofar as it is revealed through technological instruments, is real only to the extent that these instruments can measure it. Man may thus be able to control reality as long as he can control his instruments. But there may come a time when the latter will outstrip his capacity, and then he will lose his bearings altogether. More important, inasmuch as the instruments decompose nature into the simplest elements, man can synthesize them only as dead matter and not as living reality. And when he looks at his synthetic product he finds himself facing not nature but a ghost which demands its recompense for having been cut off from life.

The scientific revolution, which started with Galileo and ushered in the Age of Enlightenment, centered on the role of space and time in man's view of the world as well as in his possible control over it. The new science promised to free man from his spatio-temporal limitations, a hope cherished heretofore only by theology and metaphysics. But while the latter had promised to free him from his fetters in after-life or in another, ideal world, the former undertook to come to his aid in this life on earth. Science, thus, set out to extend the spatio-temporal horizons to their utmost limit, into infinity, while technology kept refining its tools in order to surpass each limit which science discovered at various stages of its advancement. Now, with the advent of the electric machine, man feels that technology has given him the opportunity to break through all spatio-temporal barriers and to soar without limitation to the heights of absolute freedom. However, he has failed to reckon with the cumulative power of the machine itself, which not only robs him of his freedom but also threatens his life as a human being. In his attempt to break out of his limits by means of the machine he fails to realize his human destiny as a spatio-temporal existent. The machine has shattered his real world into "bits" and converted his destiny into a blind, relentless *fatum,* which does not tolerate human qualities and crushes them whenever they try to assert themselves.

In the last century and a half the confrontation between man and the machine has built itself up to a state of crisis, and there has been no paucity of proposals about how to cope with it. However, insofar as the proposals come from science and technology, as such, they aim, for the most part, at refining the scientific and technological tools in order to overcome the very problems which these tools have created. Such, in the main, are the solutions proffered in Marxian dialectics, behavioral engineering, and the electronic and drug media. While they all start out with the proposition that the machine will help man gain his freedom, they end up with the machine determining his entire behavior, if not his total existence.

Man, Creator of His World

Modern man's drive toward individual freedom has reached a high point in his rebellious assertion against God as creator and

9

master of the world. The breathtaking achievements of science and technology have led him to believe that he can gain, or has already gained, freedom not only from church and state, but also from God Himself. "It took two centuries of crisis," says a leading philosopher of this rebellion, "—a crisis of faith and a crisis of science—for man to regain the creative freedom that Descartes placed in God, and for anyone finally to suspect the following truth: . . . man is the being as a result of whose appearance a world exists." [7] What started in the early days of Enlightenment as a plea for tolerance of religious freedom from state encroachment has gradually grown into a demand of human freedom from religion altogether, that is, a demand of independence from a transcendent Being. The modern theological question is not about the existence of such a Being but rather about the role he might play in human destiny. Even those who declared Him dead do not deny His possible influence in man's life. For the basic innovation of the radical theologians is not to dispense with the Christian faith but to reverse its order of sacrifice: Who died for whom? If, they say, man is to control the world with total effectiveness, which is the only way he can become absolutely free, he must himself be creator and master of it, or, as Sartre put it, he must "regain the creative freedom [that was] placed in God." Inevitably this leads them to an exaltation of man's powers, his deification, and ultimately the sacrifice of God for his sake.

When scientific analysis was applied to the investigation of man's knowledge of God, the question arose as to which of the human faculties might render such knowledge possible. Although Locke and Leibnitz still argued how to prove God's existence, the argument has since turned on the reliability of our knowledge of man's relation to God and on its meaning and efficacy in our quest for freedom. In this kind of analysis, man's intellectual, sensible, and emotional capacities have been put to the test. Psychology has disqualified the emotions, and the physical sciences have cast doubt on sense-perception. Theology then has taken recourse in the intellect as the only possible bridge between man

---

7. Jean-Paul Sartre, *Literary and Philosophical Essays*. Trans. by *Annette Michelson* (New York: Philosophical Library, 1962), p. 196.

and the Absolute. However, in trying to build this bridge it has lost sight of the transcendent reality of the Absolute.

The modern theologian assumes that as long as God remains transcendent to man and the world in reality, the human intellect or, in Kant's terminology, the categories of the understanding, cannot reach Him. Thus bereft of all faculties of knowing God, man can find no place for God in everyday life and sees no relevance in a belief in Him as a transcendent Being. Modern man therefore has chosen to hide from himself the real, living, transcendent God and, instead, formulated Him into a concept, an object of thought, a rational construct in relation to his own life and to the world around him. This is what Martin Buber called "the intellectual letting go of God." [8] That is, not being able to picture the living reality of the Divine Being as a thing of the imagination or feeling, as pre-scientific man did, scientific man has converted this reality into a concept, such as the Unknown, the Unlimited, or Being in general. But in doing so, the scientist-philosopher has to reconcile his God-concept with his scientific world-view as a whole, and that, as we have seen earlier, calls for an all-embracing metaphysical structure. Modern man's wrestling with the God-idea in all its theological ramifications is a struggle in the arena of metaphysics. The crisis which has ensued in this struggle is that the scientist-philosopher or his counterpart, the theologian, cannot fit his God-concept into his metaphysical scheme of things.

The problem here, as in the entire outlook of the Era of Enlightenment, is a scientific one, namely, the reconciliation of man's spatio-temporal limitations with his highest aspiration toward individual freedom or, in the language of theology, his salvation. This is especially manifest in the philosophical and theological speculations about the death of God, as promulgated by Nietzsche, Sartre, and the radical theologians. Their aim is to demonstrate the irrelevance of the God-idea or the old God, as the case may be, to modern man in his striving for moral freedom or redemption. In order to save man they sacrifice God, either by removing Him from man's world altogether or by dismembering Him so

---

8. Martin Buber, *Eclipse of God* (New York: Harper Torchbooks, 1957), p. 123.

that He may be brought into that world along with all other decomposed elements of physical nature. In the latter case, instead of having man sacrifice his spatio-temporal existence in an ascent to God, they have God sacrifice Himself by breaking the spatio-temporal barrier and descending into the human conceptualized world. In either case, they want to assure man absolute freedom to create his world and to master it. But like the physical scientists and technologists, these philosophers and theologians find themselves unable to construct a world out of their decomposed elements for man to live in securely. The more they analyze their concepts of man and God, the closer they come to the rim of Nothingness.

Our era of three hundred years of Enlightenment now appears to have run full circle. As long as it holds fast to its scientific-technological orientation it will continue to move from crisis to crisis. After scanning the horizons of this era in the following essays, we may see a new vista of man regaining his primary powers of reason and faith.

I. Building a Universe for Modern Man

Setting the Boundaries of Physics, Ethics, and Mathematics

> Is such a thing as metaphysics at all possible? For human reason is so anxious to build, that it has erected this tower [of metaphysics] already many times and then pulled it down again, in order to examine the condition of its foundation.
>
> IMMANUEL KANT,
> Vorrede, *Prolegomena*, 256

2. SCIENCE AND METAPHYSICS

When we say that modern man has become a problem unto himself we mean that he looks at his relation to the world and does not know where he stands. He does not comprehend the world as a whole and therefore feels he does not know it and cannot master it. He does not know exactly what kind of being he is himself, and he is therefore not sure whether he can know the world as it is in reality. And not being able thus to relate to the world as a whole or to know it for certain, he feels insecure in it. All these relations between man and the universe become problematic because he is aware of the fact that it is he who is unable to establish the proper relation. It is he himself who is the problem, and in order to resolve it he must first know for certain what kind of being he is and how he relates to actual existence outside of himself.

13

The fundamental human question of the modern age is whether the natural sciences are valid in man's quest for a knowledge of himself, notwithstanding the fact that scientific research has produced a wealth of information about the human species. The main difficulty man encounters with these sciences is that they represent him both as observer and as the object of his observation, as the inventor of their measuring rods and as the object of their measurement; he establishes postulates and gauges himself on their scale. But as he reexamines them constantly in the light of new experiences he questions their validity and puts himself into question. All his theories about his own nature as a human being have no common ground on which he may rest his *humanum*, for he is always a different thing to each of the different sciences. In order to see himself as a whole in relation to a universal totality he must perforce venture beyond his physical domain into speculative realms that lie on the boundary between the finite and the infinite, or in the realm of metaphysics.

Every metaphysic seeks to bring the spheres of man, the world, and God into a universal system of reality. Every metaphysic, therefore, faces the problem of relieving the tensions within each of these spheres and between them, which are manifested as opposites of becoming and being, temporal and eternal, mutable and immutable, or, in general, the finite and the infinite. This is man's quest for the One in the many, which has been his main concern since the days of Plato and Aristotle. As long as man dealt with a concept of finite space and with earth as its center, he did not have too much difficulty in holding his universe together, even though there were many gaps in it. But with the advent of modern physics his earthly habitation has been dislodged from the center of the universe and, having conceived of infinite space, he now finds himself on a tiny Globe whirling within a limitless expanse. And as he searches for new horizons he can find none in which the finite and infinite can meet. He has lost his old anchor in reality and, having been left on his own, he wonders whether he actually possesses the faculties to envision the absolute, not to speak of attaining it. Thus the scientific quest for the One in the many continues unabated.

Natural science has made tremendous strides since the early days of Enlightenment, but the problem of man's relation to reality posed in those days has remained the same in our own time. At the annual meeting of the American Physical Society in 1968, some of its leading members took note of a growing disillusionment of the young generation with physical research, because, as they suggested, it has become "more and more remote from the problems of everyday life. . . . This seeming remoteness," they felt, "makes physics less attractive to students who, in today's troubled world, seek relevance." [1] Be this as it may, the real question is whether science in general can hold out to man the promise of ever finding the kind of relevance he is seeking in life. To be sure, "physics has armed technology to revolutionize the world in which we live," and according to Dr. Fred Hoyle, who spoke at that meeting, a newly planned giant accelerator will " 'alter man's outlook for the next 1,000 years,' . . . [as it] will probe the very essence of matter." [2] But this kind of probing represents the incongruity of present-day science. The more it probes into the essence of reality the further it is removed from grasping its actual existence and thus its relevance to man's everyday life. What modern man is looking for is the living forces of the universe in which he may take his place as a human being as a whole, for this is the only way he may find relevance in the world around him.

3. ISAAC NEWTON'S METAPHYSICS

Looking back at the Age of Enlightenment in the seventeenth and eighteenth centuries when modern man launched his concerted drive toward the freedom of scientific inquiry, we may wonder why the greatest scientist-philosopher of that age, Isaac Newton, resorted to the aid of metaphysics to cap his physical world structure. It cannot be said that he just suffered from the vestiges of Scholasticism shadowing his scientific path, or that his theology was an independent speculation unrelated to his natural philosophy. Quite the contrary, it grew out of that philosophy in its universal aspects, as suggested by himself in the General Scholium of his *Principia:*

---

1. Cf. Walter Sullivan, "A 'Revolution' Against the Physicist," *The New York Times,* Sunday, Feb. 4, 1968. Science Section, p. 7E.
2. *Ibid.*

"And thus much concerning God, to discourse of whom from the appearances of things does certainly belong to natural philosophy."[3]

Scientific Mediation

Inasmuch as natural philosophy or science seeks to explain the nature of things and events, it must find such elements in the things or outside of them that will connect them with one another and form a chain of cause and effect relationships. Its highest goal is to establish this kind of interrelation throughout nature and thus construct a world-as-a-whole on universal principles of interconnectedness. This is the goal of what is known as "unified science." But whether the aim is universal or limited to a particular field, the scientist is preoccupied with the search of causes that occur *between* things, states and events—how one thing generates, produces, affects, or otherwise relates to another. As Aristotle noted at the dawn of scientific investigation, "In all our inquiries we are asking either whether there is a 'middle' or what the 'middle' is: for the 'middle' here is precisely the cause, and it is the cause that we seek in all our inquiries." [4]

Ever since Aristotle formulated the role of the "middle" in the scientific account of nature, the problem that scientists and philosophers have faced is to ascertain its locus and mode of existence. If A causes B, does the cause originally lie in A and, if so, how does it pass to B and how does it exist during the passage? And if the cause does not lie in A, what is its origin and how does it mediate between A and B? Many and varied are the answers given to these questions, depending on the different concepts of matter,

---

3. *Newton's Philosophy of Nature. Selections From His Writings.* Edited by H. S. Thayer (New York: Hafner Publishing Co., 1953), pp. 44-45. It should be noted that Newton rejects "blind metaphysical necessity"; but that does not hinder him from expounding a theological metaphysic. Cf. Max Jammer, *Concepts of Force* (New York: Harper Torchbooks, 1962), p. 141, who holds that "as far as scientific methodology was concerned [Newton] was opposed to any metaphysical or theological interpretation of gravitation. . . ." However, on p. 121 Jammer notes: "Newton's definition of impressed force [i.e., centripetal or gravitational] as changing the state of rest or uniform motion of a body is closely related to his metaphysical principle of causality."

4. Cf. Aristotle, *Post. An.*, II. 2, 90a.

energy, force, things, functions, and, especially, space and time. However, in all the answers there is always an inexplicable residue which has to do with the reality of the middle, as such, with the nature of its existence and, on the universal scale, its ultimate mode as the uncaused cause. Even those in modern science who have proposed to dispense with the principle of causality have not been able really to do away with this question but only postponed the answer. They have given the middle a different connotation, but the problem of mediation still prevails in all scientific investigation.[5]

When the scientist-philosopher pushes on to the bounds of his explanation of physical reality, he discovers that he has not succeeded in giving a full account of the locus and existence of the middle in his scheme of things. He then yields to the urge of raising a metaphysical tower and, as Kant observed, even though this tower has been torn down many times, it rises again and again on the renovated foundations of every physical theory. Such has been the destiny also of the most promising philosophies of nature, those of Newton's theory of gravitation as well as Einstein's theory of relativity. The careers of these theories are very instructive to our understanding of the role of scientific mediation in man's orientation in the world around him and in his quest to know himself as a human being.

Metaphysical Existence of Gravity

Newton posits two principles of motion, one natural, which he terms *vis inertiae,* and the other causal, which he calls a centripetal force of gravitation. He warns his readers that as far as the external force is concerned he does not seek to establish it as a physical cause or even to determine its nature, but only to use it as a principle of mathematical calculation of observed phenomena of motion. This force, he says, is not inherent in the things; but he has "not been able to discover the cause of those properties of gravity from phenomena. . . ." Yet he has no doubt "that it must proceed from a cause that penetrates to the very centers of the

---

5. Cf. Henry Margenau, *The Nature of Physical Reality* (New York: McGraw-Hill, 1950), ch. 19, on causality.

17

sun and the planets. . . ." Even though he cannot account for it, he is satisfied "that gravity does really exist and act according to the laws which we have explained, and abundantly serves to account for all the motions of the celestial bodies and of our sea." [6]

If "gravity does really exist" but is not in the things and has no "true physical sense," what kind of existence can it possibly have in Newton's world-order? It occupies the logical position of the copula or mediator—an "is" which "is not" in the subject or predicate but must be "between" the two in order to connect them. Acting at a distance between two bodies, it "is not" in either and does not touch them, but "is" somewhere between the two observed motions. Its real existence cannot therefore be explained by the physical laws of motion (or nature), because it is the underlying principle of these laws. As a physicist Newton could very well argue that he does not have to account for the existence of a cause, real or imaginary, as indeed he tried to assert. But his formulation of the concept of gravity as a universal principle of nature involves him in a logical contradiction which, of necessity, leads him to metaphysical speculations, as do all logical contradictions on a universal scale.

Gravity, for Newton, has meaning only with reference to inertia. The latter he defines as "vis insita, or *innate force of matter, . . . a power of resisting by which every body . . . continues in its present state, whether it be of rest or of moving uniformly forward in a right line.*" [7] This inertia or force of inactivity is the natural state of bodies and is manifest only "when another force, impressed upon it, endeavors to change its condition. . . ." [8] The kind of impressed force which has universal application is of a centripetal character and is called gravitation.[9] Inertia, then, signifies the state of being of a thing when no outside force is applied. By nature a thing just "is"—a changeless being, either at rest (or seemingly at rest)[10] or in motion in a straight line. Change is not-being and is thus not conceived as natural to a thing; that is, change

---

6. *Newton's Philosophy of Nature*, p. 45.
7. *Ibid.*, p. 12. Definition III (author's italics).
8. *Ibid.*, p. 13. Scholium on Definition III.

must come from the outside and cannot remain in the thing after the action is over. "For a body maintains every new state it acquires by its inertia only." [11] Newton faces here a logical contradiction which he is unable to resolve by his laws of physics and must resort to metaphysics. Inertia and gravitation contradict each other as being and not-being and cannot therefore dwell together in the same thing or in the same movement. Indeed, Newton never ascribes an inertial character (that is, "being" in the thing) to curvilinear motion caused by gravity. To maintain such motion, he says, "gravity must be caused by an agent acting constantly according to certain laws, but whether this agent is material or immaterial I have left to the consideration of my readers." [12] He may have escaped the decision as to whether this cause is "material or immaterial," but he could not avoid the question whether it is inside or outside his physical "System of the World," and he sought an answer in a metaphysical cause outside the realm of physics.[13] "To your second query," he wrote

---

9. Magnetic force does not come into consideration in this world system, as it applies only to some bodies and not in uniform degree. Cf. *ibid.*, "On Gravity, Proposition VI, Corollary V," p. 112. It is magnetic force, however, from which Einstein derives, by analogy, his concept of the "gravitational field." Cf. Albert Einstein, *Relativitätstheorie* (Braunschweig: Friedr. Vieweg & Sohn, 18. Auflage, 1960), pp. 25, 38f.

10. *Newton's Philosophy of Nature*, p. 13. "But motion and rest, as commonly conceived, are only relatively distinguished; nor are those bodies always truly at rest which commonly are taken to be so."

11. *Ibid.*, Scholium on Definition IV. If, contrary to Newton, we regard change as natural to physical reality, then inertia or not-change is really not-being, and gravity, as the active principle of change, is being. However, as an empiricist, Newton could not countenance inertia, which resides in the things, to be conceived as not-being. It assumed this form after two centuries of scientific development in Einstein's General Theory of Relativity.

12. *Ibid.*, p. 54. Note his emphatic statement against the idea of gravity being innate in the things. "That gravity should be innate, inherent, and essential to matter, . . . is to me so great an absurdity that I believe no man who has in philosophical matters a competent faculty of thinking can even fall into it."

13. Cf. Newton, *Opticks* (4th edition, London 1730. New York: Dover Publications, 1952), Question 31, p. 397. "By this Principle [*vis inertiae*] alone there never could have been any Motion in the World. Some other Principle was necessary for putting Bodies into

to Bentley, "I answer that the motions which the planets now have could not spring from any natural cause alone, but were impressed by an intelligent Agent." [14] And as he further contemplates this "wonderful Uniformity in the Planetary System," he arrives at the conclusion that it "can be the effect of nothing else than the Wisdom and Skill of a powerful ever-living Agent, who being in all Places, is more able by his Will to move the Bodies within his boundless uniform sensorium." [15]

Gravity, as the logical "between" or mediator of observed motions, is thus given a transcendent, metaphysical existence, directly associated with the "ever-living Agent." Whether or not this Agent is identical with the "agent acting constantly" to produce gravity, referred to earlier (note 12), is not germane to our thesis.[16] The important thing is that, as the cause of gravity, the agent is transcendent to the physical laws of nature. In his physico-theological argument for the existence of a Deity, Newton speaks in terms of his laws of nature; that is, his physical theory leads him to his particular kind of metaphysics.[17] Since the natural inertial, changeless movement in a straight line is infinite, it requires absolute infinite space and time in which to move; and since curvilinear motion requires a constantly acting force of

---

Motion; and now they are in Motion, some other Principle is necessary for conserving the Motion."

14. *Newton's Philosophy of Nature,* p. 47.

15. *Opticks,* p. 403. *Newton's Philosophy of Nature,* p. 42. "This most beautiful system of the sun, planets, and comets could only proceed from the counsel and dominion of an intelligent and powerful Being."

16. Cf. *Opticks,* p. 402. "For it became him who created them [the material things] to set them in order. And if he did so, it's unphilosophical to seek for any other Origin of the World, or to pretend that it might arise out of a Chaos by mere Laws of Nature; though being once form'd, it may continue by those Laws for many Ages."

17. *Newton's Philosophy of Nature,* pp. 43-44. The Agent "is not duration or space, but endures and is present, . . . and, by existing always and everywhere, he constitutes duration and space . . . in a manner utterly unknown to us. . . . We know him only by his most wise and excellent contrivances of things and final causes." See *ibid.,* pp. 52 and 57, Letters to Bentley. "I do not know any power in nature which could cause this transverse motion without the divine arm." "The diurnal rotations of the planets could not be derived from gravity, but required a divine arm to impress them."

gravity which is not in the natural state of things, there must be a transcendent cause of such gravity which fills infinite space and acts in it as if it were its "sensorium," as Newton calls it. This transcendent cause may be the Supreme Agent himself, who started the movements of the universe in their particular courses and keeps them going; or it may be the cause set up by this Agent and then allowed to act constantly on its own.

Newton's metaphysics is the logical consequence of the scientific mode of thinking that builds a system of a causally ordered world. Man can take his place in such an order only as a logical or rational being who is determined by the same laws as those of the physical order. This is also the conclusion that Kant arrived at in his *Critique of Pure Reason* after he examined the foundations of Newton's physical universe. But Kant was concerned primarily with man's freedom and he therefore had to go not only beyond the limits of physical science but also beyond his own science of ethics.

4. IMMANUEL KANT'S METAETHICS

Kant has bequeathed to us two legacies with regard to human freedom, one the primacy of the moral law over theoretical reason, and the other the absolutization of the individual. The two are mutually counteractive and counterproductive. But with these legacies he also handed down to us his critical method which introduced a new type of philosophizing man who has personified our thinking to this day, and who may be called the philosopher-scientist, in distinction from the philosopher-king of Plato's world, and the philosopher-saint of medieval times. Their difference may be found primarily in the type of questions they pose before man, nature, and God.

In his Introduction to "The Transcendental Logic" in *The Critique of Pure Reason* Kant observes that, "It is a great and necessary proof of wisdom or insight just to know what questions may be reasonably asked";[18] and he himself proves it by always

18. Immanuel Kant, *Kritik der reinen Vernunft,* B82. Note: Unless indicated otherwise, all references to Kant's works in German are in the edition of the Philosophische Bibliothek, Verlag Felix Meiner in

21

asking the proper philosophical questions. Indeed, the very essence of his critical method consists in questioning fundamental assumptions and accepted principles and dogmas. But whether he was always able to come up with the right solution depended on the manner in which he posed the problem. We may take it as an axiom of discursive reasoning that there can be no philosophical answer to a non-philosophical question, any more than there can be a mathematical solution to a non-mathematical problem. By coupling philosophy with mathematics in this respect, I mean to point out that Kant's critical questioning is in the philosophical-scientific mode of viewing reality.[19] When we speak of Kant as having wrought a Copernican revolution in modern thought or, as he conceived it, in the thinking of the Age of Enlightenment, we mean that he inaugurated the philosophical-scientific approach to the problems of modern man, which emerged in that age. To be sure, the scientific factor began to play a dominant role among his predecessors, notably, Descartes, Leibnitz and Locke, but it was Kant who established its philosophical principles and, what is more important, gave it moral justification. As is well known, in his *Critique of Pure Reason* he uncovered the philosophical ground of Newton's science of physics, and in his *Critique of Practical Reason,* together with his two other works on the same subject, he laid the philosophical foundations of a science of ethics or, as Karl Vorländer noted, he "became the Newton of Ethics." [20]

The paramount issue of the Age of Enlightenment, in which Kant lived both as its product and as one of its guiding spirits, was the problem of individual freedom against the encroachments of organized society. To resolve this issue, the social thinkers of the time adopted the scientific method of analysis whereby they sought to discover in man's nature certain faculties that would account for his drive for freedom and that could also be used as

---

Hamburg. Pages are given according to the original edition as listed in the margins. All translations are my own.

19. Kant, "Metaphysische Anfangsgründe der Naturwissenschaft," Vorrede. Kirchmann's edition of *Immanuel Kant's kleinere Schriften zur Naturphilosophie* (Berlin, 1872), p. 177.

20. *Kritik der praktischen Vernunft.* Einleitung von Karl Vorländer, p. xli.

concepts for a restructuring of society in such a way that the individual could be reconciled with his social order. It was the same method of "resolutivo and compositivo" which Galilei introduced in the physical sciences and which is still dominant in our day.[21]

Logical analysis, the new method, reduces everything to constituent parts; but then logic also becomes an instrument of constructing the parts into a new totality. An incongruity sets in when the parts assume an independent existence and refuse, so to speak, to subordinate themselves to the whole. The parts make an existential claim against the whole as they are being pressed into it. And this is the paradox of logical individualism: when individuals are reduced to independent entities, they cannot be unified into a society as a whole without being subordinated to it, that is, without losing their independence. The new logical method, based as it was on the nature of things, tried to discover principles and laws of unification either in man's nature or in the social structure, such that neither would suffer at the hands of the other. But this did not obviate the logical paradox of individual freedom, which stands in conflict with the social order in principle. Logically, the two remained irreconcilable, and to this day we still stand in the shadow of this paradox. Galilei's method worked all right in "resolutivo," in analysis, but fell far short of its goal in "compositivo" or synthesis.

When Kant looked at this problem of science, in general, he noticed that the promoters of the new method used only the analytic faculty of individual man but did not investigate his synthetic faculty; and without the latter man could not bring together, as a matter of inner necessity, what he had taken apart through analysis. Kant then reformulated Galilei's principle of "compositivo" into his famous question, "How are synthetic judgments a priori possible?" and spent his entire *Critique of Pure Reason* in deriving their possibility, function, and limitations in theoretical and speculative reason when applied as a science of nature. Then, at the end of his *Critique,* in the discussion of "The Canon of

---

21. Cf. Ernst Cassirer, *Die Philosophie der Aufklärung* (Tübingen, 1932), pp. 339f.

23

Pure Reason," he came to the following remarkable, but very disturbing, conclusion: Theoretical reason can establish a science of nature according to laws of causation, but cannot build a system of the world of nature as a whole, because the ultimate concepts for the completion of such a world are only of a speculative character, i.e., not universal and necessary.

Pure theoretical reason, Kant emphasizes repeatedly, can serve only as a "discipline for the limitations of its domain" in the objects of experience and, as such, has only negative value in that it warns man not to venture beyond this domain. Under this restraint man is left without direction in the world of reality, because his theoretical-speculative mind can tell him where not to go but cannot help him find his way to regions where he may want, nay strives, to go. The very fact that such regions—the ideas of a Supreme Being, a soul, and freedom—are being explored by man with relentless tenacity shows in itself that they play a vital role in his life, even though natural science can offer no guidance or canon of how to apply them to the world of everyday experience. Nevertheless, considering the power of this urge, there must be a special faculty of pure reason that can meet its demand, and if a philosopher is to ascertain this in a scientific manner, he must be able to establish a science of freedom by the same methods by which he established his science of nature, yet distinguishable from the latter. This is what Kant set out to do in his three major works on morality, namely, *Groundwork of the Metaphysic of Morals, Critique of Practical Reason,* and *Metaphysic of Morals.*[22]

A Science of Ethics

Science, according to Kant, is a doctrine of causal relations, and morality, in his vocabulary, is identical with free will or the will to act in complete freedom. The difference between a science of morality and one of nature, therefore, lies in their respective sources of causation; in nature it comes from outside the thing, in morality it emanates from within. A stone or animal always has

---

22. Cf. Kuno Fischer, *Immanuel Kant und seine Lehre* (Heidelberg, 1957), Zweiter Teil, pp. 53-54.

some outside force that determines its movements; a free will moves of its own accord without any outside determination at all. But both must have laws which govern their directions. In the case of natural science, the law says only what takes place; in moral science, which deals with action, it tells the will what to do. The question then is who sets the laws for free will, commanding it to act in a certain way and not in another way? This depends on what Kant means by the will being free.

We know from experience that we have a faculty of willing, but this faculty can never be free so long as it functions under limitations of spatio-temporal determinations, that is, in the phenomenal world. Kant therefore sets it free in a noumenal or intelligible world, where it does not need to relate to the intuitions of space and time or, generally, to objects of spatio-temporal experience. In the intelligible world the laws of moral action cannot be set by the categories of pure understanding, because these categories have jurisdiction only over spatio-temporal intuitions. The sole legislator of the moral law is the free will itself, which is autonomous to command unconditionally and without regard to contingencies. Its command is called the "categorical imperative," which indicates its universality and necessity as well as its non-hypothetical character. Now this issuing of an imperative by the will itself may sound like a strange business. Why does it not just act as it ought to, without going through the motion of telling itself how to act? Moreover, what certainty is there that in following an unconditional imperative man may be able to act freely in a conditioned world of experience in everyday life on earth?

In truth, Kant does not hold out much promise for real freedom here on earth. But even in the beyond he can guarantee it only if there is a Supreme Being who rules both worlds, and if the human soul is immortal so that its freedom may be attained in the fullness of eternal time. That God exists and the soul is immortal are postulates posited by Kant alongside his categorical imperative. The fact that there is such an imperative of universal and necessary dimensions, aiming at the greatest possible good, in itself shows that the aim is possible of being attained by man. "For when the moral law commands that we *ought* now to be better men," Kant says, "it follows inevitably that we must *be able* to be better men." [23] However, the magnitude of the ultimate goal is such that it cannot be reached or even sought by man without the support of a Being higher than he, and without the hope that his life will continue hereafter without end. Morality thus demands that there be a God and immortality of the soul, so that, in Kant's words, "what I may hope for" can serve as a spur to "what I ought to do." [24]

Here Kant's system of morality reaches its culmination, embracing also the ideas of theoretical reason by giving them moral necessitation. The intelligible world of ideas now assumes a greater degree of reality than the world of appearance, and consequently the law of practical reason supersedes that of theoretical, because the former, coming from the realm of noumena, governs also the phenomena, whereas the latter law is confined to the realm of phenomena only.

Thus spoke the philosopher-scientist who realized the limitations of the natural sciences and warned of their inadequacy to lead man to his true destiny of freedom. Kant's postulate about the primacy of the moral law may serve us as a reminder to beware of the scientific-technological proliferation that threatens to engulf us today. Nevertheless, and notwithstanding this timely reminder, when we look at the philosopher-scientist in historical perspective, we find that he was less able to bring the world of ideas down to us on earth than we had a right to expect, even less than Plato's philosopher-king could have done. The difficulty lies in Kant's transcendental logical individualism, which counteracts his moral principle. For when we step down for a moment from the intelligible heights into the plains of earthly existence, we begin to wonder whether or to what extent the categorical imperative can actually govern our lives. Its main weakness lies in the source from which it is derived, but even more so from the fact that it was implanted in man as an individual, making him his own autonomous lawgiver. The categorical imperative is each single man's self-directed will. There is no social imperative, or any other higher force, to direct him with equal categorical determination.

23. *Religion Within the Limits of Reason Alone* (Harper Torchbooks, 1960), p. 46.
24. *Kritik der praktischen Vernunft*, 223-226.

Yet, without such a higher power the individual will may readily lose its universal and necessary commitment and become hypothetical. Kant's imperative tells man to will to act in such a manner that the same may be willed by everyone else, and that if all willed their wills in this manner they would be on their way to freedom. It is this "if," which is implied in the moral law, that in the last analysis renders the imperative conditional and hypothetical. For if all others, or a good many others, do not will to act according to this law, the one who does may unwittingly harm not only himself but also all the others, simply because his solitary action is socially ineffective. In principle it should not matter, but in practice it does, and that is the real issue of its social import.

The Ethical Maxim and the Moral Law

If we examine Kant's formulation of the categorical imperative more closely, we shall find that it is tied to a maxim whose origin and final determination are outside the moral law, that is, not in the intelligible world but in the phenomenal one. Man may set himself any code of behavior according to his desires and goals which he strives to realize, as, for example, the pursuit of a career, the amassing of wealth, or the attainment of social status. Such a code becomes his maxim which guides him in everyday life. What the categorical imperative then says to him is that, before he applies his maxim in a given situation, he should ask himself whether it could become a universal law applicable to and by anyone under all conditions; or, as Kant formulates it, "I ought never to act except in such a way *that I can also will that my maxim should become a universal law.*" [25] Evidently, the enjoiner "to act" and "also to will" implies two wills, one setting a law for the other who tends to act according to a maxim that is not yet a law. The first will says to the other in effect: "If you want to be *free* you ought to make your maxim, which is only a hypothetical imperative, into a universal law or categorical imperative." Since neither of the two wills comes from a source outside of man, they must be identical, for man can have only one will.

---

25. *Grundlegung der Metaphysik der Sitten,* 402 (Kant's italics).

To say then that one and the same will commands itself is to identify the subject with its object, which in Kant's mode of thinking makes no philosophical sense. There must be some aspect of the will that makes it a commanding subject, and another that makes it an object receiving the command. How does this bifurcation take place? By placing the will simultaneously in two different worlds, one in a noumenal existence and the other in a phenomenal one. In the first the will acts freely by its very nature as a free existent, but in the second it is encumbered by spatio-temporal limitations. In order for the will of the second world to be as free as it is in the first world, it must obey the latter and act in conformity with its laws.

Now the maxim itself, which the will in the phenomenal world wants to follow, does not come from the noumenal world; it may only be converted by the latter into a universal law. Neither is it set as a necessary rule in its own world, for it would then have to follow its own command and would not require the categorical imperative of the other world. Furthermore, there are many maxims to choose from, and there must be a criterion for choosing the right one. From the noumenal world man only gets the command to make the maxim into a universal law but no guidance for determining what kind of maxim ought to be converted into such a law. The criterion supplied by Kant does not come from his moral law, as such, but rather from an ethical principle which he formulated in the following terms: "In all creation everything that one may want or may have in one's power, can indeed be used *only as a means;* only man, and with him every rational creature, is an end in himself." [26] This ethical principle, then, and not the moral imperative, is the real ground on which a maxim may be turned into a universal law. Stated further as a "practical imperative," it reads: *"Act in such a way that you treat the humanity in your own person as well as in the person of any other, always at the same time as an end, never just as a means"* (Kant's italics).[27] The two wills implied in the categorical im-

---

26. *Kritik der praktischen Vernunft,* 155-156.
27. *Grundlegung der Metaphysik der Sitten,* 429. The four illustrations of this imperative have the same examples as in the illustrations of universal law, earlier, 421f. Cf. Hermann Cohen, *Ethik des reinen*

perative thus assume two distinct forms, one of a moral law and the other of an ethical ground, and by placing them in two separate worlds Kant has created an "unbridgeable gap" between morality and ethics.

Dual Function of the Will as "Is" and "Ought"

Kant himself does not draw a distinction between morality and ethics directly, but we are justified in inferring it from the distinction he makes between non-purposive and purposive action. In designating the first moral and the second ethical, I mean to emphasize that Kant's fundamental concept of freedom, which he identifies with morality as such, has to do with action that is willed without purpose. It *becomes* an ethical principle when the action is directed toward a purpose, that is, ethical action is in the phenomenal world of becoming, whereas "the moral law itself" issues from "an intelligible world through the realization of the concept of freedom." [28] In other words, the principle of morality applies to man's state of being as he *is,* a rational will in a rational world, where there is no discrepancy between them. The principle of ethics, on the other hand, applies to man's action as it *ought* to be in relation to himself and others in the phenomenal world, where his will comes into conflict with inner and outer spatio-temporal contingencies.

In this dual system, morality sees man as an absolute being, a self-determining individual, whereas ethics sees him as working toward an end determined by right and wrong, or an ought, in relation to others besides himself. Morality does not presuppose such an end and does not enjoin an ought for itself. It only expresses the nature of man in his pure rational state, as *is,* and commands him, issuing from this state of higher existence, to become a better person. "This better person," Kant writes, ". . .

Willens (Berlin, 1921), p. 321, on the meaning of the categorical imperative embracing the idea of humanity as its content. Cf. Karl Vorländer, *Kant und Marx* (Tübingen, 1926), p. 119. It has been forgotten "that in the second formulation of his categorical imperative Kant declared its content to be the idea of humanity."

28. *Kritik der praktischen Vernunft,* 168. Cf. *Grundlegung,* 387-388, and *Metaphysik der Sitten,* 381.

insofar as it is a member of the intelligible world, . . . is conscious of a good will which, on his own admission, constitutes the law for his bad will as a member of the sensible world. . . ." [29] Nevertheless, what is right or good is determined by the ethical principle, formulated in the "practical imperative," as stated above. The distinction between the moral "is" and the ethical "ought," although not designated by Kant directly, is spelled out in his summary of the two principles in his *Grundlegung,* as follows: "The moral ought is thus man's own necessary willing as a member of the intelligible world, and it is conceived by him as an ought insofar as he considers himself at the same time as a member of the sensible world." [30] Clearly, in the first world there is a "will as is," and in the second a "will as ought."

Kant tried to bridge the gap between the two worlds through the mediation of the concept of a maxim, which, coming from the lower will (*Willkür*), is converted into a law by the higher will (*der reine Wille*). But, as pointed out earlier, the norm for choosing the right maxim as a possible candidate for the moral law, that is, the actual ought, is not supplied by the higher will but rather by the ethical principle in phenomenal reality. The "ought" in Kant's science of ethics does not issue from the "is" in his system of morality, as the two remain worlds apart. The latter may well be considered as the *meta-ethics* of his ethical science.

The significance of this gap between morality and ethics cannot be overestimated when we consider Kant's metaphysic of morals and the social structure he has founded on it. Like Jean-Jacques Rousseau, whom he admired greatly, Kant proposes to show how the individual may be free while being subjected to laws governing society and mankind as a whole. Both stress the idea of *moral duty* as the basic principle of freedom, meaning duty without outside coercion. But what they are really trying to do is to resolve the paradox of a free man's duty to obey others when his

---

29. *Grundlegung der Metaphysik der Sitten,* 445.
30. *Ibid.* In general, Kant separated the "ought" from the "is" in nature and established a new "is" in the moral world, where the ought may exist without hindrance, or where actually there is no ought, since in that world the "is" acts as it "ought to" by itself without an imperative.

duty in freedom is to obey only himself. This is the paradox of the absolutization of the individual as the final authority for setting his own laws and, by the same token, his social laws. Rousseau tries to find a solution in a "social contract" whereby all individual wills are fused into a general will, which becomes the sovereign or supreme legislator. It is then the moral duty of each individual to obey the general will, because the latter contains all individual wills, and each individual is thus obeying himself (patently a fallacy of a paralogism of the double meaning of will: "one will" and "multiple will").

Kant, as philosopher-scientist and astute logician, establishes the same principle of freedom through a general will, not, however, on Rousseau's empirical ground of fusion of particular wills, but on the *a priori universal* law legislated by each will, the same being true of all rational wills. He thus goes further than Rousseau in placing in the foreground individual freedom as the source from which the legislative power of the universal law emanates. That is, he posits *"the idea of the will of every rational being as a will which is a universal lawmaker"* (Kant's italics).[31] This is his moral vindication of the logic of individualism. Its practical implications may be illustrated by contrasting Plato's Greek Polis with Kant's Prussian Kingdom. Plato conjoins the king to the philosopher and is thus able to endow the combined personage with a social imperative. But Kant does not trust such a combination, as he knows that the king will corrupt the philosopher. He therefore prefers to let the latter obey the king, as long as the ruler allows him to "dare think" freely (*Sapere aude!*). And, thus, the philos-

---

31. *Ibid.,* 431. Cf. Ernst Cassirer, "Die Freiheitslehre im System des kritischen Idealismus," in his *Freiheit und Form* (Berlin: Bruno Cassirer, 1916), pp. 237-238, on the autonomy of will as lawgiver, not given in actual experience but presupposing it. Further (p. 239) he writes that, for Kant, "freedom does not follow from the intelligible being, but it posits and establishes out of itself the primary datum of this being, as such." Freedom is thus derived neither from the phenomenal-sensible world nor from the noumenal-intelligible one, but out of itself as lawgiver. It appears that, in order to avoid the gap between his two worlds, Kant took freedom out of both and posited it entirely in the individual, who, as autonomous being, is independent of both worlds.

opher-scientist is deprived of his active will and is relegated back
to theoretical speculations.

5. ALBERT EINSTEIN'S METAMATHEMATICS*

The existence of force as a cause of gravity has been the subject of scientific investigation since the days of Newton, but it has
always turned out to be an intermediate physical reality, hovering
between a mathematical function and a metaphysical agent. Whatever the nature of its existence, its role in physical theory has
been that of a "middle" or mediator between two motions.[32] It
behaves like the middle term of a syllogism, which exists as an
operator and disappears after the operation.[33] The main problem
which confronted Newton with regard to the constant action of
gravitation and for which he sought a metaphysical solution still
prevails. The physicist cannot be satisfied with the merely logical
role of force, because he needs it as a constant active agent. If it
disappeared even for a split second, his universe would collapse.
He must therefore either find a permanent abode for it beyond his
physical system or show a way whereby that system can abide
even during its absence. The first alternative leads to metaphysics;
the second has been the goal of mathematics, which reached a high
point in Einstein's general theory of relativity and has since moved
on to a unified field theory. But as mathematical physics tries to
construct a universe without metaphysics, it too has to contend
with the logical mode of physical science and, in the final analysis,
must yield to the law of contradiction, which is inherent in every
scientific system. It may succeed in discarding metaphysics only
to replace it with metamathematics.

My treatment of this subject is on the philosophical level and
not on the mathematical, which is not here my purpose nor within

---

* This chapter appeared as an article, "Einstein's Metamathematics,"
by Alexander S. Kohanski, in *Philosophia Mathematica*, Vol. 10, No.
2 (Winter 1973), pp. 165-181.
    32. Cf. Max Jammer, *Concepts of Force*, p. 242.
    33. Cf. *ibid.*, p. 244, and Henry Margenau, *The Nature of Physical
Reality*, pp. 331f. and Axiom 3, p. 339. *"The only values which measurements of an observable can yield are the eigenvalues of its operator"*
(author's italics).

my competence. By metamathematics I mean that, when physical theory is translated into terms of pure mathematics, the physico-mathematical system thus formed can be assured of an existential ground only by principles which lie beyond that system, that is by metamathematics, in the same sense as a physical system is grounded in *meta*physics. In other words, the logic of mathematics leads to *meta*mathematics as the logic of physics leads to meta-physics.[34]

Between Illusion and Reality

Einstein recognizes that the leading factor in mathematical thinking has an imaginary existence. Moreover, he emphasizes "the fictional character of fundamental principles" of modern physics in general. The question is, can mathematical physics repre-sent the real world in which man lives and communicates with his fellow man and all things around him? Einstein firmly believes that it can, nay does, represent reality. True, the principles are free inventions of the mind and cannot be deduced from elemen-tary experience. Nevertheless he asserts: "Our experience hitherto justifies us in believing that nature is the realization of the simplest conceivable mathematical ideas. . . . In a certain sense, therefore, I hold it true that pure thought can grasp reality as the ancients dreamed." [35]

To make sure that we all mean the same thing when we speak of reality, we must bear in mind that the problem of physical theory is not about the essence or nature of a thing-in-itself, but

---

34. This is attested indirectly by David Hilbert who found it neces-sary to posit transfinite metamathematics as the ground-proof for his logic of his finitistic mathematics. Cf. "Die logischen Grundlagen der Mathematik," in *Hilbertiana: Fünf Aufsätze,* von David Hilbert (Darmstadt: Wissenschaftliche Buchgesellschaft, 1964), pp. 34-35, and further, p. 42: "In our thinking occurs a finite process. . . . In my theory of proof transfinite axioms are added to the finite axioms, simi-lar to the theory of complex numbers in which the imaginary elements are added to real ones . . . the addition of the transfinite axioms is [motivated] by the sense of simplification and completion of the theory."
35. Albert Einstein, "On the Methods of Theoretical Physics," in his *Essays in Science* (translated by A. Harris. New York: Philosophi-cal Library, 1934. Quoted below as Einstein (1)), pp. 17-18.

how to construct a permanent world out of the things as they appear to us in experience, whether such experience is obtained through sense perception or through instruments of observation. Furthermore, the world structure can have permanence only if it is an ordered world, that is, if it has constant elements which operate the same way always, whether things are at rest or in motion. Should these elements change, they must do so according to a constant law. On the whole, physical theory agrees that the order of the world cannot be deduced from sense perception or, as Einstein calls it, "elementary experience." Rather, the order is introduced into this experience by the principles and calculating processes of man's thinking faculty. The question of reality is then a matter of correspondence between the order of the things of our experience and the logical order in which we have placed them. Does the order constructed by mathematical physics really represent the order of things in our sense perception? More specifically, does the mathematical world structure represent the order underlying the world of phenomena, even though we cannot sense this order through our perceptual faculties? This kind of reality, which pure thought tries to grasp, is nothing but the pure form of ordered relations or connections. Mathematical physics has singled out these connections or "betweens" of things as its proper field of investigation, regardless of the things which are being connected.[36] Instead of the thing-in-itself it seeks to know the order-in-itself of physical reality.

Only the Measurable Is Physically Real

In physical theory, we are told, reality is only that which is measurable. The basic question then is whether the physicist can know the real order-in-itself independently of the instruments of measurement which he uses to establish it. Einstein maintains that this is in fact what physical theory is aiming at. "That which appears to me to be the programmatic aim of all physics," he

---

36. Cf. Ernst Cassirer, *Das Erkenntnisproblem in der Philosophie und Wissenschaft der neueren Zeit* (Stuttgart: W. Kohlhammer Verlag, 1957), pp. 56-57. "Mathematical science proper . . . does not deal with number or magniture, but with pure *form* of connection, and it studies the laws of this form."

writes in reply to his critics, is "the complete description of any (individual) real situation (as it supposedly exists irrespective of any act of observation or substantiation)." [37] However, if only the measurable is real, what exactly does the physicist measure when he investigates reality? We find that he measures causal relations, connectives, or mediators of events by means of variables. He then tries to establish these mediators as real existents, as absolutes or invariants, independently of the variables which constitute their components. In our experience causal relations appear as temporal successions of events, that is, as variable connections which in themselves cannot be known perceptually. The empiricists, therefore, conclude with David Hume that causality cannot be known at all, not, that is, as necessary relation which has permanence and sameness. Undaunted by the sceptics, modern physicists proceed to investigate succession in temporal connection in itself with a view to establishing the sameness of its variable components and the permanence of their variations. This is the fundamental method of Einstein's theory of relativity on which his world structure rests.

The world structure of relativity is founded on the principle of a continuum of physical reality which is also a plenum.[38] To account for motion, such a continuum must contain variables which together constitute a permanent single whole without self-contradiction. It thus faces the old problem posed by Parmenides: If Being *is*, how can it move or be one and many, that is not-be, at the same time? It was Plato who suggested the method of

---

37. *Albert Einstein: Philosopher-Scientist*, ed. by Paul Arthur Schilpp (Harper Torchbooks, 1959. Quoted below as Einstein (2)), II, p. 667. Cf. *ibid.*, I, pp. 209f. "Discussion with Einstein," by Niels Bohr, who, opposing Einstein's view, implies the *"impossibility of any sharp separation between the behavior of atomic objects and the interaction with the measuring instruments which serve to define the conditions under which the phenomena appear"* (author's italics).
38. *Ibid.*, II, p. 686. "Adhering to the continuum originates with me not in a prejudice, but arises out of the fact that I have been unable to think up anything organic to take its place. How is one to conserve four-dimensionality in essence . . . and [at the same time] surrender the continuum?" Cf. *ibid.*, pp. 552-553, "Scientific and Philosophical Implications of the Special Theory of Relativity," by H. Dingle, who discusses the possibility of a parallelism of the conceptions of continuity and discontinuity in nature. Cf. N. Bohr, *ibid.*, I, pp. 210f.

solving the problem of "one and the many" which has been followed in the main by modern science. "Of all that now exists in the universe," says Socrates in *Philebus,* "let us make a two-fold division, or rather, . . . a threefold," of the limit, the unlimited, and the combined, or a mixture of the two into a new unity, according to reason. This last element, reason, is the fourth kind of thing in the division that "always rules all things" as the cause of their mixture. The method of finding the limit and the unlimited in one single form is through the investigation of intermediates which drop out in the process of unification.[39] In modern physical science the first two elements are space and time, and the mixture is a space-time continuum attained by a fourth element, which is the mathematical rule of transformation. In principle they are the same concepts as Plato's limit, unlimited, and the one, which is combined through a cause, and their method of unification, likewise, is that of progressive conceptual generalization in which the intermediates fall away by transformation into a new unity.

Modern physics seeks to establish a world structure not out of spatial and temporal percepts and so-called material causes, but out of space-time concepts derived from axioms, principles, and logical deductions.[40] Once the concepts have been formulated into a systematic whole, the shape of things can be made to fit into it. All one needs to do is choose at random the right kind of geometric configuration, bearing in mind that geometry too is not a perceptual image but a construct of axioms and rules of mathematical relations. This holds true of Euclidean three-dimensional space as much as of Minkowski's four-dimensional or Riemann's *n*-dimensional space.[41] When Einstein re-examines Newton's physics, he does not discard the latter's principle of inertial motion in a straight line or gravitational motion in a curved line. He only relates them to a new set of concepts of space, time, straight line, and distance, bringing them all together under a single, unified

39. Cf. Plato, *Philebus,* 23c-30d.
40. Einstein (1), p. 14. "A complete system of theoretical physics is made up of concepts, fundamental laws which are supposed to be valid for those concepts and conclusions to be reached by logical deduction. It is these conclusions which must correspond with our separate experiences; . . ."
41. Cf. *ibid.*

mathematical system of a certain geometric configuration. In order to achieve this he must free his mathematics of all possible perceptual encumbrances.[42] In such a system all elements which are to be measured must fall within the same kind of metric or be gauged by the same coordinates. This means that time and space, which are the structural elements of this system, must consist of commensurate units. Since they are all qualitatively different, one of the two must be converted into quantitative terms of the other. In the coordinate system of a geometrical configuration the space-like element is the dominant or real one, while the time-like element assumes a subordinate position of an imaginary spatial metric.

The physical world, whether Newton's or Einstein's, is conceptually a static space-like universe. The flow of time, insofar as it is taken into account with respect to motion, must be arrested in order to be measured in coordination with space.[43] The new concept of space-time in the theory of relativity is neither "space" nor "time" in the naive perceptual sense, but a single undifferentiated continuum of a certain geometric character. This space-time unity is an independent reality, a new kind of absolute, in which, as Minkowski views it, separated space and time "fade away into mere shadows." [44] What then constitutes this new reality, how is its unity obtained, and what kind of existence does it have as an absolute? In its totality as a world-continuum it is a geometric configuration of world-lines and distances, and its existence is that of an absolute unification of the real and imaginary, or being and not-being, like the logical copula or middle term, except that it is expressed in mathematical terms of relation. In essence, then, Einstein tries to give a mathematical solution to Newton's metaphysical

---

42. Cf. Einstein (2), pp. 673-674, where he makes a basic "distinction between 'sense-impressions' . . . and mere ideas." Cf. *ibid.*, V. F. Lenzen, "Einstein's Theory of Knowledge," pp. 373f.

43. Cf. A. d'Abro, *The Evolution of Scientific Thought—From Newton to Einstein* (New York: Dover Publications, 1950), p. 320, on stationary laws.

44. H. Minkowski, "Space and Time," in *The Principles of Relativity—A Collection of Original Memoirs, . . .* by H. A. Lorenz, A. Einstein, H. Minkowski, and H. Weyl. Trans. by W. Perrett and G. B. Jeffrey (New York: Dover Publications [1923]), p. 75. Cf. A. d'Abro, *op. cit.*, p. 191.

problem of space. His basic difficulty is to account for time, in any form, in a geometric configuration which is qualitatively spatial in character.[45]

If the continuum is made up of space-time elements which are neither space nor time, how does their hyphenated state change their character and how do they differ from space and time as such? The new elements are numerical units of mathematical space and mathematical time; that is, they combine space-like and time-like relations, such as dimension, continuity, distance, succession, and separation.[46] These relations constitute a geometry whose points and figures are the physical events in the continuum. To measure point-events, a coordinate system is introduced whereby numerical values are assigned to their mutual relations at rest or in motion. Physical events occur in space-time without differentiating space and time as separate entities affecting the occurrence in different ways. That is, the event does not take place *in* space and time, but in a continuum which has space-like and time-like properties of continuity, separation, succession, etc. But when the event is observed and measured in reference to a coordinate system specifically designed for that purpose, space and time appear as separate factors of the system. Thus, while the event does not occur in space and time, its measurements are expressed in those terms separately. The problem of the mathematical physicist is to find the appropriate numerical values that will correspond to the separate space-like and time-like properties of the continuum and at the same time represent the event as unified within the continuum as a whole. Here we must bear in mind that in mathematical space-time the event is regarded as a point, that is without dimensions, and therefore not measurable in itself. What the

---

45. The incompatibility of the two concepts shows up especially where time-instant and position of a particle in radiation cannot be accounted for by one and the same formulation. Niels Bohr proposed his well-known principle of complementarity to explain the double nature of atomic particles. Einstein did not accept it as a valid interpretation of the complete individual situation. Cf. Einstein (2), II, p. 669.

46. Cf. A. Einstein, *Über die spezielle and die allgemeine Relativitätstheorie* (18. Auflage, Braunschweig, 1960. Quoted below as Einstein (3)), p. 90, on the concept of the "space-like" as something independent of objects or bodies of everyday experience.

physicist measures is the "between" of the points or the distance within a particular geometric configuration. While the choice of geometry may be any one of a variety of structures, it is nonetheless determined by the concept of distance to be measured and by the kind of number-values which make up the metric.

The Reality of Distance

In the general theory of relativity Einstein's main task is to overcome the logical difficulty of "action at a distance," which is the basic principle of Newton's law of gravity. Such action without mediation cannot be conceived as the cause of gravitation; nor can it act of its own accord. Newton wants to locate its final cause in the realm of metaphysics. Einstein, on the other hand, tries to find it in physical reality as such, in a gravitational field. He does not deny that gravity acts at a distance, for how could there be motion if there were no distance to traverse? But he wants to account for the mediator, without which action at a distance cannot take place. Upon investigation of the nature of distance, in his general theory of relativity, Einstein concludes that the real mediator is the "between" or distance itself as a structural component of the gravitational field.[47]

The theory of a "gravitational field" has had far-reaching influence on modern physics. Hermann Weyl spoke of it as "one of the greatest examples of the power of speculative thought," adding:

> The chief support of the theory is to be found less in that lent by observation hitherto than in its inherent logical consistency, in which it far transcends that of classical mechanics, and also in the fact that it solves the perplexing problem of gravitation and of the relativity of motion at one stroke in a manner highly satisfying to our reason.[48]

To satisfy reason, Einstein needed a new concept of distance, one which would bridge the gap of the logical contradiction of simul-

---

47. *Ibid.*, p. 38. "Through a more exact study of electromagnetic phenomena one has come to the conception that there is no immediate action at a distance." Cf. Einstein (2), II, pp. 675, 677f.
48. Hermann Weyl, *Space, Time, Matter.* Trans. by H. I. Brose (New York: Dover Publications, 1952), pp. 227, 247.

taneous separation and connection of two point-events. This led
him to the adoption of Riemannian space and its tensor metric
as the ground form of his theory.[49]

The difficulty of representing physical reality in number values
is pointed out by Riemann himself in two passages of his famous
paper, *On the Hypotheses which lie at the Basis of Geometry*. He
distinguishes discrete from continuous parts of a manifold, the
first being determined by counting and the second by measuring.
He calls the former "elements" and the latter "points." [50] The
question is, when we measure the distance between two points, is
the distance discrete or continuous? That is, in determining the
magnitude of a distance, do we count its component elements
(discrete) or gauge it by rigid measuring units (continuous)? The
conceptual difference is brought out by Riemann's remark at the
end of his paper. Discussing the validity of the presuppositions of
the geometry of the infinitesimally small, he points out

> that in the discrete manifold, the principle of relations of
> measurement is contained in the very concept of this mani-
> fold, but in the continuous it must come from somewhere
> else. Therefore, either the fundamental reality of space must
> form a discrete manifold, or the ground of relations of meas-
> urement must be sought in binding forces which act on it
> from the outside.[51]

Einstein faced this dilemma when he adopted Riemannian geometry for his theory of general relativity. If the principles of the
metric are immanent in his physical system, space-time must be a
discrete manifold; if, on the other hand, space-time is a continuum,
those principles must lie outside his system. To meet the re-
quirement of continuity and at the same time posit principles of
measurement within the system, Einstein reshaped the infinitesimally small distance into a concept of an interval between two
infinitely close points, later identified by Minkowski as the "Ein-

---

49. *Ibid.*, p. 91. Cf. Einstein (1), pp. 18f. and (3), pp. 57f.
50. Bernhard Riemann, *Über die Hypothesen, welche der Geometrie
zugrunde liegen* (Darmstadt: Wissenschaftliche Buchgesellschaft,
1959), p. 9.
51. *Ibid.*, p. 23.

stein Interval." [52] This new concept expresses spatio-temporal betweenness—a separation which is constantly filled, one which "is" and "is-not," but remains independent of any object or thing that may fill it or form its terminal points.[53] The space-like factor is the one which, by its very character, separates, while the time-like factor, as a continuous flow, constantly fills the gap. How then can these two qualitatively different factors constitute one kind of quantitative metric? What kind of numerical value may designate them both as a unitary space-time element which enters into the makeup of the distance unit (ds)? Obviously, it cannot be purely spatial or purely temporal, or even a combination of the two, but must be in the nature of something that supersedes both features.

Riemann's observation that the principle of counting is inherent in discreteness indicates that a number value which represents a space-point cannot be ascribed to a time-point, because a space manifold is essentially infinitely divisible or discrete, whereas a time-point is not. There is no concept of time which does not imply a before and after. Hence there is no time-point without duration, that is without parts, as is the case with a space-point. The measurement of distance by space-time parameters is therefore a purely mathematical operation in which both space and time assume a super-spatial character. The interval is constituted of static variables.[54] This is accomplished by the fiction of the covariant tensor which is counterbalanced by the antivariant tensor.[55] Thus the real and the imaginary combine in mathematical physics in order to overcome the inner contradiction of distance as simultaneous separation and connection. If by the physically real we mean that which is measurable, then the imaginary may be

52. Hermann Weyl, *op. cit.,* p. 91, and Einstein (3), p. 57.
53. Cf. Einstein (1), p. 64. "In my opinion, this concept of the interval, detached as it is from the selection of any special body to occupy it, is the starting point of the whole concept of space."
54. On the problem of "before and after" in world time, cf. Kurt Gödel in Einstein (2), II, pp. 557-562, 687-688; H. Weyl, *op. cit.,* p. 91; G. J. Whitrow, *The Natural Philosophy of Time* (Harper Torchbooks, 1963), p. 134.
55. Cf. Riemann, *op. cit.,* p. 8; d'Abro, *op. cit.,* p. 477, on imaginary and real distance.

regarded as that which is immeasurable. Indeed, in Riemann's space, the concept of measurement extends also to non-measurables, namely, the immeasurably large and the immeasurably small. The latter, which is distance infinitesimally close to disappearance (that is, imaginary), becomes the measuring rod of distance in appearance (that is, real).[56] Distance in the general theory of relativity is thus measured by not-distance or by immeasurable space-time parameters which constitute the gravitational field. In keeping with Einstein's principle of equivalence of inertial with gravitational energy, the concept of force has been eliminated from the field entirely. All movement, whether rectilinear or curvilinear, has now become natural or free from outside forces acting on it and, as such, may be regarded as discrete and continuous without contradicting the requirements of Riemannian measurement, because the *ds* which measures it is absolute or independent of its coordinate system.[57]

No Self-Contained System

It seems that physical reality, as ascertained by the general theory of relativity, has been established as an existent which is measurable by a tool consisting of the same elements as those of the world-continuum. The physical universe thus appears as a self-contained system, and there is no need to resort to alien metaphysical causes. However, as Einstein himself realized toward the end of his career, his world structure could not close the gap to two intruders. For one, he could not remove the scaffold of coordinates, without which motion would be directionless and thus

---

56. Cf. Whitrow, *op. cit.*, p. 151; Weyl, *op. cit.*, p. 102: "Riemann's geometry goes only half-way towards attaining the goal of a pure infinitesimal geometry. It still remains to eradicate the last element of geometry 'at a distance,' a remnant of its Euclidean past."

57. The determination of motion by a single principle instead of two is Einstein's major improvement over Newton's law of gravitation. The latter calls for a dual account of motion, one the principle of inertia whereby bodies move *naturally* in a straight line, and the other, centripetal force, acting from the outside, which diverts the body into a curvilinear direction. According to the general theory of relativity, all motion, whether rectilinear or curvilinear, is *natural* to the same principle of the gravitational field in its various regions.

unable to move altogether. His invariant measuring device (*ds*) is made up entirely of variables, including the tensor g_{ik}, which depend on the coordinates; its presumed independence is derived solely from mathematical rules of transformation, which are the same for all coordinate systems. Describing the "general laws of motion" in the gravitational field, d'Abro writes:

> . . . the presence of the four-dimensional metrical field of space-time . . . acts as a *guiding influence* on bodies, constraining them along the geodesics of space-time. When, therefore, the observer partitions space-time into his space and time mesh-system, the effect of the guiding field is to direct bodies along certain paths in space and to determine their motions along these paths.[58]

Without space and time partitions, "motion would be meaningless and inconceivable." We have here a stationary world continuum similar to that of Aristotle's prime immovable mover, which influences the motion of the physical universe, without actually participating in it. Yet within this world structure, as in Aristotle's closed world, motion is inconceivable without the coordinate system of space *and* time in separation.

The second outsider which tries to get into the system is matter. But it cannot become reconciled with the space-time metric of this system, despite the fact that, according to the general theory, "The geometrical behavior of bodies and the motion of clocks rather depend on gravitational fields, which in their turn are produced by matter." [59] Einstein tried to clear the ground for some matter to enter into his system by making a distinction between "matter-energy" and "gravitation-energy," but, having left the former out of account, he did not really overcome this duality. "Our modern schema of the cosmos," he states, "recognizes two realities which are conceptually quite independent of each other even though they may be causally connected, namely the gravitational ether and the electromagnetic field or—as one might call them—space and matter." [60] Nevertheless, his concept of matter

58. Cf. d'Abro, *op. cit.*, p. 274.
59. Einstein (1), p. 58.
60. *Ibid.*, p. 110. Cf. d'Abro, *op. cit.*, 329, where, quoting Einstein, he writes: "In Einstein's own words: 'Of the energy constituting mat-

is such that it acts on the system from the outside, at least in part. Is this outside factor not a *meta-mathematical* object which overrides the mathematical system as its final cause? As Einstein himself has put the question, "Is there such a thing as a natural object which incorporates the 'natural-measuring-stick' independently of its position in four-dimensional space?" An affirmative answer would imply an external factor not accounted for by the field-equations. Einstein did not regard such a factor as logically necessary for his mathematical theory, but as long as this theory remained incomplete he made allowance for the supposition that "There are physical objects, which (in the macroscopic field) measure the invariant *ds*." [61]

Barring these physical objects for the sake of logical consistency, what, in the final analysis, does the theory of relativity account for by its metrical field? It accounts for the gravitational field which acts or influences as a *mediator* of motion *per se*. Upon reviewing the whole range of Einstein's mathematical structure and recognizing fully its theoretical magnificence, Hermann Weyl observes: "The laws of the metrical field deal less with reality itself than with the *shadowlike extended medium* that serves as a link *between* material things, and with the formal constitution of this medium that gives it the power of transmitting effects." [62] The field-medium continued to occupy Einstein's attention in his attempt to formulate a more generalized theory that would put matter and space in one "unified field." He speculated:

> It would, of course, be a great step forward if we succeeded in combining the gravitational field and the electro-magnetic field into a single structure . . . the whole of physics would become a completely enclosed intellectual system, like geometry, kinematics and the theory of gravitation, through the general theory of relativity. [63]

The same field-concept dominates physical theory today, and the

---

ter, three-quarters is to be ascribed to the electromagnetic field, and one-quarter to the gravitational field.' "

61. Einstein (2), II, p. 685.
62. Quoted by d'Abro, *op. cit.*, p. 339 (my italics).
63. Einstein (1), pp. 110-111.

search goes on for the most universal medium that would establish a single and closed intellectual world structure.[64]

A Limited World without Bounds

Einstein labored to find in the world its internal self-explanation by enclosing it within a system of a unifying general principle which sets its own limits. But all he could account for in that world is just the things that are measurable in accordance with his principle. The reality of a being, such as matter, which played a dominant role in his scheme but which would not fall under its measuring-rod, perforce remained outside—a being transcendent to his world structure. This being might have set his world's boundaries, but he would not recognize its reality unless and until it became measurable. He therefore broke the circle of his unified field in the hope of finding an all-embracing universal principle of measurement. That is, he kept extending the limits of his system, because he could not set its outer bounds through the system itself. His four-dimensional space-time continuum could close itself only in circular reasoning, within the limits of its own circle that knows no bounds. By adopting the Riemannian geometry he was able to construct a spherical or elliptical world in which all lines issuing from any point in any direction return to the same point.[65] This particular geometry sets its own *limits,* because no matter what direction a world-line may take, it lies within the same self-enclosed system. But it cannot set *boundaries* within the system, because a boundary would separate the entire sphere from something which is not the sphere and would therefore lie outside its metric system. Logically, once the principles of the general theory of relativity have been adopted, the physical world as a whole becomes a closed field of a spherical or elliptical nature, returning upon itself.[66] But

64. Cf. Ernst Cassirer, *Zur modernen Physik* (Darmstadt: Wissenschaftliche Buchgesellschaft, 1964), p. 54. "Between 'matter' and 'empty space' there now steps in a new concept of mediation, the concept of the 'field.' And it is this concept which henceforth always appears more definitely and clearly as the actual expression of the physically real, because it appears as the fully legitimate expression of the physical laws of action."
65. Einstein (3), pp. 66-70.
66. Cf. *ibid.,* p. 69. "From what has been said, it follows that closed spaces without bounds are thinkable. Among these, the spherical space

the actual realities, which are the mainspring of this world, keep breaking it up into ever-widening open fields.[67]

I have reviewed here the greatest theoretical structure of modern physics only to demonstrate the intellectual powers of man as he applies his logical mode of thinking to the construction of a world around him. Yet the problem of man, as viewed from the vantage-point of natural science, appears more pronounced today than ever before. For the scientific crisis does not stem from the unresolved riddle of the physical universe. Mathematical physics will unravel yet untold secrets of nature, and even though it may never attain its goal of a "unitary field" without resorting to metaphysics or metamathematics, it will continue to gratify man's urge toward intellectual freedom. The scientific crisis, rather, is that man is unable to find himself as a human being in the kind of world which mathematical physics is able to construct for him. The freedom which he has gained through the natural sciences is only a freedom from dogmatic conceptions tied to the vagaries of sense perception. Precious as this freedom is, it does not meet the needs of man as a human being as a whole. Man cannot live by pure reason alone; nor can he dwell in empty space. And as for his sense perceptions, he would not part with them even for a moment.

(elliptical, resp.) distinguishes itself by its simplicity, in that all its points are of equal value." Cf. d'Abro, *op. cit.*, p. 244. "In fact, . . . the complete relativity of all motion can be established only if the universe is finite."

67. Einstein did consider the possibility of an open field or an endless expansion of space on the basis of A. A. Friedmann's mathematical calculations. Cf. Einstein (3), p. 84f. and Albert Einstein, *Grundzüge der Relativitästheorie,* Anhang I: Zum "kosmologischen Problem," pp. 73, 84-87. It is noteworthy that in his observations on the cosmological problem of an expanding universe he considers its "main question [to be] whether the world in reference to space is curved positively or negatively" (p. 86). If positive, he says, the world is spherical, and pseudospherical if negative.

46

II. The Boundless Promise of Technology

> The computer, in short, promises by technology a Pentacostal condition of universal understanding and unity.
>
> MARSHALL McLUHAN
> *Understanding Media*

6. KARL MARX: MAN AND MACHINE AS MODES OF PRODUCTION

Dynamics of Dialectic Materialism

Long before the electronic age, Karl Marx recognized the conflict between man and the machine in modern industry, in which man has become a slave to his forces of production or a mere accessory to the machine which he has produced. Marx's concern, indeed, is to liberate man from his enslavement, but he is not concerned with what man is as much as with what he does as a producer of material conditions of life. Seemingly, he starts with the actual human being, but his analysis of the human productive capacity reduces man to a mode of the objective conditions which determine his existence beyond his control.. At the same time, Marx urges man to change these conditions and become his own master. This paradox of the conditioned changing the conditions that condition him Marx tries to resolve by what he designates as "dialectic materialism" or Communism. What is man's role in this process?

Marx and his followers might agree that a change in human conditions must come through man himself and not through some kind of mechanical process. However, they tie the human condition so closely to the material forces of production that unless man can gain some special power which is not subject to those forces, there is no way he can possibly liberate himself from their grip. But this is not the Marxian outlook. Instead, Marx replaces mechanical materialism with what he considers to be dynamic materialism, the kind that may generate a specifically human power out of the very material conditions of production which man is supposed to change.

The *schema* of dynamic materialism is "briefly formulated" by Marx in his preface to *A Contribution to "The Critique of Political Economy,"* as follows:

> In the social production of their means of existence men enter into definite, necessary relations which are independent of their will, productive relationships which correspond to a definite stage of development of their material productive forces. . . . The *mode of production* of the material means of existence conditions the whole process of social, political and intellectual life. . . . At a certain stage of their development the material productive forces of society come into *contradiction* with the existing productive relationships. . . ." [1]

When these relationships become oppressive, the productive forces, under new material conditions, pass into a new stage, creating "new, higher productive relationships." The new material conditions then create new antagonisms on a different, but higher, level of production. This rise and fall of different stages of productive relationships continued in a progressive line of development from time immemorial to our own day. And now comes Marx's revolutionary dictum of social dialectics: "Bourgeois productive relationships are the last antagonistic form of the social process of production—antagonistic in the sense *not of individual* antagonism, but of an antagonism arising out of *the conditions of the social life* of individuals. . . ."[2]

What interests us most in this *schema* is the source of antago-

1. *A Handbook of Marxism* (New York: International Publishers, 1935), pp. 371-373 (my italics). Note Lenin's elaboration, pp. 544f.
2. *Ibid.*

nism, for Marx wants to show that the source will eliminate itself in the dialectic process of the social relations themselves. One would surmise that the source of conflict might be in man as an elemental unit of the social relations, but that is not where Marx finds it. As his entire scheme clearly indicates, the conflict originates in "the mode of production of material means of existence," which in turn determines the social relationships and produces their inner antagonisms. It is not man as an original motive power who sets the process into motion, but the objective conditions of production which control him independently of his will. For that matter, his will and his thoughts, too, are determined by those conditions, and in this respect, Marx may speak of dialectics as "the science of the general laws of motion both of the external world and of human thinking." [3] While he sees the conflict taking place in social communication between men, he does not see man, as such, as its chief dynamic force. Accordingly, this antagonism is nothing but a contradiction between objective classes as the necessary outcome of the mode of production. Nevertheless, Marx and his followers lay great stress on the human factor in the conflict and its ultimate solution. What, then, is the role of man as a human being in this scheme of dialectic materialism? Is he completely determined by the material forces or can he add something specifically of his own *humanum* independently of those forces? The answer lies in Marx's presuppositions about the nature of man, the kind of freedom he is striving for, and his capacity to establish a free mode of communication in which he may become master over the forces of production—in a word, on Marx's answer to the question "What is man?"

Presuppositions about Individual Man

Marx regards himself as a social scientist, rather than as a philosopher in the metaphysical or ideological sense. As a scientist, he follows the Aristotelian rule that no science can be established without first principles, or, as he himself calls them, presuppositions, which cannot and need not be demonstrated by the given science. Indeed, he derides the philosophers who build ideo-

---

3. *Ibid.*, p. 542.

logical castles in presuppositionless air.[4] As a materialist he must look for his principles in observable material data, and not in thoughts, ideas, or other spiritual, metaphysical entities; nevertheless, he hopes to find them in individual man. "The economists' material," he states, "is the active, energetic life of man. . . ."[5] This presupposes the existence of individuals as producers of the material means of life, which in turn determines all other processes and forms of life. Marx's first presupposition, then, is that individual man is a category of the mode of production and that this mode is coeval with human history. There is no pre-history when man was not a producer and might have related himself to others otherwise than through his mode of production. "The first historical act," says Marx, ". . . is the production of material life itself. Furthermore, this is an historical act, a fundamental condition of all history, which must be fulfilled daily and hourly today as it was thousands of years ago, just to keep people alive."[6] The second presupposition is that individual man, as he produces the material means of life and as he reproduces himself, of necessity enters into relationships with other individuals and establishes the kind of communication that is determined by, and corresponds to, the forces of production available at a given period in the history of production. The third presupposition is that division of labor, which is determined by the social forces of production, leads to different forms of possession of property in different social orders, such as tribal, state, or feudal, and finally the capitalist order. Marx designates these three presuppositions the moments of production.

Since our concern is man, we want to know wherein lies the specifically human element in these moments. Apparently, Marx too sought a *principium humanum* in his historical *schema,* for he distinguishes men from animals by their corporeal organization insofar as it determines their mode of production of the means of life.[7] Yet the real distinction, he later suggests, is man's act of

4. Karl Marx/Friedrich Engels, *Die deutsche Ideologie.* Marx-Engels Gesamtausgabe. Erste Abteilung. Band 5. Verlagsgenossenschaft ausländischer Arbeiter in der USSR. Moskau-Leningrad, 1933, p. 442.
5. "The Poverty of Philosophy," *A Handbook of Marxism,* p. 350.
6. *Die deutsche Ideologie,* p. 17.
7. *Ibid.,* p. 10.

entering into relation. Speech and consciousness, which are characteristic of man, arise out of the necessity to communicate with other men.

> Where relation exists, it exists for me; the beast does not "relate" itself to anything and generally not at all. For the beast, its relation to others does not exist as relation. Consciousness is thus from the very start a social product and remains as such so long as men exist at all.[8]

For an instant we have here a glimpse of Marx's man as human being *sui generis,* but we lose him forthwith in the maelstrom of "the active energetic life" not of man himself but of his conditions of production. Accordingly, man enters into relation with other men of necessity, independently of his will, entirely determined by outer forces. "What [individuals] are," says Marx, "coincides with their production, with that which they produce as well as with the manner in which they produce. What the individuals are, therefore, depends upon the material conditions of their production." [9] Thus the act of relating, which stems from man's specific *humanum* and which may constitute the principal motive power in human history, is reduced by Marx to an objective, impersonal condition deprived of its inner, living drive.

Dehumanizing Effects of Division of Labor

Marx postulates that the devision of labor has undermined two major human interests, namely, freedom of the individual and the quality of his labor-power. Since his very beginnings as a producer of the means of life individual man entered into social relations with other individuals, which forced him to give up his freedom and become progressively enslaved in this relationship, as his modes of production advanced from one stage to another. As Marx explains it,

---

8. *Ibid.,* p. 20. Marx does not elaborate on this point of relation as a human capacity. Nevertheless, it is important to note that he came very near the *principium humanum* when he hit upon the concept of relation as specifically human. He lost sight of it in the subsequent course of dialectic speculations due to his materialistic blind-spot.

9. *Ibid.,* p. 11.

The social power, namely the manifold force of production which is conditioned by the common effort of different individuals in the division of labor, appears to these individuals not as their own unified power, but as an alien domination from without, because the common effort itself is not voluntary but naturally necessary. . . .[10]

The other human element, man's quality as producer, Marx holds, has also suffered grievously through the division of labor. As the modes of production have changed with the development of the means of production, the individual laborer has been deprived step by step of his specific physical and mental qualities as a human producer. That is, the advancement in tools and machines for the production of the material means of life and the concomitant changes in social relations of production have dehumanized the individual laborer.

Once more we have here an insight into man's problem as a human being who has a will to be free and to retain his human qualities, even though only as a producer of material goods. This, however, is soon lost in the Marxian dialectic of the forces of production and the relations of production, of which the human will, as a responsible free agent, is only a pale reflection.[11] This dialectic, which sees man as being fatalistically determined by the necessary conditions of production, renders him a problem unto himself. For how can he assert his human qualities over powers which are not human, when he himself is a mode of those powers?[12] Marx may well point to the machine in modern industry

---

10. *Ibid.,* p. 23.
11. Cf. Karl Marx, *Capital.* Translated from the third German edition by Samuel Moore and Edward Aveling, edited by Frederick Engels (New York: The Modern Library, 1936). Author's Preface to the First Edition, p. 15. "My standpoint, from which the evolution of the economic formation of society is viewed as a process of natural history, can less than any other make the individual responsible for relations whose creature he socially remains, however much he may subjectively raise himself above them."
12. *Ibid.,* p. 23. Author's Preface to Second Edition. "Marx treats the social movement as a process of natural history, governed by laws not only independent of human will, consciousness and intelligence." Quoted by Marx approvingly from a review of *Das Kapital* in a Russian publication of May 1872.

as the greatest dehumanizing factor of our time, but he does not find in man himself anything specifically human, outside the material forces of production, that might overcome the machine. His concept of freedom has only a negative connotation, namely, resistance to the conditions caused by the division of labor, of which the machine is man's most formidable antagonist. According to Marx, this will be resolved through the inner contradictions which the machine, as a mode of production, has created, or man will be liberated from his enslavement to the machine by the machine itself. A close look at Marx's analysis of the effects of division of labor in capitalist society, which he regards as the last stage of the conflict, will reveal that his dialectic materialism cannot overcome it of itself, as he claims it will.

Can the Source of the Conflict Abolish Itself?

Since division of labor is the source of the conflict between man and machine, it stands to reason that this conflict can be resolved only through the abolition of division of labor.[13] In Marx's concept of freedom, man is not free, because

> As the work begins to be divided, each one has a definite, exclusive sphere of activity which is imposed on him and from which he cannot get out. He is hunter, fisherman or shepherd, or critic, and must remain so if he does not want to lose his means of life. [In the communist society, which Marx prognosticates, the individual will be free to do anything at any moment], hunt in the morning, fish in the afternoon, raise cattle in the evening, write criticism after his meal, just as I please, without becoming a hunter, fisherman, shepherd, or critic.[14]

As far as the workers are concerned, Marx maintains, they have virtually become free from the division of labor, because in the modern factory system they are undifferentiated helpers of the machine which has taken over all their functions as a labor force. The only division of labor which now exists and which is becoming more and more acute in its inner antagonisms is the social

13. *Die deutsche Ideologie.* Feuerbach, p. 63.
14. *Ibid.,* p. 22.

relations of production. If this too is removed, man will have become liberated from the ills of this division altogether.

It should be noted that Marx does not consider the machine, as such, the chief culprit in man's enslavement. On the contrary, he recognizes it as a progressive means of production. The evils of modern industry, he says, are not in the machine but in its capitalist owners who deprive the workers of this instrument of labor and turn it into a "means of enslaving, exploiting, and impoverishing the laborer; the social combination and organization of labor-processes is turned into an organized mode of crushing out the workman's individual vitality, freedom, and independence." [15] Liberation may therefore come only through a revolutionary change in the social relations of production, namely, through the abolition of private property. However, revolutions are made by men, not by objective "forces of production" or "relations of production"; and if a new era is to be ushered in as the ultimate social order, as Marx envisions it, it must be such that it no longer harbors the inner contradictions which have plagued the old order. This, says Marx, will be accomplished by the modern proletariat, which has come into existence through class antagonisms of the capitalist mode of production, notably the factory system.

In order to get rid of the class antagonisms, the new social order must be free of classes or be a classless society, and this will be attained through the elimination of division of labor, which is at the root of those antagonisms. In terms of Marxian dialectics, the inner processes of production always represented a dichotomy of class interests generated by the division of labor. At each stage in human history, each class acted according to its own interests: one tried to break out of enslavement while the other tried to assert its supremacy. In this struggle each moved to new forms of a higher synthesis, such as guild craftsmen becoming shop laborers, and merchant capitalists turning into manufacturers and industrialists. But throughout this development the classes continued to perpetuate their antagonisms with ever-increasing intensity until they reached a stage in our own day when the class system, as such, is bound to break up. The inner process of the relations of

15. *Capital*, p. 555.

production will cease to generate class conflicts when "a class has formed itself which has no particular class-interests to promote against the ruling class." [16] Such a disinterested body is the proletariat whose function it is to abolish the ruling class and itself become the proprietor of the means of production. Then the second phase of division of labor, namely the antagonism caused by the capitalist social relations of production, will no longer prevail, because there will be no classes and no specific class-interests to contend against each other.

We have here a sort of inverse dynamics that will unwind the whole historical fabric of dialectic materialism. The proletariat, which has come into existence as a result of the industrial revolution and its concomitant capitalist order, must now constitute itself into a political force for the inauguration of the social revolution, which will abolish not only the capitalist class but all classes for all time. It is this political force that Marx designates as Communism, and not the society which it is to usher in, although the latter will bear its earmarks. "Communism," he emphasizes, "is for us not a state which is to be established, an *ideal* toward which reality is to direct itself. We call Communism the *actual* movement which abolishes the present state. The conditions of this movement arise out of the presently existing presupposition." [17]

The paradox of considering the proletariat a class without class-interests may be reconciled through dialectic reasoning, but hardly on the material grounds on which dialectic materialism proposes to resolve it. According to Marx's interpretation of bourgeois society, the dialectic of class struggle goes on within the bourgeois class itself, insofar as masses of its members are continually being pushed out, impoverished, and converted into "an overpowering proletariat." That is, the proletariat is that body of individuals that has been deprived of its erstwhile bourgeois

---

16. *Die deutsche Ideologie*, p. 65.
17. *Ibid.*, p. 25. On Marx's concept of the role of the proletariat in man's liberation as a human being, see Karl Löwith, *From Hegel to Nietzsche*. Trans. from the German by David E. Green (New York: Anchor Books, 1967). "Marx: Bourgeoisie and Proletariat," pp. 242-244, "Marx: Work as Man's Self-alienation," pp. 270-279, "Marx: The Proletariat as the Possibility of Collective Man,"pp. 309-313.

class-interests, and since its interests which it may have obtained as a class of laborer-producers have been taken over by the machine, it really has no class-interests whatsoever. Now, when this mass of declassed individuals becomes aware of its condition and organizes itself into a political force, it will act as a new kind of "class," but without class-interests either as owners or as producers of material means of life. And when this new class, acting with political power, will overthrow the old ruling class, the new order of a classless society will have come into existence as a matter of course, because the new class which will then rule is classless. This is presumably the dialectic process of economic power converting itself into political power, as proclaimed in *The Communist Manifesto:* "every class struggle is a political struggle." [18] But how "economic power" that ceases to be a laborer-producer (supplanted by the machine) and is not yet the owner of the means of production (which are in the hands of the bourgeois class) can become a "political power" of a material nature (and none other will do for Marx) remains a paradox of Marxian theory.

This paradox could be resolved on the human level if Marx were willing to grant man the interest and will to act independently of the forces of production, but this is contrary to his view of man. Furthermore, due to his disregard of a specific *principium humanum,* he also fails to resolve the real conflict between man and machine as modes of production. For, if we ask whether man will be free in the classless society (assuming that such a society is possible of realization), we come back to the spectre of the machine which modern industry has created and which will remain the dominant mode of production even after the social revolution. Indeed, Marx does not advocate the elimination of the machine even though under present conditions it is the laborer's

---

18. *Handbook of Marxism,* p. 33. The political character of the class struggle is further emphasized by Marx as he envisages the final stages of the dialectic process, when theory will become practice, that is, "the *Socialists* and the *Communists* [who are now] the theoreticians of the proletarian class," will become its mouthpiece in practice. (Cf. "The Poverty of Philosophy," *ibid.,* p. 369f.) Lenin considered this aspect of Marxism as the opposite side of its economic coin. (Cf. V. I. Lenin, "The Teachings of Karl Marx," *ibid.,* pp. 564-566.)

biggest enemy. Machine-breaking, he says, is reactionary as it interferes with human progress; rather, it should be socialized in the new classless society. But he does not answer the question how, in the new order, man will cope with the advanced instruments of modern industry which, as Marx himself has pictured to us, have already deprived the laborer of his human qualities and threaten to overwhelm him completely.[19]

The fact that in the new order the machine will be owned by collective society does not make it less critical as an instrument of enslavement, unless man knows how to relate with fellow men on a level which is not determined by the instruments of production. For this kind of relation man needs to know himself as man; he needs to know the nature of a relation which makes him human and renders his society a human society. Even if it were possible to remove the objective conditions of division of labor, as Marx proposes, man would still not be able to realize his personal, human capacities, unless he exercises them freely as the primary deciding factor of his existence. For as long as he has to produce and deal with "objects," there will always be "objective" conditions which will militate against his *humanum*. Only by asserting his human qualities and potencies above his material conditions, even as he regulates these conditions, will he prove his ability to establish and maintain his social relations on a human level.

In Marx's future society (and we have had more than a foretaste of it in several countries in our generation) it is quite conceivable that, when it is not constituted through proper human relations, the so-called classless society will use the instruments of production, which it will then own uncontested and absolutely,

---

19. Cf. "The Machine-wreckers of Newton's Epoch and the Present-Day Wreckers of Productive Forces," by B. Hessen, *Science at the Cross Roads* (London: Kniga Ltd., 1931), p. 204. Hessen, who was Director of the Moscow Institute of Physics at the time, says that it is "a distortion of the ideas of Marx [to maintain] . . . that the machine-wreckers of Newton's period were wiser than we." "It is not the machines which transform the workers into a blind tool of mechanism, but those social relationships which so exploit machinery, that the worker merely becomes an accessory" (pp. 206, 210). But the author glosses over the fact that the machine remains a machine and the worker remains its accessory under all circumstances and conditions of social relations.

with utter disregard of the human qualities of its members and with dire consequences to their freedom. A classless society of "free associated individuals" in which all restraints of the modes of production and of the social relations of production, including the state, will be eliminated, is just a translation of the automated machine into an automated social structure.[20] Like the machine-automaton which guides itself without interference on the part of man, except for his minimum servicing, the new classless society will regulate itself of its own accord through an automated "association of individuals"—an instrument much more formidable and destructive than the mechanical or electric automaton. What can happen to man facing such instruments in a classless society is foreshadowed by another science, not unrelated to Marxian dialectics, and that is the behavioral engineering of man, which will be considered in our next essay.

7. B. F. SKINNER: BEHAVIORAL ENGINEERING

In the Image of the Machine

Technology, Marx complained a century ago, contrived the machine for the production of commodities which, under existing social relations, has turned man into a slave. In more recent years we have witnessed the rise of a technology which purports to use the machinery of psychological laboratories to mold man along lines of predetermined behavioral patterns. This has been hailed

---

20. This was the grand scheme designed by Lenin immediately after October Revolution. As explained by his disciple N. Bukharin, whom he regarded as the best interpreter of Marxism, "The Communist method of production . . . must be an organized society . . . [and] it must be a classless society." The fundamental task of the *Communist society* is to organize production "in one vast people's workshop . . . according to a prearranged plan . . . [so that] the social order is like a well-oiled machine." And, as Marx envisaged it, Communist man will be free, because he will identify himself with a classless society which is the bearer of the interests of mankind as a whole. Cf. "The ABC of Communism," by N. Bukharin and E. Preobrazhensky, *Modern Socialism,* ed. by Massimo Salvadori (New York: Harper Torchbooks 1968), pp. 165, 169.

as a new revolutionary stage of human progress, in which man is promoted from being a mere accessory to the machine to becoming a precision instrument himself—man recreated in the image of the machine.

Testifying before a United States Subcommittee on Government Research not long ago, David Krech, psychologist at the University of California, stated: "I foresee the time when we shall have the means and therefore, inevitably, the temptation to manipulate the behavior and intellectual functioning of all people through environmental and biochemical manipulation of the brain." He based his prediction on experiments carried out on animals, but which could be extrapolated "from rat, mouse and goldfish, to man," and he warned that if we "failed to prepare ourselves for that eventuality, then we might find it too late to institute effective, carefully thought through, and humane controls." [21] While Professor Krech is thus warning about the "serious social import" of the possible manipulation of the human brain, another psychologist, Professor B. F. Skinner of Harvard University harbors no doubts about the benign results of his laboratory manipulations of human behavior or, as he calls it, "behavioral engineering." "Burrhus Frederick Skinner considers himself a man of goodwill, rather than a visionary," said one of his followers. "He merely wants a society in which people live together more effectively and more happily than they do today, and he believes he has discovered a technology of behavior that will enable them to do just that." [22]

That technology can manipulate the human brain, environment, genetics, and other factors in man's behavior is a well-founded possibility and in some measure an established fact. In discussing these problems in the following pages, I do not propose to examine the methods, findings, or validity of the various branches of the science of behavior. One may well agree with Bernard Berelson, a leading analyst in this field, that "The behavioral sciences are

---

21. "Scientist Says Control of Intelligence Is Possible," *The New York Times,* Apr. 3, 1968. Cf. "Science Seeks 'Safe Bugs' for Genetic Engineering," *ibid.,* March 3, 1975.
22. Berkeley Rice, "Skinner Agrees He Is the Most Important Influence in Psychology," *The New York Times Magazine,* March 17, 1968, p. 114.

here to stay. They have already made important contributions to our understanding of man and they will make many more." [23] My main concern is rather with the fact, as Berelson also pointed out, that these sciences "have already affected man's image of himself and permanently so." For they have generated a power of human engineering which places before us the man-instrument problem in its most crucial aspect, namely, that man himself is regarded as a machine. Since Professor Skinner is one of the chief protagonists of this view, I will examine the underlying principles of his argument.

A Social Laboratory

Skinner's laboratory for his behavioral engineering is society itself, but reconstructed by him on the basis of certain preconceived social relations, such that will enable him to carry on his experiments. He first described it in 1948 in his book *Walden Two,* which bears the subtitle "A controversial novel of morality and immorality in a scientifically-shaped Utopia." [24] The social relations in this human laboratory are patterned according to the Marxian principle of the abolition of division of labor, so that each individual may choose the kind of work he wants to do at any time and change it at will. In this laboratory also the means of production are owned collectively, private property is non-existent, and production is only for use, not for exchange. *Walden Two* is thus a cooperative enterprise of free associated individuals. What gives it a utopian character is that it functions in the Marxian dream of a classless society without state controls—the ultimate stage in social relations which, according to Marx, will come as a result of the communist revolution. Skinner, however, does not consider such a revolution as a prerequisite for his new order, for he builds Walden Two on a voluntary basis in a small rural area in the midst of the existing capitalist order in the United States of America. He hopes to propagate his idea by example and by

---

23. Bernard Berelson (editor), *The Behavioral Sciences Today* (Harper Torchbooks, 1964), p. 11.
24. B. F. Skinner, *Walden Two* (Macmillan paperback edition, 1962. Twelfth printing, 1967). This book will be quoted below only by page number in parentheses in my text.

peacefully spreading similar communities throughout the land. At the same time, the Marxian conditions of the abolition of division of labor, private property, and the system of exchange value are fundamental to the success of Skinner's enterprise.

Another important feature of Walden Two is that it is a planned society. Marx's main contention against the bourgeois order is that it is conditioned by a natural process of the division of labor and is not planned according to the needs of free will, which makes it oppressive to the individual producer. With the abolition of this order the individuals will be able to form a free, planned association. Such is the character of the voluntary association of individuals in Walden Two.

Granted then that the prerequisite conditions of the mode of production and social relations exist in Skinner's new order, what are the human factors which enable it to function to the satisfaction of all of its members without state controls? More specifically, what are its interhuman relations which will guarantee freedom to all individuals? In answer to this question, Skinner adopts the method of positive science; that is, he proposes to examine such a social structure in fact and show how its underlying factors lead to success (pp. 179, 192). But this method proves to be a major flaw in his argument. The use of Utopia as a model society may be convincing only to the degree that its underlying principles are consistent within a philosophical frame of reference, whether from a religious, sociological, or similar world view. A Utopia may thus serve as an ideological model, but is not a real case-study for positive science, which presumes to draw its conclusions not from principles but from actual events. The author of *Walden Two* seems to struggle with this incongruity in his entire presentation, as he tries to avoid coming to grips with principles and only enters upon them reluctantly toward the end of his story. His protagonist Frazier simply has no use for them (pp. 192-193, 242, 276-277).

Technology versus Freedom

The fundamental question is, how does man emerge in this Utopia, is he still a human being or just a functional element of a social engine? For when a person submits himself, even voluntarily, to be reshaped by the behavioral engineer, he is in the same helpless situation as when a patient gives his consent to be operated on by a surgeon. In either case, the candidate has no part in the operation of shaping or reshaping himself, with this ominous difference: the surgeon operates only on a given part of the patient's body to suit the patient, whereas the behavioral engineer reshapes him totally to suit a preconceived social plan determined by scientific experimentation. The key issue here is one of scientific determinism against human freedom. Skinner's first principle of his science of human behavior is that freedom as a human potency does not exist.

> If man is free [Frazier asserts] then the technology of behavior is impossible. . . . I deny that freedom exists at all. I must deny it—or my program would be absurd. You can't have a science about a subject matter which hops capriciously about. Perhaps we can never *prove* that man isn't free; it's an assumption. But the increasing success of a science of behavior makes it more and more plausible (pp. 256-257).[25]

Skinner's reliance on natural determinism to prove his case is further complicated by his operational determinism. His Managers in Walden Two are comparable to the mathematical "operators" in the science of physics.[26] His Scientists-Planners first set up a social structure according to predetermined specifications and then seek individual members who will function in line with their pattern. They even go further than the physical scientists because, while the latter try to *find* a formulation for objects under observation that will fit their Operator's specifications, the behavioral

---

25. Cf. the statement by Richard Herrnstein, a former graduate student under Skinner: "The real issue is not, can you be controlled? Of course you can. There's no question about it. The real issue is one of determination and free will." And he adds: "I feel we are machines. I couldn't be a behavioral scientist if I didn't." *The New York Times Magazine,* March 17, 1968, p. 114.

26. Cf. Henry Margenau, *The Nature of Physical Reality* (New York: McGraw-Hill Book Company, 1950), pp. 331-333, concerning operators which determine existence by acting on a function which supplies the object. The physical situation is to find a *function* which will satisfy the *operator,* as specified in advance.

Planners manipulate their objects (the individuals) and *make* them function as prescribed by the Operators. To say that the "increasing success" of this science proves or makes it plausible "that man isn't free" is a case of circular reasoning which is the fate of all scientific theory that ventures to prove its own first principles. Skinner starts with the principle of determinism (no freedom) as a basis for his behavioral science and then uses this science to show that only determinism and not freedom exists. While he may still harbor some misgivings about the procedure of his proof, he is nevertheless convinced that his conclusion cannot be otherwise. At the end of his discourse on the scientific operation of human behavior he states with considered finality: "If science does not confirm the assumption of freedom, initiative, and responsibility in the behavior of the individual, these assumptions will not ultimately be effective either as motivating devices or as goals in the design of culture." [27]

In this deterministic vein, Skinner assumes that what is generally regarded as human freedom has no universal and necessary cause, but is only of a spurious, contingent character. At best, freedom manifests itself as a negative reaction to force or the threat of force used by the state (p. 258). But the state, he holds, is an historically contingent and unnecessary factor in human behavior, which can be negated. Therefore, if the state and its use of force were abolished, the whole question of freedom would cease to exist. The behavioral engineer could then manipulate the individual objects of his scientific society and make them fit into his planned social structure without encountering the conflicts that now exist between the individuals and the state; "in that

---

27. B. F. Skinner, *Science and Human Behavior* (New York: Free Press Paperabck, 1966), p. 449. Skinner, apparently, takes "freedom" to be an assumption or hypothesis that ought to be verified by experimental procedure. In fact, however, his experimentation is conducted on the presupposition that freedom does not exist even in hypothesis. In his later book *Beyond Freedom and Dignity* (New York: Knopf, 1971), Skinner tries to defend his negative stand on human freedom, but his entire argument is a rewording of the behavioral technological vocabulary he used in his other writings. For one who considers man merely as a function of a planned social order, as Skinner does, cannot find in him any kind of autonomous behavior, least of all the autonomy of freedom.

case, *the question of freedom never arises"* (p. 262, author's
ital.).

The determinism underlying this science far surpasses that of
physical science in its unmitigated law of necessity. The physicist
may yet be deterred in his experimentation by the unruly objects
under his observation when they refuse, so to speak, to comply
with his theories. Not so in the case of the behavioral engineer.
There is nothing in his objects to deter him from his course,
because he manipulates them directly and deliberately and makes
them comply. The physicist may still deal with God's creation,
wondering why it sometimes does not behave according to physical
law. The behavioral scientist creates his own objects, such that
they must comply with his scientific rules of behavior. This leads
us to some theological aspects of man's place in Skinner's social
structure.

Technological Application of "Love Your Enemy"

The other fundamental concept of behavioral engineering is of
a religious character, derived from Christian theology but centered on man instead of God. "Frazier's program," we are told in
Walden Two (p. 308), "was essentially a religious movement
freed of any dallying with the supernatural and inspired by a determination to build heaven on earth. What could stop him?" We
hear an echo of this religious overtone as the author approaches
the end of his journey in Utopia. The central personage of the
new society, Frazier, is given the features of Jesus, if not in tem-
perament, at least in physical appearance. In his last encounter
with the works of his hand, he ascends the Throne—a ledge from
which "practically all of Walden Two can be seen." "His beard
made him look a little like Christ. Then . . . he assumed the position of crucifixion." He didn't quite think he was God, but "there's
a curious similarity," he said. With this Calvary-like setting, the
author no doubt thought he had borne witness to a new Gospel
for the salvation of man. The Christ is here not God-Man but
Scientist-Man, who replaces and even surpasses God in the power
of shaping the human kind in his own image. Scanning over his

"creation" through a small telescope, Frazier mused: "I look upon my work and, behold, it is good" (pp. 295-296).

Though eschewing theology, Skinner draws from Christianity the concept of law as it manifests itself in the form of a principle and a method. In principle, he seems to accept Paul's view that law is some kind of source of sin. In Paul's treatment, law is not the real cause of sin but it arouses in counteraction a sense of sinfulness. Since law is not the real cause, it does not go to the root of sin (which does not stem from individual responsibility but from the progenitor of mankind), and cannot therefore lead man to his salvation. Hence, law serves only a temporary purpose and can be dispensed with as a negative force. Skinner regards law in the same negative sense, except that he draws from it the logical conclusion that the abolition of law will dispose of the question of sin, or the will to sin, altogether, a conclusion which Paul struggled to avoid.[28] But Skinner would still agree with Paul that man suffers from weaknesses of anti-social behavior and needs treatment, for which there must be a better method of using power than that offered by the state.[29] Such a method, Skinner holds, is the Christian concept of "love your enemy." Jesus, he says, discovered it by accident, but his followers have not been able to apply it because, like the discovery, the application has been unscientific and hence ineffectual. Not only that, but the whole theological view of creation and salvation has miscarried. God the creator had no plan, and God-Man, His Son, who chanced upon the proper method of salvation, did not possess the proper techniques of implementing it. Now Scientist-Man, who replaces them both, has discovered a technique through scientific experimentation which will carry the method into effect with unfailing success. For, says Frazier, "What is love . . . except another name for the use of positive reinforcement?" (p. 300).

Skinner's translation of "love your enemy" into a scientific method is in itself an interesting piece of behavioral engineering: love as "positive reinforcement" of behavior and hate as "oppres-

---

28. Cf. *Romans*, 3:20-31, 7:4-11.
29. *Walden Two,* p. 104. "Each of us has interests which conflict with the interests of everybody else. That's our original sin, and it can't be helped."

sion." In order to apply this method to a given individual, the Planner must have charge over him, and Walden Two is so planned that anyone joining it (voluntarily, to be sure), must accept its Code of Laws and abide by it. If an individual does not comply, he may as well leave, even if he has nowhere to go. This is clearly a case of punishment for non-compliance, or of hating your enemy. How is this to be reconciled with the intent of the method? That is, how can the behavioral engineer guarantee that his method, because it is based on scientific experimentation, is bound to work in all cases, even on the most flagrant violators of the Code? Skinner tries to persuade us that in banishing the violator he is not actually punishing the person involved, but only the enemy in him. This is what the logician calls a parologism of reasoning, using the word "enemy" in one sense in the major premise and in another sense in the minor premise, thus arriving at a double conclusion of punishing the enemy, yet not punishing him. In Skinner's view of man, the enemy is not the individual but his anti-social behavior for which he is not responsible.[30] "Love your enemy" may thus be applied to the anti-social behavior as the enemy, while hate is meted out to the individual as enemy of the Code. The second meaning of "enemy," to be sure, refers for the time being to those who refuse to join the new society or, having joined, do not abide by its Code of Laws. But when Walden Two shall have extended its economic sway over surrounding areas, if anyone does not want to join it, "All we can do," says Frazier, "is make his personal demise as painless as possible, unless he's intelligent enough to adjust to the new order" (p. 231). "Love your enemy," then, is turned into full hatred.

Power Is the Basis of the New Order

The most important thing about the new order is that it does not eliminate power as a means of government but, on the contrary, enhances it to a degree never dreamed of in pre-scientific culture. "When you have once grasped the principle of positive reinforcement," Frazier asserts, "you can enjoy a sense of un-

---

30. Cf. *Romans*, 7.17. "So then it is no longer I that do it, but sin which dwells within me."

limited power. It's enough to satisfy the thirstiest tyrant" (p. 264). To say then that the power of positive reinforcement is love and not an oppressive force is an argument by reduction. The behavioral engineer reduces man to a modality of pure anti-social behavior which he can then modify through positive reinforcement. In Skinner's words, a person or "a self is simply a device for representing *a functionally unified system of responses.*" [31] By reducing man to a neutral element of the social plan (no personal will, no responsibility, no initiative, no independent thinking), the behavioral engineer may exercise over him unmitigated, absolute power. There is no appeal from it, because the individual is made to want to do what he does or rather what he is supposed to do. Skinner thinks that by negating the negation of human wants (abolishing force and the threat of force) he can liberate those wants. What he actually proposes is to remove the natural human wants from the individual by a behavioral surgical operation and to replace them with the kind of wants the Planner has designed for him. Man becomes a "transplant" of wants. That is how Skinner comes to the paradoxical conclusion that he is going to preserve freedom for individuals while denying its existence to begin with (p. 264).

The planned new order in Walden Two enmeshes man into a "social engine" constructed and kept in operation by the Planners, but eventually to be so perfected that it will run by itself. The Planners too will be negated by the very power which their engines will have generated. When this engineered power becomes absolute, it will be self-generative and render the temporary power of the Planners unnecessary (p. 272). This may come in "the end of days"—a goal to strive for, though never attainable. Just the same, the goal is a social engine that will be turned into a Superorganism with supreme powers (pp. 290, 293).

---

31. *Science and Human Behavior,* p. 285 (author's italics). Cf. *ibid.,* p. 254. Generally speaking, scientific reductionism, whether in psychology, sociology, or behaviorism, has contributed to a concept of man which is derived from his abnormal states—mental illness, criminal acts, biological and physiological deviations. Hence, what was heretofore regarded as abnormal has now become the norm for gauging human relations. This influence is manifest also in commercial (notably in advertising), social, and artistic standards.

This is how materialistic dialectic determines the fate of man when he is confronted by his own technological devices. The modern instruments of production have dehumanized man by depriving him of his intellectual and technical powers as laborer-producer. His special skills of planning, devising, even manufacturing tools and using them have been transferred to the machine. Now the behavioral engineers also propose to turn man's social relations into a machine. In industrial engineering man's productive capacities are taken over by the machine and incorporated as part of the factory system. In behavioral engineering man himself becomes a machine, tooled and geared as part of the social engine. If man is not a free agent, as the behaviorists and some theologians maintain, then there is no hope for his salvation technologically or theologically. No instrument acting on human relations, whether conceived scientifically or mythologically, is self-regulative in purpose and operation for good or for evil. It is up to man as a human being to use the forces he developed in himself and through his technology with responsibility toward fellow-men and other beings. And for that he must know himself as he is: the kind of being who can relate in a free, responsive, and responsible way.

8. MARSHALL McLUHAN: THE DILEMMA OF UNDERSTANDING MEDIA

The Problem and the Method

Man's confrontation with the machine as a medium of communication places him in a dilemma. The more the machine takes over his functions, the more he becomes fragmented and dehumanized. How, then, can the machine become the kind of medium that may help him regain his human qualities and enable him to see himself as a whole? Marshall McLuhan undertakes to resolve this dilemma by posing it as a problem of understanding the nature of the machine as a medium of communication which also entails the knowledge of man as a human being. Man can find himself in reality through the electric machine as a form of communication without regard to content, because change in the social order occurs as pure form rather than content. "Societies," McLuhan writes, "have always been shaped more by the nature of the media by which men communicate than by the content of communication," or, as he puts it in one phrase, "the medium is the message." [32] According to this thesis, modern man has failed to heed the message of the medium, because he does not understand that the medium, as such, is only an extension of his human self; instead, he sees in it some other force which threatens his existence. This happens whenever he faces new technological media which drastically disturb his sense-ratios, as, for example, when the sense of sight is greatly amplified by a new medium. In order to relieve the strain of this amplification, man amputates the offending sense and extends it outside himself as if it were not his own.

When a given sense is thus extended, man forms around it a closed system in which the outside world is perceived through that sense alone or predominantly so. For example, as print technology amplifies our sense of vision, we see the world in visual images, fragmented, systematized, in linear perspective. Our space is visual space; our thinking is in concepts of visual relations. We see the world around us as an outer constellation, not recognizing that it is actually the reflection of our extended sense of vision. McLuhan calls it the print or Gutenberg galaxy. Now the important aspect of this occurrence is that, while the technological medium makes it happen, it does not make man aware of it. The event takes place subliminally and man walks in a daze without being able to find himself.

With the advent of electronic communication, all senses tend to become involved in the medium at once, so that in order to

---

32. Marshall McLuhan and Quentin Fiore, *The Medium Is the Massage. An Inventory of Effects* (New York: Bantam Books, 1967), p. 8. Note on references. The following books by McLuhan will be quoted below by their initials and page numbers in parentheses in my text: MM—*The Medium is the Massage;* UM—*Understanding Media* (A Signet Book, 1964); GG—*The Gutenberg Galaxy. The Making of Typographical Man* (University of Toronto Press. First U.S.A. Edition, 1965. Reprinted 1967); EC—*Exploration in Communication,* edited by Edmund Carpenter and Marshall McLuhan (Boston: Beacon Press, 1966).

protect himself man amputates his entire nervous system and extends it outside himself. That is, he becomes totally self-amputated and, because he doesn't understand the nature of the new medium, he is unaware that what is extended out there is nothing but himself, his own senses; he becomes completely disoriented, numbed, shocked out of existence in reality. What will bring him back to his senses, or rather what will bring his senses back to him, says McLuhan, are the same electric media, for these media can also make one conscious of the unconscious. "With our central nervous system strategically numbed," McLuhan states, "the tasks of conscious awareness and order are transferred to the physical life of man, so that for the first time he has become aware of technology as an extension of his physical body" (UM 56). It means the physical perceptual organs act as protectors of the nervous system. If man would only understand that the technological media are only extensions of these organs, he would see the media as his protectors and would not feign numbness against them. He would not amputate his sense organs and put them out of himself, but would see them and himself in the media and understand their message. "We can, if we choose, think things out before we put them out" (UM 57). However, if man knows only what he perceives through his senses and if his entire nervous system has been extended outside himself into the medium, what agent is there that will shock him out of his numbness or make him conscious of the unconscious? Apparently, it must come from the outside, that is, from the self which entered into the medium. McLuhan therefore advises the extended self to listen carefully to the information coming from the electric medium and thereby cognize himself through its message. Man's liberation from the overwhelming power of the machine will thus come through the machine itself.

If this argument appears unconvincing, as it does to me, McLuhan says it is because the reader has failed to grasp his mode of expression, which presents no argument and does not try to convince. The method of argumentation, he says, belongs to literate, typographical man who writes for a visual-oriented society. Not so his own method which speaks to oral man, molded in the new electric media. In order to convey their dynamism—action

70

rather than conviction—McLuhan has chosen the form of aphorism and disjointed citation of evidence. His praise of Harold Innis' style may well apply to his own manner of writing. Instead of arranging his "evidence in perspective packages of inert, static components . . . he is setting up a mosaic configuration or galaxy for insight. . . . [He] makes no effort to 'spell out' the interrelations between the components in his galaxy. [He does not present a point of view but] insight into causal dynamics" (GG 216-217).

The typical form of oral cultures, McLuhan points out, is the "disjointed sentence" and the aphorism. Therefore, as part of his "mosaic of *The Gutenberg Galaxy*," he needs "the proverb, the maxim, the aphorism, as an indispensable mode of oral society" (GG 103-104). He applies it, in a manner which may be designated as an "extended aphorism," that is, in copious quotations from literary, scientific, and philosophical writings in the history of Western culture as a record of events under observation. In other words, his evidence is culled from the sources of literary, visual-oriented man. His only innovation is in presenting it as a random record of happenings, a do-it-yourself-kit, in which the reader is expected to become "involved" and construe the causes himself.

Although McLuhan disavows the methods of philosophical speculation and scientific experimentation, he brings together a confluence of well-known philosophical and scientific terms and meanings of terms in a modernized art-form which resembles a Pollack painting—pure randomness—aimed at producing a unifying effect.[33] From this effect I shall try to trace his concept of pure cause, from which he ultimately derives his other meanings and to which they all come back.

---

33. To stretch the comparison with modernistic art a little further, many of McLuhan's picture-presentations do not render an organic *Gestalt,* as he claims, but rather a jagged *collage*—cutouts of poetry, science, philosophy, and cultural history pasted together in a pattern of aphorisms—very illuminating at times but not always enlightening. Cf. GG, Introductory Note, opposite page 1. *"The Gutenberg Galaxy* develops a mosaic or field approach to its problems. Such a mosaic image of numerous data and quotations in evidence offers the only practical means of revealing causal operations in history." Cf. *ibid.,* p. 265.

Determinism Through the Electric Machine

McLuhan says he is "far from being deterministic" but rather hopes by his method of observation to "elucidate a principal factor in social changes which may lead to a genuine increase of human autonomy" (GG 3). Yet when he speaks of understanding media he means understanding them as real causes of social change. He has to square the possibility of human autonomy with his theory that man becomes identified with the automated electric medium. To say, as he does, that a technological reversal through electric media will make man aware of himself as a being as a whole is tantamount to saying that the automated machine can produce an autonomous man. This is in essence material determinism, no matter how much McLuhan may try to spiritualize his new medium.

McLuhan makes a qualitative distinction between the mechanical machine, which goes back to the days of Newton, and the automated machine, which is the specific mode of modern electronics. As an extension of man's perceptual faculties, the special feature of the mechanical machine is that it takes over one sense at a time, thus augmenting man's experience in a fragmented manner and disturbing the sense ratio of his natural faculties. This, for example, takes place in the visual mode of the Gutenberg type of technology. The visual sense ordinarily functions together with all other senses in an interplay of experiences synthesized by the tactile sense, keeping mind and body in equilibrium. But when the visual sense by itself is outered into the mechanical medium, the ratio of the senses gets out of balance, and the externalized visual sense is beheld as a closed-in fragment of man alienated from his self. His imagination or synthesizing factor is broken, and when he looks at the world through the alienated sense, he himself becomes like it, fragmented into many selves following each other in succession (GG 265-266). It means that man is divided between himself and his outered sense which has been taken over by the medium, and he cannot find himself as a whole in either. This takes place subliminally. In order to preserve his identity and integrity, man amputates the offended sense, sinks into a state of somnambulism, and remains unconscious of its effects. Unless this outered closed-in system is broken, it may become the most serious menace to the human self. On the other hand, the electric medium takes over all senses simultaneously and can therefore return them to man in a unifying experience, in total synthesis, making him aware of himself as a whole, or making him conscious of his unconscious self-extension. What exactly are the powers of this new medium of communication, and what are the failings of the old medium in this respect?

Perhaps we ought to ask first, what exactly is man expected to bring to his consciousness in order to save himself from disaster, and why does the mechanical machine stand in his way or is at best unable to help him? We must remember that McLuhan, in agreement with physical and biological sciences, observes not things but relations between things. That is, he observes the *medium* or mediator itself and hopes to find in it the pure cause. But then he runs into the problem of scepticism which Hume faced when he discovered that mere sequence does not reveal causality. Man, who seeks to communicate with the world, must be able to apprehend its causes, and if he finds that he has no way of attaining them, he falls into despair. This, I presume, is McLuhan's concern about the disaster man is facing in his state of somnambulism induced by the Gutenberg galaxy. By looking at things through his amputated visual faculty, outered by the mechanical machine, man sees the world as an order of spatio-temporal succession, but not its connective causes; and since the medium itself is the cause, man cannot perceive it as an entity when it operates in successive visual steps. This, says McLuhan, has been overcome by the modern media which operate instantaneously and thus render causality empirically perceivable. The situation now is that,

> as David Hume showed in the eighteenth century, there is no principle of causality in a mere sequence. That one thing follows another accounts for nothing. . . . So the greatest of all reversals occurred with electricity, that ended sequence by making things instant. With instant speed the causes of things began to emerge to awareness again, as they had not done with things in sequence and in concatenation accordingly (UM 27).

73

Instantaneous awareness, McLuhan holds, is made possible especially through the medium of television, as it involves man in its "mesh by a convulsive sensuous participation that is profoundly kinetic, because tactility is the interplay of the senses, rather than isolated contact of skin with object" (UM 273). But most important, TV is able to accomplish unification because it operates as a massive extension of man's central nervous system and thus develops him "in a daily session of synesthesia" (UM 275). The same effect is obtained through the automated machine and its instant information. This is the age of information, McLuhan reminds us, meaning that work and subject-matter are reduced to a system of transmission, processing, and utilization of information, all of which occur simultaneously through automation. Work is no longer a specialized function of the individual but a universal process of the medium, extending like the nervous system over a global network and bringing man into a single unified field of experience. It is an organic process involving man as a whole and the world as a whole without being affected by the content on which it operates, that is, without affecting man as subject or producer. "Energy and production now tend to fuse with information . . ." (UM 304). Yet it involves man's faculties insofar as they are extended into the medium, for "the age of information demands the simultaneous use of all our faculties" (UM 301).

If we reformulate the problem of determinism *versus* freedom stated above, we may now ask, is man entirely conditioned by his environment or does he have an autonomous role in shaping it as well as his own behavior? McLuhan proposes to establish man's autonomy through automation. When he comes to the end of *The Medium Is the Massage,* he has a member of the young generation, to whom he presumably addresses the "message," explain to his Dad emphatically (author's italics):

> *"You see, Dad, Professor McLuhan says the environment that man creates becomes his medium for defining his role in it. The invention of type created linear, or sequential, thought, separating thought from action. Now, with TV and folk singing, thought and action are closer and social involvement is greater. We again live in a village. Get it?"* (MM 157).

74

Yes, we get it; but it ain't necessarily so! It might appear from the message that man himself decides his interhuman relations coming through the medium. That is, since he produces the technological media which are only extensions of himself, and since these media *are* his environment, whatever participating role this environment assigns to him subsequently is nothing but the role which he has created for himself. But all this self-determination is only an illusion, for it is the electric machine through its superior powers that determines man's conduct by involving him against his will, as it disregards the content of the message. In human affairs it is content that is of paramount importance, insofar as it is decided by man himself, who becomes involved in it of his own accord.

Admittedly, McLuhan assures us that man as a whole is involved in the electric medium: "Television demands participation and involvement in depth of the whole being. . . . It engages you." And he notes: "Perhaps this is why so many people feel that their identity has been threatened" (MM 125). He passes over this notation without getting its message. Of course, they feel threatened, because, first, the involvement is against their will, and, second, its tendency is to fuse them with something which is not-human, be that a thing or a collective, so-called modernized village brought home to them by TV. Indeed, McLuhan drives his full message home when he declares: "The new media are not ways of relating us to the old 'real' world; they *are* the real world, and they reshape what remains of the old world at will" (EC 182). If these electric media should ever become the real world, man would have good reason to be frightened by them. To be assigned a *role* can be as oppressive as to be assigned a *goal,* as long as one is drawn into it against his will by an outside force. It is of little consolation to man to be told that that force is actually an extension of himself and that he should therefore not be a Narcissus and go numb because he thinks it is not himself. The superior power McLuhan ascribes to the electric medium rests on the fallacy of reciprocal reduction. First he reduces man to an electric model which is supposed to function organically as if it were a human nervous system, then he reduces the model back to an extension of the nervous system as it actually functions

75

organically. No wonder man is numbed by this extension, for he does not recognize himself as man.

A Happening in Vanishing Space

McLuhan ascribes organic unity to the instantaneous electric medium because it functions as an organized whole and seemingly overcomes space and time. As he conceives it, "ours is a brand-new world of allatonceness. 'Time' has ceased, 'space' has vanished. We now live in a global village . . . a simultaneous happening" (MM 63). Now in the scientific account of what happens in electronics, space does not vanish. That is, the principle of spatial separation and fragmentation has not been overcome, and organic unity has not been achieved in electric media. What does happen is that distance, which is the basic concept of modern physics, is shortened to such an extent that it becomes immeasurably small, and for purposes of calculation, movement over such a distance is regarded as simultaneous.[34] But happenings in the modern four-dimensional world are neither instantaneous nor simultaneous, as the universe is still very much spatio-temporal in character and conception. It is even more so in its conception through the principle of relativity, according to which simultaneity at different places is impossible.[35] Time and space have not abdicated. On the contrary, they have conspired to transform the world more strictly into their own image, and space has taken the upper hand in this enterprise. Because space does not tolerate all-at-onceness, it has converted time into its own mode of gauging reality, so that they can now both coordinate their efforts to lend all happenings, far and near, an extended existence.[36]

---

34. Cf. Leon Brillouin, "The Problem of Very Small Distances," in his *Science and Information Theory* (New York: Academic Press, 1967), pp. 321ff.

35. Cf. Mortimer Taube, *Computers and Common Sense* (New York: Columbia University Press, 1961), p. 86. See above, chapter 5, "The Reality of Distance."

36. Cf. Charles Porteus Steinmetz, *Four Lectures on Relativity and Space* (New York: Dover Edition, 1967), pp. 32-34. A four-dimensional time-space can be brought under one coordinate system by expressing both time and space in terms of units of distance. Cf. G. J. Whitrow, *The Natural Philosophy of Time* (Harper Torchbooks,

In all our experiences separateness is a prevailing factor. Distance has been overcome only in the sense that we cannot talk about it when we cannot measure it; but its effects on man's sensibility have not been eliminated. There is spatial separateness in a mosaic pattern as much as in linear succession. If one chooses to pay attention only to certain parts of the pattern, neglecting the rest, the pattern will not appear as a unified whole. Automation, contrary to McLuhan's contention, is as much subject to the principle of fragmentation and separation as are mechanical operations (cf. UM 302). What may give the automated pattern its unity is man's unifying faculties and not those of the medium.[37] And even that unity is at best an organized unity, not an organic one, unless the thing communicated with is an organic unity in its own right. Hence, the fact that the electric medium functions as an *organized* unit does not render it an *organic* whole. The two concepts are not the same, and to equate them, as McLuhan does, is to confuse the "organic" with the "organized." This fallacy calls for some further clearance, in view of its central role in this context.

According to McLuhan, "Organic interdependence means that disruption of any part of the organism can prove fatal to the whole" (UM 306). This does not say what kind of interdependence constitutes an organic function. If the disruption of any part

---

1963), pp. 3f., on "the tendency to subordinate the temporal to the spatial" and its historical background in the last century.

37. Cf. Michael Polanyi, "Experience and the Perception of Pattern," *The Modeling of Mind,* edited by Kenneth M. Sayre and Frederick J. Crosson (New York: A Clarion Book, 1968), p. 210. "So we see that while communication theory does make the distinctiveness of certain patterns vividly explicit, it brings out also clearly that this quality is the result of an informal act of our own." Cf. Arthur Koestler, *The Ghost in the Machine* (New York: The Macmillan Company, 1967), p. 203-204, on man's independent choice of reaction. He cites the neurologist Wilder Penfield, who comments on his own experiments as follows: "Behind the 'brain action' of one hemisphere was the patient's mind. Behind the action of the other hemisphere was the electrode. . . . There are, as you see, many demonstrable mechanisms [in the brain]. They work for the purposes of the mind automatically when called upon. . . . But what agency is it that calls upon these mechanisms, choosing one rather than another? . . . To declare that these two things are one does not make them so."

proves fatal to the whole, it is characteristic of a machine rather than of a living organism. Any key bolt removed from an airplane, or any band disrupted in an automaton, will put one as well as the other entirely out of commission. This is because the whole of the machine is equivalent to the sum of its parts, and if any part is removed, the machine can no longer function as a whole.[38] This is true of the mechanical as well as the electric machine; qualitatively, the kind of information transmitted by one does not differ from that of the other.[39] But an organic whole is always more than the sum of its parts. Hence, even if one part is removed, the organism continues to function as a whole, other parts compensating for the one removed. That is, the main characteristic of an organic unit is that its parts depend on the whole, and not the other way around.

Pure Information: Real or Simulated Cause

The information transmitted by the electric media is a product of the modern mathematical structure of the world, and to this extent it may well dispense with content. As Bertrand Russell puts it enigmatically, "Thus mathematics may be defined as the subject in which we never know what we are talking about, nor whether what we are saying is true." [40] The emphasis is, of course, on the "what," meaning the content. Electric information does not deal with content but is conceived as a force that causes a change of action, or rather reaction, in an organic or inorganic body

---

38. Cf. *The Modeling of Mind,* pp. 269-270. For a machine to be able to do more than what it was modeled to do, it must have another part added to it, and it thus becomes a different machine.

39. It is interesting to note that in modern physics both mechanical and electric energy are termed "high grade energy," as compared with heat which is "low grade energy." Since the grade of energy corresponds to negative entropy, which is related to information, the mechanical and electric machines transmit the same grade of information. Cf. Brillouin, *op. cit.,* pp. 114, 152ff., and Mortimer Taube, *op. cit.,* p. 74, on the lack of a significant distinction between mechanical and electric machines as exemplified in digital computers of both types.

40. Bertrand Russell, *Mysticism and Logic* (London, 1917; New York: Anchor Books, n.d.), p. 71.

which takes in the information and puts it out. What does this information do generally?

Conceived scientifically as a concept of pure causality (since content is left out of account), its function is to restore order out of disorder. This gives it universal scope, for regardless of the content or source of the disorder, information acts promptly to rectify it. If we designate disorder as entropy, in accordance with the second law of thermodynamics, the function of information is that of negative entropy or negentropy. Both are measured in terms of entropy units and expressed in the same physico-mathematical formulation.[41] Now the question is, does information act as a real force, the same as other forces do in our experiences in nature, or is it merely a mathematical-statistical formulation, an abstraction of a complex of factors, the operation of which defies true knowledge? To put it in terms of man's reaction to electric media, the question is, does man *experience* the information of these media the same as he experiences other forces in everyday life, consciously or unconsciously?[42] Is the information "fed" to man through the media a special kind of diet which produces organic reactions? As Anatol Rapoport, a leading scientist in this field, states the problem: We know that food is used as a source of heat, locomotion, and mechanical energy for growth, all of which are constantly dissipated and restored by the organism. "Can it be," he asks, "that besides energy in the form of food and sunlight, organisms also feed on something called 'information,' which serves to *restore the order*. . . ?" If we take the mathematical equivalence between entropy and information as actual, how does the organism convert one into the other?

---

41. Cf. Brillouin, *op. cit.*, p. 3. See also p. 116 on the use of the term negentropy and its application in mechanical and electric systems.

42. On the notion of experiencing statistical forces, a comment by P. W. Bridgman is worth noting: "It seems to me that the extrapolation we make in statistical mechanics is really not an extrapolation of everyday experience, but of the mathematics of everyday experience." See his *Nature of Thermodynamics* (Harper Torchbooks, 1961), p. 159. Cf. Brillouin, *op. cit.*, pp. 152f., on the statistical basis of the definition of information in its relation "to the physical entropy of thermodynamics."

If there is such a conversion factor, how do the information receiving, information transmitting, and information storing organs operate to convert information into negative entropy or its concomitant "free energy" and, perhaps, vice versa?[43]

Technology leaves this question wide open; but humanism, looking through the gap, sees it in a different galaxy. What strikes us in this entire complexity of the principle of information as a function of restoring order out of chaos is its dialectic character of negation of a negation, conceived logico-mathematically. The negative factor of entropy, as "a measure of disorder in a physical system," is negated by information as a quantitative expression of the restoration of order; one quantity is negated by another quantity. Man, who is a qualitative being, cannot be restored to his human self through this kind of dialectic.

The Message of Negation

In Goethe's *Faust*, Mephistopheles introduces himself to man, whose soul he is about to ensnare, by saying: *Ich bin der Geist der stets verneint*—"I am the spirit that always negates." Coming from the devil, it is high comedy, because the devil cannot be tragic. But when Faust begins to play the role of negator, he becomes a tragic figure. And this is Western man's Faustian tragedy. From the days of Hesiod's mythical *Chaos* and Plato's *mē-ón,* through Hegel's ideal and Marx's material *antithesis,* to our own day of atomic *antimatter* and thermodynamic *entropy,* the negations have always beckoned to man out of the abyss, luring him toward the hidden, but threatening to engulf him. And man has always struggled to keep his balance on the edge of the precipice by negating the negations. McLuhan's suggestion that man now create his environment out of pure information of the electric media is just another desperate attempt on the part of *homo sapiens* to create his real world out of nothing—a feat reserved in the past only for the Divine Creator. For when man, who is

---

43. Anatol Rapoport, "Technological Models of the Nervous System," *The Modeling of Mind*, p. 37.

himself but a creature of that primordial nothing, ventures to recreate himself and the world out of it, he can only negate the negation.

9. ALDOUS HUXLEY: SELF-TRANSCENDENCE THROUGH DRUGS

With some reservations, Aldous Huxley agrees with Rousseau that man's individuality is his natural state of being and that his social restraints are imposed on him by civilization.[44] But, unlike Rousseau, he does not seek to sublimate the social order into a higher moral state but rather wants to help the individual escape it into a superhuman fusion with the All by propelling him toward the highest condition of bliss, which, he says, can be attained through the use of mescaline. Huxley bears witness to the efficacy of this drug from personal experience.[45] Half an hour after he had had an appropriate dose of it, he "became aware of a slow dance of golden lights." He looked at ordinary objects in his room, a vase of flowers, the legs of a table or a chair, books on the shelves, his flannel trousers. They lost their spatial appearance. His "mind was perceiving the world in terms of other than spatial categories." The point is that the category of space was not abolished but lost its predominance, and that there was "an even more complete indifference to time." He felt he saw in all those things, in their objective reality, an Is-ness, "a transcendence that was yet eternal life, a perceptual perishing that was at the same time pure Being. . . ."[46]

---

44. Aldous Huxley, *Brave New World Revisited* (New York: Harper & Brothers Publishers, 1958), pp. 29-30. "Biologically speaking, man is a moderately gregarious not completely social animal." Civilization transformed the primitive human packs into "an analogue of . . . the social insects' organic communities." Rousseau, it will be recalled, denied even gregariousness to natural man.

45. Aldous Huxley, "The Door of Perception," *Collected Essays* (Harper & Brothers Publishers, 1959), pp. 327-336. Mescaline, it is noted there, is an alkaloid isolated from a desert cactus and can also be synthesized. The root of this cactus, called peyote, was eaten at primitive religious rites by Indians in Mexico and the American Southwest. Taken in suitable doses it changes consciousness, yet is not toxic.

46. *Ibid.*, pp. 329-330.

Such is the description of Huxley's vision under the influence of mescaline when his eyes responded to something of another order of reality. Then comes his interpretation of the vision as a metaphysical identification of the individual with the All. When he looked at the legs of the chair he felt "being them," or, more accurately, being his "Not-self in the Not-self which was the chair." It was an absorption of the individual self into the Not-self, as taught in Buddhist teachings, to which he refers. It is rather significant that he became unaware of persons around him. As he explains it, his identification with the Not-self of things left no room for persons, who are selves, for he "was now a Not-self, simultaneously perceiving and being the Not-self of the things around me." He was in a state of complete release from his surrounding world, especially from responsibility toward fellow men, which left him in "no state," so that his own self and other selves became irrelevant. He saw "the Absolute in the folds of a pair of flannel trousers!" [47]

Huxley's interpretation of his vision under the influence of the drug is a philosophy of individualism raised to its ultimate possibility of escaping everyday reality and all interhuman communication. Such an escape by means of a technological device is nothing but an attempt to save the individual from his own individuality to the point where the human element, even as individual, becomes non-existent. While in the trance, Huxley could not tolerate even the semblance of a real person which was presented to him in the self-portrait of Cézanne. "For relief," he says, "I turned back to the folds of my trousers," insisting "these are the sort of things one ought to look at." "The nearest approach to this," he further notes, "would be a Vermeer . . . the greatest painter of human still lives. . . ." [48] Yes, "still lives" but not active human lives. Huxley overlooks here the reality, which he does not deny

---

47. *Ibid.*, pp. 333-334.
48. *Ibid.*, p. 334. In a sober moment Huxley made a contrary statement about the drug: "Peyote produces self-transcendence in two ways—it introduces the taker into the other world of visionary experience, and it gives him a sense of solidarity with his fellow worshippers." Cf. *ibid.*, "Drugs That Shape Men's Minds," p. 343. Perhaps the sense of fellowship is due to the situation of worship rather than

elsewhere, that the individual is a human being only to the extent that he is in active interrelationship with other human beings.[49]

10. R. E. L. MASTERS AND JEAN HOUSTON: PSYCHEDELIC SELF-REALIZATION

While Huxley tries to wed the drug experience to Eastern mysticism, R. E. L. Masters and Jean Houston keep it mostly on a scientific plane of discourse within the confines of Western civilization. Over a period of fifteen years, these two investigators have piled up what they consider to be a substantial body of evidence from two hundred and six of their own cases and from many others on a wide range of psychedelic experiences. Though they claim to have done only "pioneering" work of a "crude and tentative" nature, they nevertheless feel that psychedelic drugs have brought about "a revolution in the study of mind." [50] They are also convinced that the drug-state affords a positive transformation of person and, in certain limited cases, an authentic religious experience described as a "confrontation with God," which "does have the power to transform" (p. 301).

In recent studies of man's relation to his environment, an attempt has been made to reconcile the conflict between psychology and technology by placing them both within a unified science. But no matter how well adjusted the two may appear within a dynamic or organic theory of physical reality, man cannot be reduced to a composite of elements taken from his environment. Consequently, any technological device contrived to help him realize himself as a human being must remain alien to his nature. His self-realization must come mainly from within himself. This view, which is predominant among psychologists, is now being challenged by experimenters with the use of drugs, who claim

---

to a situationlessness induced by mescaline. As Huxley remarks later in the same essay (p. 344), the drug is "neither necessary nor sufficient for salvation," but can help those who need it.

49. "What Can Be Done?" *Brave New World Revisited,* ch. xii.

50. R. E. L. Masters and Jean Houston, *The Varieties of Psychedelic Experience* (New York: Holt, Rinehart and Winston, 1966), pp. 314, 316. This book will be referred to below as *The Varieties* and will be quoted only by page number in parentheses in my text.

that the drug-state they are able to induce puts man in a condition similar to the psychic state revealed in psychoanalysis, but with far greater efficacy than the latter. At the same time, their theories are derived from well-known schools of psychology, and it appears that the authors of *The Varieties* have derived their views from the school of Carl G. Jung. Although it is not my purpose to deal with this school, as such, I will sketch its fundamental theses in order to establish the psychological principles and goal which underlie the psychedelic experiments.

On the psychological level, the question is, what psychic state will help man to relate himself to the world around him and to find his place in it? According to Carl G. Jung and his school, it is the state of mind when man feels integrated as a human being within himself that enables him to relate to the outside most effectively and with greatest satisfaction. Man's goal in life is to realize himself as man. But this goal, Jung teaches, lies entirely within the individual human psyche, which is by nature a dual entity consisting of innerly conflicting opposites, such as male and female, good and bad, or, in general, its bright and dark sides. The origin of this duality remains unknown, yet it is embedded in man's unconscious and personified through its all-embracing Self as the innermost nucleus of the psyche. Its mode of expression is the dream and its language the symbol.[51] Man's self-realization is a striving to overcome his duality through a process of becoming conscious of the true nature of the Self. That is, by becoming aware of the two opposite aspects of the Self and its dual "relatedness to the surroundings," man can integrate its bright and dark sides into his being-as-a-whole and face the outer world in its brightness as well as its darkness.[52] The guiding and protecting spirit in this process is the unconscious, which has the faculty of producing symbols manifested in dreams. The

---

51. Cf. Carl G. Jung, "Approaching the Unconscious," *Man and His Symbols*. Edited by Carl G. Jung (New York: Dell Publishing Co., 1964), p. 3. By symbol Jung means "a term, a name or even a picture that may be familiar in daily life, yet that possesses specific connotations in addition to its conventional and obvious meaning." In contrast, a "sign is always less than the concept it represents," or when applied to things, "signs . . . do no more than denote the objects to which they are attached."

dreams always carry some message to man's consciousness called the Ego, and it is for the latter to heed the message and understand, that is interpret, its import. The main thing is that "the unconscious and the conscious must be integrally connected and thus move on parallel lines. If they are split apart or 'dissociated,' psychological disturbance follows." [53]

This entire drama of self-realization is played out or, as Jung would say, "lived out" in the psyche of each individual, who is the only human reality. It is "the process of individuation" in which one grows to maturity. As long as it works only subliminally in the unconscious, man is not yet the integrated human being that he is destined to be. It is when the conscious ego pays attention to its guiding "partner," the unconscious, that the human totality is realized through the proper relation with the Self. As Marie-Louise von Franz puts it, "It is the ego that seems to light up the entire system, allowing it to become conscious and thus be realized." [54] Yet the conscious ego can only carry out the demands of the unconscious Self without as much as being able to influence it, not to speak of changing its course.

This lofty goal of man—his self-realization as a human being-as-a-whole—is to give meaning to his life, save him from "a terrible emptiness and boredom," with which he is afflicted in this technological wonder-world. We can readily accept this goal as worthy of our highest aspiration, but we may question the transcendental powers that Jungian psychology ascribes to the faculty of individual unconsciousness to guide each of us in this direction inexorably, all alone. Jung is undoubtedly the greatest interpreter of the age of Enlightenment insofar as man strives to realize himself as an individual with the aid of the science of psychology. "The individuation process," which he and his followers find in man's growth to maturity, expresses the passion for individualism that has characterized our era since its inception. Now all the powers of this passion are placed in the individual psyche, which assumes both a mystic and mythical character. The psychologist

---

52. Cf. *ibid.*, p. 17.
53. *Ibid.*, p. 37.
54. M-L von Franz, "The Process of Individuation," *Man and His Symbols*, p. 163. See also pp. 215, 221, 228.

may play only the role of interpreter of the messages sent to man by his unconscious Self through the symbols of dreams; but the all-powerful mediator in this process is the Self or its "shadow," in whatever form it may choose to appear.[55]

Based on this fabric of mythical and mystic symbolism, the experimenters in psychedelic drugs propose to substitute a technological device for the methods used by the practitioners of psychology. This, in the final analysis, is what the authors of *The Varieties* may claim as their major accomplishments. "Psychedelic" means mind-manifestation, as such, and its application as a method is another attempt to reconcile psychology with technology by inducing the psyche to reveal its mysteries through a technological contrivance, in this case, through the use of a drug. As the authors state at the very outset of their book, they "hope to make entirely credible [their] belief that the psychedelic drugs afford the best access yet to the contents and processes of the human mind" (p. 3, also p. 314).

Creating a Psychedelic World

Like Jungian dream analysis, the drug-state experiment is purposive, teleological, hence directional, except that in the former the goal is subliminal and revealed to consciousness by the unconscious Self, whereas in the latter it is planned in advance by the subject and his guide. In both, the experience is enacted in a world of symbols, but in the former the symbols are produced in natural dreams, whereas in the latter they are induced by a drug potion. Both maintain that the mind has the faculty of producing symbols which may be interpreted as messages of personal significance to the life of the individual, but in the one the interpretation

---

55. *Ibid.*, pp. 90, 159, 220, On the "shadow" see pp. 110-112. In his book *The Undivided Self* (Translated from the German by F. C. Hull. A Mentor Book, 1958), C. G. Jung makes a passionate plea for the individuation of man through a return to the origin of religion which, he says, is embodied instinctively in the unconscious. Neither the organized state nor the institutional church can help man heal the split in his psyche, which is at the root of his present crisis. This can be done only by the psychiatrists, that is, by those individuals who understand the human psyche and are able and willing to lead out of the crisis.

flows entirely out of the phenomena which appear to the subject in his dream, while in the other it comes from actual things placed by design in his physical surrounding.[56] Of decisive importance in the drug-state experiment are the experimenter's concept of mind and the goal set by him and the subject prior to the session. And since the experimenter chooses only subjects above average intelligence (mostly college graduates and with higher academic degrees), the subject's concept of mind and his preconceived ideas of himself and mankind also play a decisive role in the outcome of the session.

The drug-state experience, though involving sensory and emotional disturbances, seems to act itself out on the ideational level; symbols are turned into ideas mostly related to current social and scientific concepts as well as to mystic and mythical notions entertained by the subject in the past. It appears that the main purpose of inducing a psychedelic state is to enable the subject to play with his ideas more freely than he would under normal conditions. The drug removes his perceptual and conceptual inhibitions and lets his imagination roam all over the wide universe, even in its innermost crevices, in which he finds the desired symbols of his own personality. But the universe he thus envisages and his personal relationships with it are nothing but conglomerates of his own fancies, rather than confrontations with reality in everyday life. For the experimenters insist that before the session the subject must be willing "to suspend or abandon his ordinary, everyday ways of thinking and 'looking at things.' " He must relinquish his usual controls in advance (pp. 139, 177). In the drug-state, then, "real world" categories fall away and the subject moves in the midst of phenomena which are creatures of his psychedelic world. There, of course, he can see what he wants to see, even though actually it may be otherwise (p. 152).[57]

---

56. For example, in a given psychedelic session, the guide puts a stone into the hand of the subject and the latter, identifying himself with this object, feels that "it matters" and finds that "in the heart of creation I . . . matter." Cf. *The Varieties*, pp. 146-147. In a case of Jungian psychoanalysis, "the dark oval stone" appeared in the subject's dream, and "probably symbolizes the dreamer's innermost being, his true personality." Cf. *Man and His Symbols*, p. 217.

57. Cf. *ibid.*, pp. 112-113, on the subject's LSD empathy with his female friend, while she was actually rejecting him.

The authors of *The Varieties* do not subscribe to all esoteric notions which have grown around the Psychedelic Movement, but interpret their own experiments and other cases as "depth-sounding" of the human mind. It is obvious from what has already been described here that the drug itself (peyote and mostly LSD which were used by the experimenters) acts only as an opener of portals to the deeper levels of the psyche. What do we find upon entering those levels? How deep may one go, and can the subject make the journey by himself or only with the aid of a guide? If the latter is the case, to what extent does the guide determine the goal to be sought, or chart the road to be taken? Since the ultimate goal is individual self-realization, what does one realize while in the drug-state and what is left when one steps out of it? Before these questions may be answered by the results of the experiments, we must look into the theoretical assumptions about the human mind on which these experiments are based.

The authors posit four faculties of the human psyche, each built on top of the other in an ascending order of increased potency, the deepest being all-embracing and the most potent of all. These levels are identified as sensory, recollective-analytic, symbolic, and integral (p. 142). In traditional psychology, they correspond roughly to the faculties of sensation, conception, imagination, and higher intuition. The authors assume that in natural everyday experience each level acts as a sort of shield or inhibiting layer on the one below it and thus hinders man from utilizing all his faculties to his best advantage. The lower, that is, the more important levels, may only seep through the ones above them, and when they appear on the surface of the sensory level they are enfeebled by the latter's spatio-temporal vision of reality. Without the benefit of the deeper faculties, especially the integral one, man finds himself fragmented, dissociated and disoriented in relation to his own self, to fellow men, and to things in general. The most pernicious influence in this respect comes from the sensory and recollective-analytic levels, which are the hardest to break through in everyday experience. Man's goal in life, therefore, is to realize himself as a human being-as-a-whole in whom all faculties are coordinated and act in full harmony in relation to reality. This may be attained in large measure at the symbolic stage, but can

88

be consummated only with the aid of the integral faculty. These, in substance, are the basic assumptions of the depth-sounding approach, as it appears from the authors' analysis and interpretation of their own cases and the records of others.

We said earlier that the word "psychedelic" means mind-manifestation, and we can see now how this entire *schema* is patterned after Plato's famous "divided line" between the two lower sensible faculties and the two higher noetic ones, as described in the *Republic* (Book vi). The goal is also the same as Plato's, namely, to free man from the chains of the shadowy fragmentation of the "things of the eye" and enable him to penetrate the realm of Ideas or the "things of the mind." Finally, the authors' concept of the human self is also derived from Plato's view that man is essentially pure mind held in chains by his body. Be this as it may, the fundamental issue before our psychedelic experimenters is whether the drug potion can raise man to his purely spiritual state and bring him in direct communication with absolute spirit, which the experimenters set as his ultimate goal of self-realization.

The Main Factors of Psychedelic Experience

There are three factors in the induction of the drug-state, namely, the subject, the guide, and the setting of the session. The drug has only a catalytic function, that is, to help the subject break up one layer after another as he decides to descend to the deeper levels. What, then, produces self-realization? The answer is to be sought in all three factors working jointly. We shall consider the GUIDE first, because he is the chief agent in determining more elements in the entire process than the authors may be willing to admit. His personal qualifications are stringent in character, mental and emotional stability, educational and cultural background, and in training for his specific tasks in the psychedelic session. He is comparable to the ancient priest, shaman, seer, or sybil, and his powers are described as God-like (pp. 93, 130). While he must be very careful not to dominate the situation, he must gain the subject's fullest confidence not only as to his technical ability but also as to his wisdom and unerring capacity to lead the subject to his desired goal. Even more than the drug, the guide actually induces the subject to pierce through the crusts of the various levels and to unveil the hidden signs of the psychedelic world. Most important to the outcome of the session is the choice of subject and his preparation for the session which are determined entirely by the guide; if he errs in these two functions, he has to abandon the session (p. 138).

THE SUBJECT, as stated, is chosen for his suitability to the experiment. He must be of sound mind and body, above average intelligence, with no mental illness or existing psychotic disturbance, and not be involved in major conflicts for the duration of the session. He is usually a person able to articulate his ideas with ease and some literary skill. Those actually selected by the experimenters included many "persons of superior intelligence and considerable education. Moreover, many were educators, clergymen, attorneys, and other such persons whose day-to-day work demands a fairly high degree of verbal facility" (p. 7). The subject ostensibly sets his own goal, but actually he and the guide agree on it in advance, and he rarely determines the course of the session in detail. Furthermore, the guide may also have other goals unknown to the subject which enter into the structuring of the session (pp. 140-141).

THE SETTING for the psychedelic experience, its natural surroundings, the cultural and artistic milieu, certain objects for arousing desirable perceptual and ideational reactions and for a relaxed, comfortable atmosphere are all carefully planned by the guide in advance. Some objects used for acclimatization to the psychedelic condition are pictures, flowers, music, sea shells, stones, fruits and vegetables, and especially the "cork as substance." These are all chosen with a view to producing eidetic images, arousing symbolic, mythical ideas, and generally getting the subject to step out of his everyday manner of looking at things. "Such a major role does the physical environment play in determining the course of a subject's experience that it would be difficult to overemphasize the need for this objective climate to be favorable" (p. 136). In the course of the session the guide may rearrange the setting or introduce new things in order to encourage the subject to proceed toward his pre-determined goal. The determinate character of the setting is further emphasized by the authors' insistence that the guide must know in advance the goals as well as the techniques he is going to employ, and he must reexamine the goals during the session and stress those he considers worthwhile (p. 140).

Encounter with the Self, No Actual Other

All three factors—the guide, the subject, and the setting—work together toward the end of releasing man from his sensory and recollective ties with things around him in everyday life so that he may descend to the deeper level of symbolism and from there still deeper to the level of integration. The authors maintain that, as the subject passes through the first two stages of the psychedelic experience, he does not really discard his perceptual awareness but incorporates it into the deeper stages in a purified form as "a cumulative expansion of insights." He goes through "a process of phenomenological progression through the sensory, recollective-analytic and symbolic levels before passing into the integral" (p. 267). In the final stage he reaches "the deep integral level wherein lies the possibility of confrontation with a Presence variously described as God, Spirit, Ground . . . or Fundamental Reality" (p. 266). This confrontation is designated as a self-transformation through an "authentic religious experience." But this is so only insofar as the guide, who mediates the process (although he says he does not go along on the integral level), sets the stage and interprets the phenomena, and to the extent that the subject has agreed in advance and at every stage to allow himself to be taken on the journey (p. 150).[58]

The first goal which the guide sets for the subject is to shed

---

58. The guide's "activity stops on the threshold of the *integral* level and the subject experiences the final integration unassisted and alone." Yet, the guide urges the subject repeatedly to enter the "authentic rligious experience" with promptings such as, "Go down still deeper," "down to a level where you might meet God," or suggests that the Devil may have no power over the subject (p. 290). When the subject, already on that level, once felt that God withdrew in disgust, the guide urged again, "Go back and tell God you are sorry." Then, the guide reported, the subject "experienced the Presence of God for the second time, and on this occasion with much greater emotion than before" (p. 294).

his ordinary sensory-perceptive and analytic faculties which are considered a hindrance on his way to the deeper levels. The effect of the drug is to *discredit* the sensory-rational world by completely distorting it and thus prepare the ground "for the free psyche to function in such a way as to result in beneficial transformation and self-realization of the individual" (p. 152). The authors do not explain how this shedding of the first two faculties may be reconciled with their contention that these faculties are incorporated in the subject's experience on the deeper levels, unless they mean to imply that they become so purified of the spatio-temporal taint that they transform themselves into some spiritual form. But to continue with the descent, when the subject "lets go" of the real world, he is thrown entirely on his own inner "self" without communication with an actual other, such as he may encounter in normal everyday life. The guide does not even attempt to take the place of that "other"; he merely serves as a prompter or stimulator to get the subject deeper and deeper into his own psyche. It is noteworthy that in the drug-state the subject reacts best to things rather than to persons around him, for things, particularly those placed in his surroundings by the guide, readily lend themselves to a transformation into the kind of symbols the subject desires to see. He thus moves in a new world of his own creation, or presumably so, constructed out of symbols which are acted out in his individual psyche. Self-realization means here the Self realizing himself by becoming a total individual within himself. His confrontation in the psychedelic session is between two aspects of his inner duality, but not between him as-a-whole and an actual other outside himself. This is a Jungian "process of individuation" which leaves the subject standing all alone, abandoned to his limited psychic powers, except for the promptings from his guide. There is no living other to communicate with.

Is the Self-Integration Real?

The supreme test of the entire process occurs when the subject descends into the final stage in which he is supposed to attain "authentic religious experiences" and thus realize himself as a human being-as-a-whole. Very few cases under review reached this stage. The authors evaluate only five percent of the subjects as having involved themselves in a radical transformation on the integral level. But even if we accept the testimony of the most prominent case (a successful psychologist) who is described as having attained such experience, it appears that what he went through in the drug-state was an intellectual debate with himself in the nature of a theological argument. He had always conceived of himself as being Lucifer and saw his "whole life as a recapitulation of Lucifer's struggle with God" (p. 279). When he realized that the conflict was too much for him to bear, his so-called hunger for God became a hunger "to devour God, . . . to become God." To preserve his ego he "must wage war against God. . . . Either I meet God on equal terms or I cannot meet him at all." He could not stand being defeated by God, which is "an Idea greater than himself." He felt the fight would be equal if God would assume human proportions, "come into the human sphere, . . . dwindle down and make himself human" (p. 277). These theological-metaphysical speculations, interwoven with mythological motifs and certain psychological ideas about man's nature and destiny (reminiscent of Nietzsche's struggle with God), had occupied the subject's mind for years, and, we are told, he was about to resolve them more or less prior to the psychedelic session. The drug-state only served to "free" his imagination and to induce him to articulate his ideas in vivid symbolic forms with which he had been familiar through reading and schooling from childhood on.

This case and others like it only demonstrate that the entire psychedelic act is a juggling of ideas and notions which the subject had entertained through life as part of his cultural-religious background and which the guide, who knows this in advance, only helps him to conceptualize. When, for example, in the case under discussion the subject was on the threshold of the integral level, he summarized the data he had collected on the preceding levels and remarked: "Once certain premises are accepted as in some way true, then everything makes perfect sense" (p. 292). This about sums up the Lucifer-God argument the subject was having with himself. Whether this may be considered as an actual religious experience of man's encounter with God in reality is very dubious indeed. Even the authors of *The Varieties* do not vouch for its authenticity. "To comment first of all on the preceding chapter," they say in their Epilogue, "it should be clearly understood that we make no judgment as to whether confrontation or union with a literal God has occurred in the experience described. Such a determination could have no foundation other than our own wishes and personal beliefs" (p. 314). If so, what has the drug-state accomplished? If it has not affected their beliefs in the slightest, how can the authors assert in their evaluation that "the encounter does take place—in an atmosphere charged with intense affect," or conclude that, after some promptings by the guide, the "subject then experienced the Presence of God for a second time, and on this occasion with greater emotion than before" (pp. 266, 294)? An inner psychic conflict between a Lucifer-idea and a God-idea is not an actual confrontation with the living God in reality. A God who serves as substitute for the Devil is only a surrogate god who really never overcomes the devil but who agrees to dwell side by side with him—in the subject's mind. For if there is no faith, what can the drug do? And if there is faith, what is the drug for?

Considering the great risks of mental derangement involved in subjecting oneself to a psychedelic experience, which the authors themselves warn against, on what ground can they claim that even a purposeful and controlled drug session can be "beneficial to the person" (p. 4, also p. 63)? With all their sincerity and sound advice on the possible misuse of drugs by the uninitiated, the authors of *The Varieties* might succeed only in making the Drug Movement a respectable cult; but they cannot warrant the high promise they hold for its power of liberation or therapeutic value (p. 201). Like every other popular cult, the belief grows that only a select few, those endowed with unusual gifts and willing to undergo a carefully designed ritual of initiation and preparation, are destined to attain the blissful state. This is virtually the conclusion the authors reached at the end of their very interesting and, I should say, illuminating experiments. As for their goal of man's self-realization, it can hardly be said that it has ever been, or ever will be, accomplished through psychedelic experience.

III. Breaking Through the Human Bounds

God-Is-Dead Theologoumena

> There can be endless kinds of ability-to-be-different, even the ability-to-be-God.
>
> NIETZSCHE,
> *The Will to Power* 1005

11. FRIEDRICH NIETZSCHE: THE NEW GODS

In Quest of the True Philosopher

In a moment of desperation in search for the divine, Nietzsche exclaimed through the mouth of Zarathustra, *Wenn es Götter gäbe, wie hielte ich's aus, kein Gott zu sein!*—"If there were gods, how could I stand it not to be a god!" [1] This was after he had emerged from his "romantic pessimism," as he termed his early period of groping, and was "overwhelmed" by a vision of the new human type. The next moment (it took him only ten days to write the first part of *Zarathustra*) he declared with greater assurance, *Tot sind alle Götter: nun wollen wir, dass der Übermensch lebe. . . .*—

---

1. Friedrich Nietzsche, *Thus Spoke Zarathustra* II. "Upon the Blessed Isles." All my references to Nietzsche's works, unless indicated otherwise, are to the German original in Kröner's Taschenausgabe, *Sämtliche Werke*, 1964-1965, *Der Nachlass* I and II, 1956. All quotations are in my own translation, giving the titles of the works (in English) and the numbers of the aphorisms or sections, as the case may be. Since these numbers are standard, the reader may refer to the same titles in Walter Kaufmann's English translation of the corresponding works.

"All the gods are dead: now we want that the Supreme Man shall live. . . ." [2] What did he mean by these pithy statements regarding the existence of God? And what did he mean by his aphorisms and epigrams on morality, such as, "life has just not been contrived by morality; it wants deception . . ." "to admit untruth as a condition of life," or "We live by lying and forgery?" [3] Ordinarily, one does not evaluate a philosopher by his aphorisms; but Nietzsche is different, he abounds in them and relishes their pungency. Yet we must be on guard not to overrate their disparate importance but rather search for their intrinsic meaning in his other, more expository and discursive writings.

In my reading of Nietzsche's works I have tried to follow his

2. *Ibid.*, end of first part. I translate Nietzsche's "Übermensch" as Supreme Man, rather than the common word Superman or the technical term "Overman," the latter suggested by Walter Kaufmann (*Nietzsche. Third* ed., 1968, pp. 307-310). While the German word *über* corresponds to the English "over," the combination *Übermensch* does not lend itself to the same combination in the English "Overman." In the latter the substantive (*man*) does not blend with the preposition (over) to form a new, if only elevated, substantive, as intended by the German word *Übermensch*. Kaufmann's interpretation of this concept as implying *Überwindung,* that is *over*coming, is well taken, but somehow the prepositional verb "overcome" does not transform itself into a prepositional noun "overman." However, this is just a matter of word coinage. More important is the philosopher's idea of *Übermensch,* as such. Nietzsche teaches "that there are superior and inferior men" who exist now and will continue to exist in eternal recurrence. What he is looking for is the supreme type of man who is yet to come, not just the greatest among men who have been thus far. "Verily," says Zarathustra, "there were [men] greater and of higher birth than those whom the folk call redeemers. . . . But even by greater ones than all the redeemers ones, my brothers, must be redeemed. . . . Never yet has there been a Supreme Man. . . . Verily, even the greatest I have found—all too human" (*Thus Spoke Zarathustra* II. "On Priests.") On the use of the term *Übermensch* in Lucian and in German literature prior to Nietzsche, see Walter Kaufmann, *op. cit.,* pp. 307-308. Paul Tillich suggests that "superior man" is perhaps the best translation, but he takes this to mean "the development of mankind in the Darwinian sense," which is hardly in keeping with Nietzsche's anti-Darwin pronouncements or his doctrine of eternal recurrence, in which the inferior as well as the superior recur. Cf. Paul Tillich, *Perspectives on 19th and 20th Century Protestant Theology* (Harper & Row Publishers, 1967), p. 202.

3. *Human, All-too-Human* 1, Preface, 1; *Beyond Good and Evil,* 4; *Der Nachlass* II, 795. ,

advice on how to relate his aphorisms to systematic thinking. Nietzsche was averse to systems of any kind, particularly philosophical,[4] but he was not unaware of the need of an overall coherence of his philosophical mode of thinking. For he considered himself first and foremost a philosopher. Indeed, his striving for the Supreme Man was in essence a quest of the true philosopher on whom he pinned all hope for human self-realization unto eternity —a theme and variation of Kant's Eternal Peace in Philosophy.[5]

Nietzsche found in "the aphorism, the sententious sentence . . . the form of 'eternity' " and chose this form for his *Zarathustra,* which he regarded as "the profoundest book" ever given to humanity.[6] After the *Zarathustra* we find him at work in discursive philosophical style, as he was trying to explain the inner structure of his earlier thought, to which he still held fast. These thoughts, he said, grew out of him like the fruits of a tree, "related and all in all interconnected, and are witnesses of one will, one wholesomeness, one earthly domain, one sun. Whether these fruits are to your taste?—But what does it matter to the trees. What does it matter to us, us philosophers! . . ."[7] In this brief self-revelation we may find the key to our philosopher's ideas and what holds them together, not as a system but, perhaps, what may be designated as a thought-coherence. The key is his concept of the philosopher as a certain type of man and of philosophy as typological thinking.

The mode of thinking by type is based on the existential idea

---

4. Cf. *Twilight of the Idols,* Maxims, 26. "I mistrust all systematizers, and I get out of their way. The will to a system is lack of fortrightness." Cf. *Nachlass* I, 1249. "I am not sufficiently narrow-minded for a system—and not even for my system. . . ."

5. Cf. Immanuel Kant, *Verkündigung des nahen Abschlusses eines Tractats zum ewigen Frieden in der Philosophie* (1796), on the "lowest level of the living nature of man to that of its highest, philosophy." In contrast to Nietzsche's concept of the philosophical lie, it is well to note Kant's formulation of it and his admonition (at the conclusion of that essay), that "to accept intrinsically the commandment Thou shalt not lie (even with the most pious intention) as the basic rule of philosophy as a doctrine of wisdom, will in itself not only influence eternal peace in philosophy, but also assure its future."

6. *Twilight of the Idols.* "Skirmishes," 51.

7. *Genealogy of Morals.* Preface 2.

that man does not think by reason alone but with his being as a whole. To know a person's thoughts, therefore, we must know what kind of man he is, and this may assume an ontological form of a category of being differentiated from other creatures, or an ideological form which differentiates types of men on a principle of valuation. Nietzsche chose the second form.[8] In order to understand his philosophy, then, we must trace the characteristics of the type of man he envisions as the "true philosopher"—the one who thinks, hopes, and acts, sets values, judges, and behaves according to his specific type, whom Nietzsche designates "Typus Zarathustra." When he speaks of "us philosophers," out of whom all sundry ideas grow like fruits from a tree, out of a common root, "related and all in all interconnected," he has in mind a particular kind of man that he has constructed through observation and revaluation into a philosopher-god or a Dionysos-philosopher.[9] Whether or not Nietzsche himself may be identified with this type should not concern us here, as that is a problem for biography, not philosophy. What is important for us here is that his thoughts, expressed in various forms of dithyramb, aphorism, argument, or plain discourse, converge into a philosophical coherence which is incarnate in the Typus Zarathustra. No doubt he saw his own philosophical destiny in this type, as we read in *Ecce Homo* ("Why I am a Destiny" 8): "Have I been understood? I have

---

8. Cf. Helmut Schoeck, *Nietzsche's Philosophie des "Menschlich-Allzumenschlichen"* (Tübingen: Verlag J. C. B. Mohr, 1948). "Nietzsches Bedeutung für eine Ideologienlehre," p. 72, "Der Idealtypus bei Nietzsche und Max Weber," pp. 83-86. Cf. Nicolai Hartmann, *Der Aufbau der realen Welt* (Berlin: Walter de Gruyter & Co., 1964), p. 18. Hartmann calls this mode of thinking "Typologismus," and points to its consequent relativism of being and truth.

9. Cf. *Beyond Good and Evil*, 295. "Merely that Dionysos is a philosopher, and hence that gods, too, philosophize, seems to me to be a novelty which is not without danger, and which perhaps might arouse suspicion just among philosophers." Cf. Carl G. Jung, *Psychology and Religion* (Yale University Press, 1938), p. 103. "Nietzsche was no atheist, but his God was dead. The result was that Nietzsche himself split and he felt himself forced to call the other self 'Zarathustra' or, at other times, 'Dionysos.' In his fatal illness he signed his letters 'Zagreus,' the dismembered Dionysos of the Thracians. The tragedy of *Zarathustra* is that, because his God died, Nietzsche himself became a god; and this happened because he was no atheist."

just said not one word which I would not have said five years ago through the mouth of Zarathustra." Now this new anthropos has a metaphysic behind him; the two cannot be separated in Nietzsche's thinking. We may grant that Nietzsche, as a philosopher who thinks out of the depth of his being, treats the problem of man existentially, but we must also recognize that the type of man he presents as the "true philosopher" is founded on a certain metaphysical anthropology which is also the foundation of his religious-moral outlook.

Good and Evil or Good and Bad

The main burden of Nietzsche's typological thinking is that he sees many types of men and classifies them in an order of degrees of the will to power or in ranks of superiority-inferiority. "I teach," he says, "that there are superior and inferior men." "The cleavage between man and man, status and status, the plurality of types, the will to be oneself, to stand out—what I call the *pathos of distance,* that is characteristic of every strong age." Accordingly, each type sets its own "norm of sociological value-judgment." [10] And since there are superior and inferior types, there are also superior and inferior norms of value. But the real value-setter who is true to life and nature is the superior type whose will to power reaches the highest stage in the Supreme Man. He is as he is, and his norm is valid for mankind as a whole. What for him is existential being becomes for others an ethical ought. He is the man of the future, the one who is to "become what he is," and all acts he may perform in the process of realizing himself are considered ethical. That is, the Supreme Man sets his own norms out of his being as he is and renders them ethical insofar as they enable him to become what he is.

Nietzsche does not ask about the good life or the good deed, but about the good man. After long observation and contemplation since childhood, he said, he found that the difference in

10. Cf. *Will to Power* IV, 997, and *Twilight,* "Skirmishes," 37. Cf. *Nachlass* II, 753, "Zur Rangordnung," for a table of inequalities among men of different rank. Cf. his use of the term "ein inferiorer Mensch," *ibid.,* 763.

ethical standards rests on a distinction between two mutually opposed normative word-pairs or values, "good and bad" and "good and evil." [11] The meaning of good in the first pair is not the same as in the second, because "bad" and "evil" are not the same. Both word-pairs represent a relationship between master and slave, the first pair expressing the natural state of the master who is "good" and the slave who is "bad," thus giving the right to the master to set ethical norms for both himself and the slave. But when the two "do not want to come to terms with each other," the slave revaluates the relationship, calling the master "evil" and establishes a morality of "good and evil." The master has no part in it, because he is "beyond good and evil." Nietzsche offers an extensive list of traits which identify the good and the bad characters, or, as he also calls them, the "noble type" and the common man, or "ignoble type," respectively. This is their

> ultimate basic difference: the desire for freedom, the instinct for happiness and the subtleties of feeling for freedom necessarily belong to slave-morals and slave-morality, even as art and zeal in reverence, in self-denial, are the normal symptom of the aristocratic manner of thought and valuation. [12]

In sum, whatever the noble type does, even with a measure of hatred and vengeance, he does nobly; the same acts performed by the common man, even with compassion and love, are ignoble.

Such is our philosopher's *Vorbereitung zu einer Typenlehre der Moral*—"propaedeutic to a typology of morals." [13] His vocabulary clearly reflects his ethical double-standard. The weak type "hates"

---

11. *Genealogy*, Preface, 3, and Part I, 16. I use the term "word-pair" advisedly, as Nietzsche dwells also on the etymological significance of the words "good" and "bad." Cf. *ibid.*, 4-5, and "Anmerkung" at the end of that essay, where he poses the following question for study by some philosophical faculty: "What suggestion does the science of language, especially etymological research, offer for the history of the development of moral concepts?"
12. *Beyond Good and Evil*, 260. Cf. *The Antichrist*, end of 57. "What is *bad*? But I have already said it: everything that stems from weakness, from envy, from vengeance." Cf. *Nachlass* II, 466. ". . . when you felt disgust there arose 'the bad.' "
13. *Ibid.*, 186. "Typenlehre" should perhaps be rendered as "doctrine of types," to indicate its theoretical, contemplative connotation,

and that is bad, but the strong type "despises" and that is good and noble. "Cruelty" in the weak is bad, but in the strong it is good. Even *ressentiment,* the most accursed earmark of the bad man (whom he calls "the man of ressentiment"), turns into a virtue in the noble soul. "Ressentiment itself, when aroused in the noble man, consummates and exhausts itself in an immediate reaction; hence it is not poison. . . ." [14] Small people who want "that nobody should hurt them" are "cowards," but great men have a "natural" right to hurt the small.[15]

Esthetic Morality

We may wonder what kind of morality Nietzsche is aiming at in his revaluation of morals. We shall not find a satisfactory answer in a recitation of all shades, nuances and intricate meanings of the term morality, whether sociological, psychological or otherwise, used by him in all his writings. Rather, it must be sought in his fundamental concept of man in relation to the world, to the All, on one hand, and in his interhuman relations, on the other. Nietzsche views man from the naturalist-esthetic angle, not from the ethical. The moral issue he raises is about what man *is* by nature and how he may realize himself toward the Supreme Man, and not about his conduct in relation to his fellow man, which is the ethical issue. True, his man is a man of action, but

---

rather than an actual division of mankind into two opposite types. For Nietzsche recognizes intermediate stages between the two types and also a mixture of them (cf. *ibid.,* 260). However, it is not so much the *theorein* that should interest us as the characteristics of noble and common which Nietzsche derives from what he regards to be an essential distinction between men according to rank in the order of superior-inferior. In such an order there can be no ethical norm. Nietzsche's valuation of character is of an esthetic nature.

14. *Genealogy* I, 10.
15. *Zarathustra* II. "On Virtue that Makes Small," 2. Frederick the Great of Prussia howled at his soldiers whom he led in battle at Kunesdorf (1759), "On, you dogs! Will you live for ever?" History has judged that year as a turning point in the fortunes of Prussia. It must be said for Frederick that he carried poison on him and was himself ready to die during those fateful days. Yet he would die as the noble prince, and his loyal, disciplined soldiers only as dogs. Nietzsche admired this king greatly. Cf. R. J. White, *Europe in the Eighteenth Century* (New York: St. Martin's Press, 1965), pp. 158f.

the way he sees him, his man does what he is and forms himself in his own image, whereas the ethical man is what he does and forms his image through his relation with others. Nietzsche's denial of free will and, with it, responsibility in God only betrays his fatalistic naturalism: the totality of man's being belongs to the fatality of the All—it is a necessity, a heap of fate, a whole, and there is nothing outside of him to be responsible to. "We deny God," he proclaims, "we deny responsibility in God: only thus do we redeem the world." [16]

Seen in this fatalistic light, the noble type may be acting out of his being, but he really has no active role as a human being, as a free agent. The philosopher who contemplates this type of being and the artist who creates an image of him see the noble character as an esthetic expression of the fullness of life. The good type is beautiful, the bad one is ugly. "In the beautiful man posits himself as the measure of perfection," and "nothing is beautiful, only man is beautiful." This is our philosopher's first truth of esthetics, and he adds immediately the second truth: "Nothing is ugly but the degenerate man." [17]

How is this esthetic view of man reflected in Nietzsche's philosophy and particularly in his revaluation of morals? Nicolai Hartmann's observation on this point may fit our philosopher: "One can well live without being affected by the problematic of

---

16. *Twilight,* "The Four Great Errors," 8.
17. *Ibid.,* "Skirmishes," 19-20. Cf. *Genealogy* I, 4. The German word *schlecht* (bad) is identical with *schlimm* (ordinary, common). Cf. *Twilight,* "The Case of Socrates," 3, on ugliness as degeneration. Nietzsche derives his *ethos,* meaning character, from Greek tragedy, from Aristotle's *Poetics* rather than from his *Nicomachean Ethics.* He might agree with the Stagirite that virtue is "a state of character" or a disposition, but not with his teaching that it is a disposition to choose the mean between extremes and to refrain from conduct which is wrong in any degree. (Cf. *Nicomachean Ethics* II, "Moral Virtue," 1105-1107a.) Cf. Walter Kaufmann, *Basic Writings of Nietzsche* (The Modern Library, 1968), p. 328, note 35. "Aristotle's discussion of greatness of soul . . . evidently influenced Nietzsche." Kaufmann finds this "relevant and extremely interesting" to Nietzsche's "long discussion of 'what is noble.'" One should note, however, that while there is a similarity in their concept of "noble soul," there is a vast difference in their ethical evaluation of "great deed," and that is the point at issue.

the arts, but one cannot philosophize without being seized by it." [18] Nietzsche the philosopher was indeed seized by the esthetic problem to the core of his being and he tried to sublimate it to a new metaphysic of morals, if we can call it that. It expressed his creative, contemplative passion. If we accept his own dictum on the genesis of "metaphysical suppositions," his tragic physical and spiritual suffering became his life-interest and molded his innermost human drive, which "seeks to dominate and, as such, tries to philosophize." [19] By this I do not mean to indulge in psychologizing, but only to emphasize the esthetic character of our philosopher's morality.

Revaluating the Metaphysic of Morals

Nietzsche does not revaluate morals but the metaphysic of morals. He directs his metaphysical arrows against Kant more than against any other of his predecessors. Kant, he says, came to the odd conclusion that the intelligible world is unintelligible, that is, the "true world" which Kant postulated beyond the sensible phenomena—the world of noumena or conceptual world—is inaccessible to the concepts of the understanding. Accordingly, "there is a realm of truth and of being, but reason in particular is excluded from it! . . . ('intelligible character' thus means for Kant a sort of quality of things of which the intellect conceives just so much, that to the intellect—it is entirely inconceivable)." [20] To

---

18. Nicolai Hartmann, *Zur Grundlegung der Ontologie* (Berlin: Walter de Gruyter & Co., 1965), p. 22.
19. *Beyond Good and Evil*, 6.
20. *Genealogy* III, 12. Nietzsche misunderstood the real meaning of Kant's assertion. The intelligible world of noumena, says Kant, is not known through man's understanding not because the latter cannot possibly know it, but because its present categories cannot operate without a perceptual content, and that content is not part of the noumena. That is, the understanding cannot grasp the intelligible world of noumena in its purity. For this, man would need an understanding of a purer order. By "becoming intelligible" Kant means becoming an object of the existing categories of the understanding. Generally, his basic test of knowledge is whether there is an object known. The thing-in-itself (noumenon) cannot become the object of man's categories of the understanding for the reason stated; hence there is no knowledge of it and it is unintelligible in that sense. But this, says

resolve this paradox, Nietzsche takes two bold steps: he denies the existence of a world of noumena and he downgrades the value of the understanding as an instrument of real knowledge of the world of phenomena; he shakes the foundations of Kant's "real" world and unhinges his categories of the understanding which are fastened to the world of appearance. What kind of reality and what means of knowledge does Nietzsche substitute for Kant's dual kingdom? "The true world," he says, "we have abolished; which world has remained? perhaps the phenomenal?— Not so! With the true world we have also abolished the phenomenal one!" [21] But with that he did not abolish metaphysics, any more than Kant did. Both only revaluated the old into a new world-orientation.

Fundamentally, Nietzsche as well as Kant tries to set limits to a scientific account of reality by placing the physical sciences within a philosophical frame of reference. Both recognize that science is a useful tool of cognition and action but also that, in a sense, it falsifies reality. Their metaphysical difference stem from their different concepts of the nature of physical science and the sense in which it falsifies the "true world." If Kant fails to give direction in the world of being, Nietzsche limits himself to finding direction in the world of becoming. As for their respective scientific outlooks, Kant built his on the foundations of Newton's physics, whereas Nietzsche, by a stroke of genius, projected his into the principles of modern nuclear physics. He did not leave us a finished work on a metaphysic of nature, as Kant did, but there is no mistake about his outlook on physical nature.

I shall resist the temptation to draw a parallel between

Kant, does not preclude the possibility of a human faculty of pure understanding (not tied to sensible percepts) which could have the noumenon for its object. As it stands, there is no such faculty in evidence, and there is therefore no objective noumenon in man's intelligible world; it is only a limiting concept. Cf. Kant, *Kritik der reinen Vernunft*, B295, 307, 311.

21. *Twilight*, "How the 'True World' Finally Became a Legend," item 6. Cf. Frederick Copleston, *A History of Philosophy* (Garden City, N. Y.: Image Books, 1965), Vol. 7, Part II, p. 166. In the second phase of his writings (after 1876), Nietzsche "prefers science to poetry . . . and pretty well plays the part of a rationalistic philosopher of the French Enlightenment."

Nietzsche's "interpretation" of the world and modern theories of mathematical physics, as this would take me far outside the limits of my present study. I will only indicate how some of his concepts project themselves into those theories. On the general concept of "points of force" which prevails in modern physics, he writes:

> The mathematical physicists cannot use atom-lumps for their science: hence they construct for themselves a world of points of force which may be reckoned with. Roughly, this is exactly what men and all organic creatures have done: that is, arranged the world, ordered it in thought and imagination, until they could use it, until it could be "reckoned" with.[22]

On giving up the principle of causality, as is now being advocated by the Copenhagen school of quantum mechanics, and generally on the use of sign-language to describe rather than explain physical states, he says:

> The development of the mechanistic-atomistic mode of thinking is today not yet aware of its necessary goal:—that is my impression after I have long enough looked at its adherents between the fingers. It will end up with the creation of a system of signs: it will forego explanation and will give up the concept of "cause and effect." [23]

Many of his other observations anticipated modern concepts of movement, atomic structure, disregard of the singular, contingency of combination, law of probability, relative character of simultaneity, and the like, which are the building blocks, cement, and scaffolding of today's mathematical structure of the universe. He even dared to think of the physicist's concept of motion not as action at a distance but as "symptoms of an inner occurrence," and of the concept of "time as a property of space." [24]

---

22. *Nachlass* II, 271.
23. *Ibid.*, 273. Cf. also 230.
24. *Will to Power*, 619, 862. Cf. *Nachlass* II, 101-102, 204, 331, 257, 261, 281, and 282, on movement, the atom and molecule, probability, simultaneity, force, and space. Nietzsche was familiar with the new developments in scientific theories of his time, notably in mathematics, physics, and psychology. Cf. Alwin Mittasch, *Friedrich Nietzsche als Naturphilosoph* (Stuttgart: Verlag Alfred Kröner, 1952).

The World as Perspective Interpretation

Is everything in the physical world an illusion, a lie? Yes, says Nietzsche, and necessarily so, because life itself demands that it be so. If we ask "what" moves within the whole? his answer is not a "thing," for there is no thing just as there is no movement in itself. There is only "interpretation" relative to a given "perspective." There are many perspectives, each issuing from a certain drive, and there are many interpretations.[25] Nietzsche's "perspective interpretations" are analogous to coordinates in modern physics. Both are innumerable, and anyone who wants to make use of them must choose from among their endless possibilities. However, since there is no purpose or goal in Nietzsche's world of nature, as there is none in modern physical theory, there is no way of deciding on a given perspective interpretation in preference to any other. Modern physics has circumvented this problem by adopting a certain geometry as a basis for its coordinates. How does our philosopher get around it, when he advises man to choose to "become what he is"? What kind of perspective interpretation will enable man to move in that direction? For, as we recall, Nietzsche's primary task is to give direction in a world of sheer becoming. Without some constant guideline man will be totally disoriented in the becoming, will be unable to hit upon the right perspective, and will remain in the condition of nihilism, from which Nietzsche tried to save him through his revaluation of all values. What are his new horizons?

In the past, Nietzsche says, man interpreted the world from the narrow perspective of a belief in God as the creator and preserver of the universe which, while it served certain life needs, has now become untenable. Actually, he does not deny God, only the Christian doctrine of a supernatural, transcendent Being who demands a given morality. Such an interpretation of human life, he finds, is inconsistent with the new emerging view of reality.

---

25. *Genealogy* III, 12. "There is only a perspective seeing (*perspektivisches Sehen*), only a perspective 'cognition': and the more drives we allow to come to expression over a thing . . . the more complete will be our 'concept,' our 'objectivity' of that thing." Cf. *The Gay Science* V, 374, on the possibility of endless perspectives and interpretations.

"The refutation of God:—actually only the *moral* God is refuted." [26] That is, Nietzsche denies the life-giving values of Christian theology and its metaphysic of morals, which are grounded in a dual world of being and appearance, such as the philosophers, notably Kant, had built up in the past. If now he wants to revaluate those values and, as he claims, not to abolish them, he must establish new religious concepts, a new metaphysics or theology, which will support his own view of the world of nature and man. This should not be too difficult if only he could find a guideline for choosing the right "perspective" for a new interpretation; that is like choosing the proper geometry for a new set of coordinates.

The real problem that our philosopher faces is to establish the meaning of being in reality when all there is is becoming. Any being that one might ascribe to it would be only an interpretation, but reality is an interpretation of becoming. It is "the *interpretative* character of all occurrence. There is no event in itself. What occurs is a group of appearances, *selected* and comprehended through an interpreting being." [27] And here we come to Nietzsche's paradox: If there is such a being apart from the interpretation, he is unreal, because a being in reality arises only through interpretation. Having dethroned the principle of causality, Nietzsche may deny the need of an Aristotelian "prime mover," but he cannot forego the first principle of a prime interpreter.

As if in anticipation of this difficulty, Nietzsche forewarns: "One should not ask: 'who then interprets?' for the interpreting itself, as a form of the will to power, has existence (not, however, as a 'being' but as a process, a becoming) as an affect." [28] Nonetheless, we still want to know who or what is this will that can do all these things. Nietzsche's "will to power" is a metaphysical first principle, not a hypothesis. It is a duality in oneness posited by our philosopher in place of the Kantian dualism of two separate worlds. Its two terms, *will* and *power,* are inseparable from each

---

26. *Nachlass* II, 994. Cf. Karl Jaspers, *Nietzsche. Einführung in das Verständnis seines Philosophierens.* Dritte unveränderte Auflage (Berlin: Walter de Gruyter & Co., 1950), pp. 290-330, for a detailed analysis of Nietzsche's view of the world as interpretation.
27. *Ibid.,* 245. "Der *interpretative* Charakter alles Geshehens."
28. *Will to Power,* 556.

other. The first term, taken by itself, even in its most determinate form, says Nietzsche, is only a vague abstraction or illusion, and "to reduce everything to will [is] a very naive distortion!" [29] He therefore proposes to abolish it as "the dying God" that "crumbles in the individualities" [30] and to replace it with a new kind of will that is not an individual human capacity or quality of reason trying to grasp its object, the thing-in-itself (as Kant did), but a universal striving toward self-realization. He avoids the logical separation of subject and object by changing the static connective (a middle "is") into a dynamic relation (a middle "to") of becoming (*Geschehen*). Thus, his first principle is expressed as an assertion, not a definition. But the assertion is not that "will *is* power," "will *has* power," or "will *wills* power"—all constituting a duality that cannot be brought into oneness. The assertion is "will *to* power," which represents a oneness of inner conflict, an original *dynamis* or, as he calls it, "not a being, not a becoming, but a *pathos*, . . . the most elemental reality (*Tatsache*), out of which a becoming, an action, first arises—." [31] It is causality-in-itself. Everything in it is in an inchoate state of becoming, assuming various forms of organic and inorganic nature, of life and man, unto the highest form, the supreme man. This will to power speaks out of all its forms through the self-interpretation of its drives.

The second term, power, is also inseparable from the oneness, will-to-power. In itself, like will it is conceivable only as an abstract force, a law of mechanical causality of attraction and repulsion—"a total fiction: a word." [32] Nietzsche's "power" makes its own laws which are expressed spontaneously in its effect. It is a oneness of a basic immanent duality, splitting itself into subdualities (like Plato's principle of *dichotomy*): two kinds of will,

---

29. *Nachlass* II, 83. Cf. 321, 331.
30. *Ibid.* I, 61.
31. *Will to Power*, 635. *Beyond Good and Evil*, 36. Cf. Plato, *The Sophist*, 219d-221c, 253d, on separation and participation of subject and object through dichotomy. Cf. Ernst Hoffman, *Platonismus und christliche Philosophie* (Zürich: Artemis Verlag, 1960), p. 49, on Plato's use of the copula "is."
32. *Ibid.*, 627.

two kinds of power, two types of man, two kinds of philosopher, and so on, in endless self-interpretation. This may be inferred from the very concept of interpretation which presupposes a duality of meaning, whether of interiority or exteriority.[33] This oneness of interpretation, like every coordinate mesh, requires at least two elements at cross purposes or directions: " 'Purpose and means,' 'cause and effect,' 'subject and object,' 'action and passion,' 'thing-in-itself and appearance,' as interpretations (not as facts) . . . all in the sense of a 'will to power.' " [34] Nietzsche follows here the methodology of the philosopher-scientist who tries to establish a unified science by positing one and only one all-embracing functioning principle as the interpreter of the world of becoming. As he says, "it is dictated by the conscience of method," or "it is a morality of method, . . . it follows 'from its definition,' as a mathematician would say." For if the principle "will to power" interprets everything, then, he says, we have "the right to determine univocally all active forces as: will to power. The world seen from within, the world determined and designated as to its 'intelligible character'—just 'will to power' and nothing be-

---

33. Cf. Karl Jaspers, *Nietzsche* (Berlin: Walter de Gruyter & Co., 1950), pp. 303ff. "Aber die Macht ist zweideutig" (But power has a dual meaning). Cf. Walter Kaufmann, *From Shakespeare to Existentialism* (Garden City N. Y.: Doubleday, 1960). "Jaspers' Relation to Nietzsche." *"Summary of criticism,"* p. 312. Kaufmann objects that "Jaspers' frequent references to Nietzsche's 'ambiguity' are misleading." But his objection, it appears, is due primarily to his own translation of the word *Zweideutigkeit* as ambiguity. He is correct in saying that Jaspers does not use ambiguity in "the usual meaning of the word, equivocality"; but he does not recognize that Jaspers does not intend to use the word ambiguity at all. His term *Zweideutigkeit* should be rendered in English in the sense in which he uses it, namely, as duality of meaning. "Ambiguous" means "doubtful, not clearly defined, . . . equivocal, . . . not to be trusted" (*The Shorter Oxford Dictionary*). Jaspers does not impute these allegations to Nietzsche, but rather points out that his term power has a clear, unmistakable duality of meaning. Cf. Karl Löwith, *From Hegel to Nietzsche*. Transl. by David E. Green (Garden City, N. Y.: Doubleday, 1967), p. 189. "This ambiguity of Nietzsche's philosophical existence also characterizes his relationship to time [which] . . . enabled him to interpret his present philosophically."
34. *Will to Power,* 589.

sides." [35] "Granted that this too is only interpretation . . .—then, the better.—" [36]

The New Gods: Philosophers-Lawgivers

Having established his first principle in the manner of the philosopher-scientist, Nietzsche went beyond this type of philosophizing in search of the "true philosopher" who must be "a lawgiver" of evaluation.[37] Through this philosopher "speaks the sovereign drive, which is stronger than man." [38] He is "man becoming what he is," the will to power not yet realized but striving for the highest interpretation, toward the utmost state, the Supreme Man. His manifest destiny is to sublimate himself to artist-philosopher becoming a god.[39] Thus Nietzsche hoped to overcome the nihilism of his generation, indeed for a thousand years to come, by setting a new goal and purpose for the human race, namely, the production of supreme man. "These Lords of the Earth shall now replace God and attain for themselves the deep, unconditional trust of those who are ruled." [40]

When Nietzsche proclaimed "All the gods are dead," he postulated with Zarathustra, as he also did with the Madman in *The Gay Science,* that it is possible for God to die or, more correctly, for man to kill him. At any rate, this is how he posed the problem: "Either we die of this . . . artificially inoculated religion, . . . or religion dies of us. I believe in the old Germanic word: all gods must die." [41] However, he intended by this act to save mankind from nihilism, that is, not to leave it without a supreme being. He therefore would not have ventured to kill God, unless he

---

35. *Beyond Good and Evil,* 36.
36. *Ibid.,* 22.
37. *Will to Power,* 972, 979. See also 464, 465.
38. *Nachlass* II, 717.
39. Originally, Nietzsche had three types of supreme men, the artist, the philosopher, and the saint. But after he eliminated the Kantian-Christian "real world," he had no place to put the saint and he therefore left him out of the final reckoning. Cf. Kaufmann, *Nietzsche* (1968), p. 285. "The saint has dropped out of the picture. . . ." See also p. 322. "Nietzsche was not primarily a moral philosopher at all. . . ."
40. *Nachlass* II, 1414.
41. *Nachlass* I, 1.

110

assumed that man had created him and could now kill him and create new gods in his stead. "And how many new gods are still possible!" "Type of god according to the type of the creative spirits, of the 'great men.' " [42] The old God, he said, was fashioned out of weakness: "One has named God that which weakens, teaches weakness, infects weakness . . ." which caused the crisis of nihilism.[43] The new gods, the philosophers sublimated into Supreme Men, will come forth as the self-interpretation of the Will to Power.

Nietzsche's doctrine of sublimation does not set a goal for man, as such, or for mankind as a whole, but for select individuals, the great, superior men, for whom the entire human species is to sacrifice everything needed in order to bring them into fruition. "Humanity on the whole has no goals. . . ." [44] Its task is to produce individual great men; its goal lies not in an end, but in its highest specimens. For "man is a bridge and not an end: to count himself blessed that noon and evening are a road to new dawns." [45] The great men are to become "the Lords of the Earth," to whom even the governing forces are to be subordinated.

Beyond the governors, relieved of all ties, live the highest men: and in the governors they have their tools. . . . Not "humanity" but *Supreme Man* is the goal! . . . Not to make men "better," not to speak to them about some kind of morals, as if there were "morality in itself," or an ideal kind of man, in general: but to create conditions under which stronger men are needed, who on their part will use morals . . . which make strong, and who will therefore have such morals. . . . The great passion [which wants something great] . . . has the courage also for unholy means. . . . [For] the destiny of mankind lies in the attainment of its highest type.[46] . . . All virtue and self-overcoming have meaning only as preparation of the ruler![47]

42. *Will to Power*, 1038. Cf. *Nachlass* II, 927. "Men have created God, there is no doubt. . . ."
43. *Ibid.*, 54.
44. *Human All Too Human* I, 33.
45. *Zarathustra III, "On Old and New Tablets,"* 3.
46. *Will to Power*, 998, 1001, 981, 963, 987.
47. *Nachlass* II, 1279.

One could cite many more passages in the same vein, all of which intersect in the following entry: "About the ruling types.— The 'Shepherd' in contrast to the 'Lord' (—the former a means to sustain the herd; the latter, end for which there is the herd)." [48] The "Lords" form a breed of philosopher-gods who are detached from the rest of mankind, assuming a sort of transcendence within a universal immanence, removed on a new Olympus, and from its clouds flash the words *noli me tangere!* No wonder our philosopher himself was awed by his new creation. "When I created the Supreme Man," he said, "I arranged the great veil of becoming around him and let the sun stand over him at noon." "When he [Zarathustra] leaves the people, he turns back unto himself. It retreats from him like a cloud. Type of how the Supreme Man must live: like an Epicurean god." [49]

As the highest interpretation, as the self-realization of the will to power, this philosopher-god "is a man who constantly experiences extraordinary things, . . . who is himself perhaps a thunderstorm pregnant with new lightning; a fateful man around whom there is always peeling, growling and yelping, and things go weird. . . ." [50] Such is Nietzsche's Supreme Man—like a storm without an ethic. He may be the sublimated manifestation of nature, but he is not the man who will bring salvation to his fellow men, no matter how sublime the heights to which he himself may climb. Man regarded as "nature" (Nietzsche often speaks of *die Pflanze Mensch*—the plant humanum, which exists only to produce the topmost, finest fruits), whatever metaphysical soil he may grow from, cannot be elevated to the state of an ethical being. That is why Nietzsche sees "Morality as Anti-Nature," and "The single human being [as] a piece of *fatum* from the front and from the rear, one law more, one necessity more for all that is yet to come and to be." [51]

48. *Will to Power,* 902.
49. *Nachlass* II, 1273, 1359.
50. *Beyond Good and Evil,* 292.
51. *Twilight of the Idols.* "Morality as Anti-Nature," 6.

12. JEAN-PAUL SARTRE: THE LONELY SELF

Absolute Freedom

One of Sartre's characters, Goetz, muses before another character, Heinrich the priest, in the play *The Devil and the Good
Lord:* "If God exists, man is nothing; if man exists"—here his
sentence breaks off, and then he goes on—"Heinrich, I am going
to tell you a colossal joke: God doesn't exist." In the following
scene, when Goetz is faced with deciding on a matter of life and
death, he tries to fathom the consequence of God's non-existence:
"I killed God because He divided me from mankind, and now I
see that His death has isolated me even more surely." The play
ends with the hero's resolve "I shall not flinch," but without re-
solving the problem of his newly discovered loneliness: "I shall
remain alone with this empty sky over my head, since I have no
other way of being among men." [52]

Sartre, unlike Nietzsche, conceives of the death of God as a
necessary condition of man's very existence, which is at the root
of his anthropological question as he developed it in his major
work *Being and Nothingness*.[53] The real issue he is trying to
resolve is the possibility of individual man's freedom in confrontation with the world of things and with fellow men insofar as the
latter are also represented as things. He accepts the Cartesian idea
of absolute freedom, but since he denies the existence of God,
he must find a new kind of absolute that will enable man to
become the sole source of his own freedom. Ultimately, this is a

---

52. Jean-Paul Sartre, *The Devil and the Good Lord*. Trans. by
Kitty Black (New York: Vintage Books, 1962), Act III, scene x and
xi, pp. 141, 147, 149. Goetz's pronouncements echo similar statements
by Zarathustra and the Madman in Nietzsche's works. The latter's
influence on Sartre has been dealt with by Walter Kaufmann in several
essays. Cf. Maurice Natanson, "Jean-Paul Sartre's Philosophy of Freedom," *Social Research, XIX*, p. 368. "Sartre accepts Nietzsche's proc-
lamation, 'God is dead,' and seeks to find the final expression of this
dictum." Cf. Martin Buber, *Eclipse of God* (Harper Torchbooks,
1959), pp. 69f., on Sartre's and Nietzsche's doing away with God.
53. Jean-Paul Sartre, *Being and Nothingness: An Essay on Phenomenological Ontology*. Trans. by Hazel Barnes (New York: Philosophical Library, 1956). This work will be quoted below only by page number in parentheses in my text.

philosophical problem of setting values in certain ends or, as Kant poses the question, "What ought I to do?" and "What may I hope?" [54] Kant seeks to answer the first question by morality and the second by religion. Sartre, on the other hand, tries to combine them into one question of morality, urging man to seek both answers in himself alone. This leads Sartre, as it does Kant, to the anthropological question, "What is Man?"

My purpose here is not to evaluate Sartre's philosophy as a whole, but only to bring to light his treatment of the theological issue in man's relation to the Absolute. Why does he feel constrained to deny God's existence which Descartes has posited as a prerequisite of the existence of man?[55] Why cannot both be real existents? Only after "killing" God does Goetz see the reality of Hilda. Only then is he able to take her in his arms and say to her, "How real you have become since He no longer exists." Before that he loathed even to touch her; she filled him with nausea; her "body is disgusting," her "Beauty is Evil." Then when he is left with his accuser, who is but one half of himself against the other half, he says to him: ". . . search me to the depth of my being, since it is my being that is on trial." [56] What is his being?

Sartre does not pose the question "What is Man" directly, but, rather, asks, "What must man be like in order to exist as an absolutely independent being?" His problem of absolute freedom is enmeshed in the problem of how man can become absolutely independent: being free is identical with man's very being or, rather, his becoming man. He eliminates God from his scheme of things, because the God-idea, as he conceives it, destroys his concept of man. He sees the concept of man-God or God-man as a

---

54. Immanuel Kant, *Introduction to Logic*. Transl. by Thomas Kingsmill Abbott (New York: Philosophical Library, 1963), p. 15.

55. Cf. *Descartes Selections*. Edited by Ralph M. Eaton (New York: Charles Scribner's Sons, 1955). "Meditations" II, p. 109f.

56. *The Devil and the Good Lord*, pp. 131ff., 143. There are some Gnostic overtones in Sartre, and "the Good Lord" may just be an allusion to the Gnostic "Good God." Similarly, Marcion, the second century Gnostic and Christian heretic, was filled with *nausea* at the mere thought of the sexual method of reproduction and a woman's pain at childbirth. Cf. Henry Chadwick, *The Early Church* (Baltimore: Penguin Books, 1973), p. 39.

self-destructive entity, and therefore one must die in order that the other may live. That man may be saved only through divine sacrifice is a basic tenet of Christian theology, but Sartre, with his "destructive philosophy," wants to show that man can be saved not through the sacrifice and resurrection of the Son but through the total sacrifice of the Father Himself. He may well find the prototype of his theology in the Patripassians of the second century whose leader, Noetus, taught "that Christ was the Father Himself, and that the Father Himself was born and suffered and died." [57] In his godless theology Sartre is concerned with the same theologoumena as are found in doctrinal theology, namely, creation out of nothing, salvation from sin of the body, transcendence, incarnation, transubstantiation, and resurrection, only he posits them all in man's existence whose self-created essence is absolute freedom. And this is the point of issue in his circuit of nothingness.

Sartre starts with the concept of "creative freedom 'ex nihilo' " as a primary experience.[58] Upon examining this concept he finds, or rather decides, that the "nihil" must be no other than man himself; otherwise man's creative action could not be free. Man's being *is* freedom in that he is a *nihil* creating himself *ex-nihilo,* or a self-creating nothingness. If God exists, He stands in man's way to self-creation, for in God's presence, Sartre argues, man is a nothing, capable of doing nothing. Sartre issues from the Cartesian concept of freedom as a power of "absolute autonomy" and the free act as an "absolutely new production," but instead of bestowing this power on God, as Descartes does, he wants to wrest it from the Divine Being and bestow it on man. He says,

> It took two centuries of crisis—a crisis of Faith and a crisis of Science—for man to regain the creative freedom that

---

57. Cf. Williston Walker, *A History of the Christian Church* (New York: Charles Scribner's Sons, 1918), p. 73. Tertullian said of Praxeas who spread this doctrine in Rome: "Praxeas did two works of the devil in Rome. He drove out prophecy and introduced heresy. He put to flight the Holy Spirit and crucified the Father." One wonders whether this was not the background for Sartre's "The Devil and the Good Lord."

58. Cf. Jean-Paul Sartre, *Literary and Philosophical Essays.* Trans. *by Annette Michelson* (New York: Collier Books, 1962), p. 180.

Descartes placed in God, and for anyone finally to suspect the following truth, which is an essential basis of humanism: man is the being as a result of whose appearance a world exists.[59]

In terms of "creatio ex nihilo," "Man is the being through whom nothingness comes to the world," and the question is, "What must man be in his being in order that through him nothingness may come to being?" (pp. 24-25). Furthermore, the problem is how to do away with God so that man may escape His infinite fullness and take over His creative powers. For, unlike Nietzsche, Sartre does not elevate man to a state of godhood. On the contrary, he holds that man cannot be God, but must become totally independent of Him. Thus a new ontology arises in which man is not encountered by God at all, but by Being, as such, from which he escapes through his own creative act. In Sartre's terminology, it is a confrontation between the "for-itself" (man) and the "in-itself" (being), and God is dead because He stands in the way of the "for-itself" to become what it is. We may designate this doctrine as a type of negative theology or metaphysical atheism, inasmuch as the God-idea is considered here ontologically self-contradictory and metaphysically unnecessary.[60]

The Ontological Structure

The province of ontology, Sartre tells us, is not to explain why being is the way it is, but to describe its structure so that it may be recognized in its actual manifestations. As we follow him on a tour through his new edifice, we shall find he has introduced certain structural elements which he is trying to hide from our sight but which serve him as props for his metaphysical speculations. We will be especially on the lookout for some elements of logical causality that lie deep in its foundations. We shall also find that he keeps God out of his edifice, because if he allowed Him in He would bring it down on man by the power of His infinite fullness.

---

59. *Ibid.*, p. 196.
60. Jean Wahl has called Sartre an advocate of *neontology*. Cf. H. Spiegelberg, *The Phenomenological Movement* (The Hague: Martinus Nijhoff, Second edition, 1965), II, p. 503.

Sartre's ontological building is structured out of pure space as a principle of separation both internal and external, or as he calls it, interiority and exteriority. His "pure negation" (not-in-itself) is an adoption of Plato's space as *mē ón* or not-being. Like Plato, Sartre is trying to overcome the Eleatic doctrine that only being is and that not-being is-not, by demonstrating that not-being also is.[61] Obviously, the word "is" cannot have the same meaning in both cases. Moreover, whatever its meaning, there must be a locus for *not-is* in relation to *is* and a separation between them. A more troublesome problem is that of becoming, which is the main stumbling block in Sartre's world structure. Plato, not being able to give a rational account of space, lets it hover between heaven and earth as a primary independent principle that serves to hinder the world of appearance from becoming real. Space is here a privative "third principle" which stands between Becoming and Being as the former strives to become the latter.[62] This abstract, static view of space or not-being does not satisfy Sartre's dynamic ontology. Such a space can hinder but cannot produce. To make it productive in a non-causal way, it must function as an immanent principle of becoming. We now have being, becoming, and not-being all placed in the same house. How do they dwell together? As one existent, says Sartre, as separation separating or, in his own hyphenated terminology, as nihilation-nihilating. Its locus in the intra-mundane realm of phenomena is consciousness which exists as self-consciousness.[63] Referring to Plato's discussion of not-being as otherness, Sartre writes: "For the only way in

---

61. This is especially the burden of the Stranger in Plato's *The Sophist,* as for example, 256d. "Then it unquestionably follows that *non-being* is, throughout. . . ."

62. Cf. Plato, *Timaeus* 52d. ". . . my verdict is that being and space and generation, these three, existed in their three ways before the heaven. . . ."

63. Cf. *Being and Nothingness,* p. 18, on the source of this intra-mundane nothingness. Whether or not Sartre follows strictly the phenomenological method of structuring his ontology, as he apparently claims in the subtitle of his book *Being and Nothingness: An Essay on Phenomenological Ontology,* is not pertinent to our discussion. This matter has been thoroughly examined by S. Spiegelberg, "The Phenomenology of Jean-Paul Sartre," in his book *The Phenomenological Movement,* II, ch. X, pp. 445-515.

which the other can exist as other is to be consciousness (of) being other. Otherness is, in fact, an internal negation, and only a consciousness can be constituted as an internal negation" (p. 618).[64]

Now, what Sartre is trying to accomplish by his immanent negation is to establish an absolute separation between man and the rest of being (between the for-itself and the in-itself), not however, through a pre-ordained act of divine creation, but through the free action of man himself. This is the new or "non-substantial absolute" which stands for man's absolute freedom, his very existence, inasmuch as he is to withdraw or separate himself from being. Without going into an elaborate discussion of Sartre's for-itself, in-itself, reflecting-reflection, etc., let us review the relationship he establishes between man (the for-itself) and being (the in-itself), from which the former separates himself or, as Sartre says, is "condemned" to separate himself. What does our philosopher mean by "human reality," "human freedom," man who is "nothingness" but not "emptiness," the appearance of man as an "absolute event," or "a world [which] exists" as a result of man's appearance (pp. 84, 85)? Even at a glance we can recognize the scheme of *creatio ex nihilo,* such that man is the creator who fashions himself and his world out of his own nothingness.

Many questions will arise in the course of our analysis of this scheme. I will pose a few of them in advance, in order to set the

---

64. It is interesting to note that Sartre refers to Plato's *The Sophist,* where the "other than being" or "not-being" is considered from a dialectical point of view with reference to a doctrine of true and false judgment, and he does not mention the *Timaeus,* where not-being is viewed as an ontological principle. In *The Sophist* 257b ff., the Stranger specifically points out that by "otherness," which he calls not-being, is meant something different from being (of a particular thing), and not what Sartre understands it to be, a nihilation. Sartre writes (BN, p. 618): "We may recall the fine description which the Stranger in the *Sophist* gives of this 'other,' which can be apprehended only 'as in a dream,' which has no being except its being-other. . . ." Sartre undoubtedly means the *mē ón* or space of the *Timaeus,* for his description of "the other" appears in this dialogue 52b and not in the *Sophist.* It says there: "And there is a third nature, which is space and is eternal, . . . and is hardly real—which we, beholding as in a dream, say of all existence that it must of necessity be in some place and occupy a space, but that what is neither in heaven nor in earth has no existence" (Jowett's translation).

stage for Sartre's quest of human freedom in an immanent-transcendent structure which is an "intra-mundane nothingness." Where does this nothingness come from and how is it related to being and to man? How does our philosopher account for "is" and "is-not" in the process of "becoming?" How can man come out of being, which is a fullness and can do nothing, unless somehow nothingness or an is-not is generated in it? If so, who generates this nothingness, what is its nature and its locus? And if man is the one who generates it in being, how does he escape its fullness, which is not diminished, and become an independent, existing "for-itself?" Moreover, what happens then to the nothingness?

The Act of Separation: Being, Self, Nothingness

Before we proceed with this analysis, we ought to clear up the the significance of the hyphen in Sartre's word coinage, which is inherent in his philosophical system. The hyphen serves him as a sign of separation of multiples which in reality are a comprehensive unity, that is, it is a sign both of separation and of unity in the same process. This is not to be viewed as a conceptual analysis and synthesis, but rather as a process that separates without breaking the unity. It breaks but does not break up or, as Sartre would say, it is a "detotalizing totality," an "evanescent unity" (p. 82). At the same time, separation means for him an act of nihilation of something in order to create a hiatus or distance within a totality. In order to obviate an absolute break, he inserts the hyphen between the elements to indicate that their separation is a nothingness and that the unity is thus preserved. Such, for example, is the hyphen in the "for-itself" implying an "itself" and in the "in-itself" signifying that after nihilation "it is a fullness." When a term cannot conveniently take a hyphen, he inserts a preposition in parentheses, such as, "the consciousness (of) belief," which *is* belief (p. 75). The only absolute break he allows is between the for-itself and the in-itself, because there the act of separation is "the absolute event." And even there he does not preclude the possibility, though an unrealizable one, of bringing the two together, also through a hyphen, in the *for-itself-in-itself*. In reality, that is in the realm of possibilities, there is no un-

119

hyphenated ground. All possible existence is a process of separation and unification.

In order to keep this discussion on a concrete humanistic level, I will henceforth, wherever possible, use the term "self" or "man" instead of "for-itself," and being instead of "in-itself." There is no essential difference in this nomenclature, except perhaps that Sartre's "for-itself" may mean a kind of primordial man, an *Adam Kadmon,* who is the original upsurge from being and who forms the foundation of man's coming into existence. But since, as we shall see, the "in-itself" can do nothing in this process, it must come altogether through a self, which is none other than the for-itself.

Sartre conceived of BEING (or in-itself) as a plenum, a total fullness without any spatio-temporal elements of distance, separation, or movement in succession. It "is full of itself, and no more total plenitude can be imagined. . . . There is not the slightest emptiness in being, not the tiniest crack through which nothingness might slip in" (p. 74).[65] Being just *is,* without activity or production, and "cannot provide the foundation for anything" (p. 82).

The SELF (or for-itself) is the active, creative principle in Sartre's ontology. Since there is no separation, distance, or foundation for anything in being, all these functions must be derived from the self, or man. It founds the foundation for itself as well as for everything else in the world. This is the meaning of Sartre's assertion that "man is the being as a result of whose appearance a world exists" (see above, note 52). How does the self or man accomplish this? Sartre resorts to the Cartesian logic of doubt and certainty and combines it with a dialectic of the negation of negation. Descartes established that doubt is the only possible certainty, because everything can be doubted. Thus doubt becomes the foundation of possibility. To be sure, doubt is a negation, but it is only through negation that we can arrive at the concept of possibility; the very fact of doubting something implies the possibility of its existence or non-existence.

---

65. We shall see later that the in-itself or being is not entirely free from nothingness.

In this line of reasoning, Sartre establishes that reality is possibility resulting from questioning, which is realizable only through man as the being who questions. Therefore, man or the self is the founder of all possible existence, which comes into being through his act of separation of the possible from the impossible. The prime act of questioning introduces "a certain negative element in the world," a nothingness, and by negating this negation the self becomes possible or real; "thus the for-itself [man] must be its own nothingness" (p. 78). This does not mean, Sartre notes, that the self founds any being, but it creates the foundation of its own and the world's becoming, which is their real existence. That is, the self founds not its being (whatever it is), but its becoming, which is not-being. This will elucidate some of Sartre's enigmatic statements, such as, "For man to be able to question, he must be capable of being his own nothingness . . ." or his often repeated designation of the *for-itself* "as being what it is not and not being what it is" (pp. 45, lxv). They all resolve themselves into the basic dictum of his "philosophy of destruction," that "human reality is before all else its own nothingness" or "it is the unique foundation of nothingness at the heart of being" (pp. 79, 88).

NOTHINGNESS, says Sartre, also *is*; and yet he seems to be greatly disturbed by this man-founded nothingness, for if it actually is what it is, then nothing begets nothing. He therefore modifies it as something that is which is not, namely it is not emptiness. Now he has to account for a new *is* (of) nothingness, which *is* not-emptiness, and this leads him back to his plenum of "Being-in-itself [which] is never either possible or impossible. It *is*" (p. lxvi).

The Logic of "Bad Faith"

By introducing the concept of not-emptiness as distinguished from nothingness, Sartre places the act of separation in the womb of being, but without the latter's participating in, or being affected by, this act. Since the self (for-itself) is the only agent capable of action, it must act in such a manner that the fullness of being is not diminished or disturbed through separation; that is, in founding its nothingness, the self must not cause an emptiness in being,

121

and yet it has to establish itself as a duality of "being and nothingness." To resolve this paradox, Sartre uses the method of logical inversion of the terms "is" and "is-not."

In formal logic it is permissible to draw an inference by inversion, such as, if All A is B then Some not-A is not B. However, as John Neville Keynes noted long ago, this is not altogether legitimate, because the rule requires that the predicate must retain the same distributive character in both propositions. But in the above, B is undistributed in the first proposition (All A is B) and distributed in the second (Some not-A is not B). To legitimize the inversion, one may assume that in the original proposition there exists not only the predicate B but also its contradictory not-B. That is, when we say "All A is B," we also imply the existence of some things which are not-B or other-than-A, which then appear in the partial inversion in the same distributive manner as in the original proposition. This is what happens when Sartre arrives from his proposition "being is fullness" to the conclusion "the self is not-fullness" in the womb of being. He assumes that the proposition "being is fullness" contains also a being which is not fullness, namely, the self or "a particular being" which is not-being. From this he infers, by partial inversion, that the "self [some not-being] is not fullness." As Sartre himself stated in his Introduction (lxvii), he posited these "two types of being" to start with.

This type of reasoning to establish an "is" through the negation of negation is what Sartre himself would designate as "bad faith." "And what is the goal of bad faith," he asks? "To cause me *to be what I am,* in the mode of 'not being what one is,' or *not to be what I am* in the mode of 'being what one is.' " Translated in terms of being, it means "the *ontological characteristic* of the world of bad faith with which the subject suddenly surrounds himself is this: that here being is what it *is not,* and is not what it *is.*" But then he turns around and tries to find "the 'faith' of bad faith," such that "if bad faith is faith and if it includes in its original project its own negation . . . then . . . a faith which wishes itself to be not quite convinced must be possible," in other words, questioning or negation makes for possibility of existence (pp. 66, 68, my italics). This is how he establishes self-questioning faith as a

122

certain kind of being, which is not fullness of being. Moving in this logical circle, which "includes in its original project its own negation," he still has to devise a means of extricating the for-itself from the in-itself in order to make the former absolutely independent.

The Upsurge of the Self

To break this magic circle, Sartre engages in speculations about "the origin of the for-itself" which, he says, is a metaphysical question inasmuch as it seeks to ascertain the existence of an existent (p. 619). The for-itself or self, as stated, is an existent which is the foundation of its own nothingness, but not of its being. But neither is the in-itself or being the foundation of the self's being, because being-in-itself cannot be a foundation at all. The self is therefore a "being which exists by itself," and the question which our philosopher himself raises is, "since the for-itself—in so far as it is—is not its own being (i.e., not the foundation of it), how can it as for-itself, be the foundation of its own nothingness?" (p. 80). More specifically, he is asking for the origin of the self or, how the self as nothingness can move out of being, when the latter just is and cannot cause or "cannot provide the foundation for anything."

The self, Sartre asserts, is an upsurge of being insofar as the latter fails to be its own foundation; that is, the self is being's failure, which is a certain *lack* or nothingness. He calls this upsurge an ontological act of an absolute event in which being *degenerates* into the self, as if to say, being is there for the sake of *falling* into a state of not-being or into the possibility of becoming. "It *is,* in order to lose itself in a for-itself" (p. 81). The fall appears like "a hole in the heart of being." "Thus nothingness is this hole of being, this fall of the in-itself toward the self, the fall by which the for-itself is constituted" (pp. 78-79).[66] This is Sartre's version of the doctrine of the "fall of man" through man's own negation or sin.

---

66. The concept that the "hole in being" and not the plenum represents reality is current in modern physical theory, as suggested by Paul A. M. Dirac in his book *The Principle of Quantum Mechanics*

We still have to account for the act of nihilation in the original upsurge. Since being cannot nihilate, what does it mean to say that it "degenerates" unless it has the possibility of degenerating. This possibility, according to Sartre, can be none other than the self (for-itself), which lies in the womb of being awaiting its upsurge. Its appearance "is the absolute event which comes into being" but not through being-in-itself but through the self by itself. This self is like a chick that pecks the "hole in the heart of being" and separates itself from it by simply falling out of it. What all this amounts to is that being not only *is* but also *fails to be,* and its failure is nothing but the self or man. "The for-itself is *effectively* a perpetual project of founding itself qua being and a perpetual failure of this project" (620).

By assigning to being a negative role—failure—in the upsurge of the self, Sartre actually posits nothingness in being, as such. Through its failure to be the foundation of the self, being turns itself into the self that sets the foundation. Being's failure may be designated as negative creation, which Sartre converts into "creative negation" of the self. "Why is it that *there is* being?" he asks. To account for it he would have to posit an act of becoming in being, as such, which would be self-contradictory. Therefore, he prefers to have being "fail" to act, but makes it somehow turn itself into a self that can assume the responsibility of action. "It is only by making itself for-itself that being can aspire to be the cause of itself" (p. 620). The self, as the active agent, can never become fully being, but must remain its failure (or, to use a theological term, its fallenness). If it ever succeeded in reverting to its original source, it would cease to exist as a separation. It therefore "perpetually founds its nothingness-in-being." The "absolute event which is the appearance of the foundation or upsurge of the for-itself . . . is contingent in its very being" (pp. 619, 82).

_____

(Oxford, 1930). The "hole" is also spoken of as "anti-matter" which some physicists say exists in the universe. All this goes back to Plato's space or not-being "as the mother of all things visible." As an example, anti-matter was produced and photographed by the Bevatron at the University of California, in April, 1958. More recently, Soviet physicists identified nuclei of anti-helium, which fit into the concept of anti-matter or the "hole" in being. (See *The New York Times,* Feb. 24, 1970.)

If, as we have seen, being (or its failure) is immanent in the self, how does it ever get to be transcendent to it? This problem arises in Sartre's account of human consciousness, which must be conscious of something, that something being nothing else but being as negated by the self (pp. 79f., "Immediate Structure of the For-Itself"). "The concrete, real in-itself is wholly present in the heart of consciousness as that which consciousness determines itself not to be" (p. 85). It is as if the self said to being (in its consciousness), "I am not going to be this being" and by thus annihilating it, the self now *lacks* being or determines itself as "a lack of being." This does not actually remove being from consciousness, but only lets it be an "out-of-reach presence" or a "transcendence of the for-itself." Now what, exactly, is the nature of this transcendence? Sartre says, "it is conceived as the original bond between the for-itself and the in-itself," and when this bond is innihilated by the self (in its upsurge from being), it turns into a transcendence. But what is the nature of the bond and who establishes it, to begin with? Sartre places it as "the original connection" represented in the nihilation, or transcendence is the nothingness caused by nihilation acting as a bond between being and the self. Nihilation, as the cause, may be represented as the middle term in the following syllogism: Nihilation is transcendence. The bond is nihilation. Hence the bond is transcendence.

This logical triad of bond-nihilation-transcendence may be illustrated by a diagram of two concentric circles which represent being and the self. Let (B) stand for being, and (S) for the self. Placing B in S (S⨀) the two intersect having (B) as their common subset. But (S) refuses to be (B) and nihilates it. Yet (B) remains in (S) but separated from it by a line which is neither B nor S, that is, by a null-set or nothingness which now constitutes the bond between being and the self. This kind of bond is the only meaning one may ascribe to what Sartre calls "absolute transcendence in absolute immanence" (p. 91), or his claim that "Nothingness [the null-set] carries being in its heart" (p. 18).

By reversing the order of the circles (S⨀), we obtain Sartre's statements "Nothingness [the null-set] must be given at the heart of Being" or "the hole in being in the heart of being," and "Nothingness lies coiled in the heart of being—like a worm" (pp. 22, 21). Finally, "a total immanence which is achieved in total transcendence" (p. 91) can be realized only through a null-set that is neither B nor S, that is, nothingness. Sartre's reply to his own question "Where does nothingness come from?" is that being neither includes nor excludes it; "Being lacks all relation with it" (p. 22). In sum, the bond is transcendent to being because the bond is nihilation, and nihilation is nothingness.[67]

Morality and the Individual Self

When Sartre turns his logical triad into a metaphysic, there emerges a trinity of being-nothingness-self, patterned after the Christian Trinity but without the living God. Being makes itself into man (Sartre's version of Incarnation) in order that the latter may found himself through the mediation of nothingness and in order that with his appearance the world may come into existence (instead of creation of man and the world through Christ). We shall examine how this godless metaphysic has been transformed into ethics and morals.

A trinity, Sartre observes, has meaning only within totality as unity (p. 86). In Christian theology, whatever explanation is given of the Trinity, its ultimate meaning rests in the living God. In Sartre's meaning, man realizes himself entirely by himself in that he determines himself as a lack and strives to surpass what he lacks and become a totality (p. 89). This, in essence, is our philosopher's conception of man's moral goal—the attainment of total personality. While Sartre dispenses with God in this process, he nevertheless takes cognizance of what he regards to be man's passion to be God or to fuse with the absolute totality, and he warns that man must be cured of this passion. "Ontology" and existential psychoanalysis," he says, "must reveal to the moral

67. Albert Camus builds a triad of Absurdity, Man-Absurdity-World, similar to Sartre's triad of Nothingness. Camus posits absurdity as the only bond between man and the world, a bond which causes a separation or gap between the two and belongs to neither one of them. Cf. Rolf Denker, *Individualismus und mündige Gesellschaft* (Stuttgart: W. Kohlhammer Verlag, 1967), pp. 59-60.

agent that he is *the being by whom values exist*" (pp. 626-627, italics in original). Just as the world comes into existence by the appearance of man, so does value arise in the world through human reality (p. 93). As founder of his own existence man also founds his values, and this is his freedom. But what, in the final analysis, is the nature of this value? Once more, Sartre resorts to the "ontological act" of the upsurge of the self in which he introduces a concept of "lack" as its ground of value. That is, value, like the self, originates through an act of nihilation. For value really lies in being, as all values must, and the self retrieves it from there in its upsurge. "In value the for-itself becomes itself by surpassing and by founding its being; there is a recovery of the in-itself by the self" (p. 119). Yet it is not being, as such, that enters into the self as its value, but what the self makes of it through negation.

How does value, which lies in being, come to the self, which does not want to be being? Sartre conceives of value as an ontological act whereby being sacrifices itself in order that the self may exist (an allusion to Divine sacrifice for the sake of man's salvation). This value is taken over by the self as a lack or a special kind of being which the self founds as its foundation. "In this upsurge of the for-others, value is given as the upsurge of the for-itself although in a different mode of being" (p. 95). This lack with which the self merges is the bearer of a trinitarian dialectic process. As Sartre explains,

> A lack presupposes a trinity: that which is missing or "the lacking," that which misses what is lacking or "the existing," and a totality which has been broken by the lacking and which would be restored by the synthesis of "the lacking" and "the existing"—that is "the lacked" (p. 86).

The lack has the same position and function as nothingness in the triad of being-nothingness-self. In its upsurge from being the self comes out with a lack, because it nihilated being. But in order to assure its own existence, the self must perpetuate the lack; otherwise it would fall back into the fullness of being and cease to exist. The lack now becomes the self's value or the goal toward which it strives, namely, to escape fusion with being. "This being

127

of the self . . . is to be value; that is, not-to-be being" (pp. 92-93).

Out of this trinity of "the lack" man emerges as a duality of "self" and "value" (the synthesis of "the existing" and "the lacking") or what Sartre designates as the "insoluble dyad, Being and Nothingness" (120). In order to preserve this duality and at the same time complete itself as a totality, the self, as a lack, must surpass itself "toward what it lacks," that is, become "the lacked" or the "individual self." In actual existence, then, man turns his duality back into a trinity, as the concept of lack presupposes. In this dialectic fashion, Sartre has transformed the Divine Trinity into a functional trinity of human self-existence.

The Circuit of Selfness: Man Is Alone

As we now look back at Sartre's scheme of self, nothingness, and being, we find that these stand, respectively, for man, value, and the world of things (including others as things). Inasmuch as being is in the heart of nothingness, man realizes himself as a dyad (or duality) of self and value, i.e., Being and Nothingness. He can surpass himself toward his goal through his communication with others (things and fellow men) as objects of his goal. He is always at a distance from others, as he himself is perpetual separation. Without the distance, Sartre warns him, he would fuse with being (the others) and cease to be a self. Man's salvation, we may therefore say, is his nothingness, which keeps him from total annihilation. But in his existence in relationship with others in the world, he makes himself into a triad of subject-copula-object "in the mode of reflective-reflected on," instead of "the mode of the dyad reflection-reflecting." That is, as man, I am "engaged in the circuit of my selfness" (153).

In the final reckoning, the nothingness of Sartre's ontology constitutes his metaphysical ground for the being of the self. It all hinges on the specific being of the for-itself. To his first metaphysical question "why being is other," Sartre replies, "the question can have meaning only within the limits of a for-itself and that it even supposes the ontological priority of nothingness over being." And to the second metaphysical question "Why is it that *there is* being?" he answers with logical circularity, " 'There is' being because the for-itself is such that there is being" (619). The word "such" stands for the "priority of nothingness" which is the real cause; that is to say, there is being *because* the for-itself founds itself in nothingness.

The moral and ethical implications of Sartre's metaphysical atheism is that man is left completely alone in his incompleteness to found his own foundation of values and ethical conduct in relation to fellow men. It is Sartre's great merit that he has placed his ethics on the level of action, decision, and responsibility. The freedom which he identifies with morality is a freedom of action, not just of being. But his concept of responsibility is entirely individualistic, without an ethical imperative, human or divine— pure activism of the individual self toward its goal of personal totality. This is not the same as ethical responsibility, and it may even go contrary to it. According to Sartre, man is responsible for every situation he may find himself in, because he alone is its founding foundation. By the same token, he is responsible *for others,* because he projects "the other" in his own freedom of self-realization. Thus, each individual is responsible for his situation, including the world and the people with whom he lives in everyday contacts, because he alone totalizes them as he totalizes himself through these contacts. "I have to realize the meaning of the world and of my essence; I make my decision concerning them —without justification and without excuse" (p. 39). Sartre then is telling the incomplete self to be completely responsible *for* everything and everyone, but *to* no one. If this spells absolute freedom, then the inordinate burden it places on man can crush the stoutest of hearts and splinter the "self" into bits, and Sartre may indeed be right when he says, "man is *condemned* to be free." His promise of salvation through this kind of freedom allows man only to escape from fusion with being, which would at best be an escape from a logical-dialectic identity; that is, if the dialectician were to take "nothingness" out of the middle between being and self, the two would coalesce. Sartre tells man he need not fear such a possibility, because possibility itself is only human, and since man is a duality who creates his own possibility, his unification with being is excluded *ipso facto.* The only thing man *cannot* do is *not* to create his own possibility, that is, cease to be a dyad of Being and Nothingness, and that is why, again, he is condemned to be free.

On "the ethical plane," Sartre has not yet produced the "future work" which he indicated at the end of his book *Being and Nothingness*. Suffice it here to pose the ethical question which he himself raised in the final stages of that book, and that is the question of freedom as it grew out of his metaphysical speculations. If man rejects the supreme value of *ens causa sui* or God (as Sartre conceives of God) and human freedom becomes "conscious of itself . . . as a unique source of value and the nothingness by which the world exists," will freedom "be able to put an end to the reign of this value" of the *ens causa sui,* that is, God? More important is the question, what does freedom signify if it means escape—"to flee itself, not to coincide with itself but to be always at a distance *from* itself"? Will the "self," who is this freedom, "escape all situations" or stay situated "and accept more fully its responsibility as an existent by whom the world comes into being" (pp. 627-628)? Without a guideline from our philosopher, and barring any revelation from a higher source, we must leave these questions exactly as he left them—wide open.

13. RADICAL THEOLOGY: SALVATION WITHOUT GOD

Radical theology does away with the God-idea because it finds it contrary to the principle of individual freedom. But the radical theologian, reared in Kantian-Protestant transcendental reason or in Hegelian-Protestant dialectics, deals with two worlds, and the question is, in which of these worlds does he propose to dispense with God? That depends on his view of man's essence. Kant, who regarded pure reason as the essence of man, could show, at least to his own satisfaction, that the God-idea could not be a necessary and universal concept in the phenomenal world of the understanding, nor a necessary principle in the noumenal world of freedom. Yet he found a need for it in the realm of morals and advised man to act so as if there were a God and another world, or that, as a matter of practical religion, man may will that there be a God and immortality for his own sake.[68] The radical theologian, on the other hand, who deals not just with pure reason but with man as a whole, questions this human need altogether. Contrary to Kant, he finds that man, for his own sake, must will the death of God rather than His existence. At the same time, as a theologian for whom "the death of God is an actual historical event," he too views the problem under the aspects of a dual world. If God "must be negated by the word of faith," and if, as Altizer demands, "It is the Christian who must murder God," [69] the question then is whether this is a Christian "must" only for this world of mundane life or also for the super-mundane, other-worldly life. I will discuss the views of two radical theologians who have spoken quite clearly on this subject, one, William Hamilton, on the mundane aspect, and the other, Thomas J. J. Altizer, on the super-mundane.

a. *William Hamilton's Dual Salvation*

Hamilton focuses his attention on man as he stands in communication with fellow men in a world without God, or in a secular world without religion, if by religion is meant man's relation to God. There is no need for religion in interhuman relation, he avers, even though there may still be a need for it insofar as individual man may seek his way to God. But then, he says, the role of God in human life would have to be totally different from what traditional theologians have pictured it to be in the past. "The breakdown of the religious *a priori*," he writes, "means that there is no way, ontological, cultural or psychological, to locate a part in the self or a part of human experience that needs God. There is no God-shaped blank within man" (RT 40). Thus, while Kant finds no faculty for the God-idea in pure reason, Hamilton denies it a place in human experience altogether, and yet he admits the existence of God as "one of the possibles in a radically pluralistic

---

68. Cf. Immanuel Kant, *Kritik der praktischen Vernunft*, 223f. See 226: "It is morally necessary to assume the existence of God."

69. Thomas J. J. Altizer and William Hamilton, *Radical Theology and the Death of God* (New York: Bobbs-Merrill Company, 1966), p. 135. This book will be quoted below by its initials RT and page number in parentheses in my text.

spiritual and intellectual milieu." The only place for such a possibility would be the other world, for in this world, Hamilton says, God is not needed in the mundane life of man at all; the mundane world has nothing to do with religion. "God, if he is to be for us at all, must come in some other role," and that is in the role of a dead God. In Hamilton's confession, "This combination of a certain kind of God-rejection with a certain kind of world-affirmation, is the point where I join the death of God movement" (RT 40-41).

Hamilton's main approach to the God-idea in man's world is a pragmatic one:—does it work? and his answer is, No, we can do best by ourselves without it. Whatever pertains to this world, the world itself "is qualified to do," and there is no call for "God to meet a need or to solve a problem, even the problem of not having a God." On the positive side, the affirmation of God's death, according to Hamilton, is that it clears the way for a Christological ethic, which is exemplified in the life and teachings of Jesus. "We turn from the problem of faith to the reality of love," he says. Man's ethical existence in love, his concern with his neighbor in an actual, concrete world of things, is the content of the new theology, and man is admonished to find Jesus in the world, find him "in your neighbor," become "Jesus in and to the world," live an ethic of love (RT 40-41, 47, 49).

No Christian, it would seem, could object to this ethic, but he would want to know more about the Jesus Christ which our theologian has in mind. "The radical theologian," we are told, "has a strange but compelling interest in the figure of Jesus . . . who appears in conjunction with the death of God." The strangeness comes to the surface when we learn that the radical theologian views Jesus not as Person but as an ethical experience. Thus Hamilton writes:

> In Christology, the theologian is sometimes inclined to suspect that Jesus Christ is best understood as neither the object nor the ground of faith, neither as person, event or community, but simply as a place to be, a standpoint. That place is, of course, alongside the neighbor, being for him. This may be the meaning of Jesus' true humanity and it may even be the meaning of his dignity, and thus of divinity itself (RT 92).

Although the absent God died, man is urged to wait for his resurrection, "trusting in waiting, silence, and in a kind of prayer for the losses to be returned" (RT 92). These losses and their return have nothing to do with this world but are reserved only for the other world. Indeed, Hamilton arrives at the idea of a dual salvation in two different worlds. It doesn't really matter where he might locate the other world, here or above; what matters is that he cuts it off entirely from man's everyday needs and experiences. In this "worldly world" he has man seek salvation through a Christological ethic in a locus named Jesus Christ without God; in another world, if there is one, man may seek additional individual salvation in or through God. In keeping with the tradition of salvation through divine sacrifice, Hamilton advises that the true Christian must kill God or affirm his death, and then wait patiently in silence for his resurrection, that is, if he should choose to "come in some other role." He envisages salvation in God as enjoyment in the Divine Being, but not in the sensible world, where man has no need of him, but in another world, after man will have lost his sensible pleasures or perhaps in old age or after his death, when he will have only God to look to.

This new American theology, as Hamilton calls it, is without faith in the past or hope for the future, only holding on to the moment of the present. "We should not only acknowledge, but will faithlessness," he suggests (RT 87). And what about waiting and praying "for the losses to be returned," which he promises? Upon careful examination, we shall find that it is really not a return to God but, of all things, to middle-class urban man and his "new faith" in the reality of science and technology which has been "made inevitable by the scientific revolution of the seventeenth century . . ." (RT 47). We are fully aware of the illusions of the "scientific revolution" when man is left all alone in this world. We shall now turn to some of the metaphysical speculations of the new theology.

b. *Thomas J. J. Altizer's Salvation in Resurrection of the Nothing*

Altizer and Hamilton have stated jointly:

133

The aim of the new theology is not simply to seek relevance or contemporaneity for its own sake but to strive for a whole new way of theological understanding. Thus it is a theological venture in the strict sense . . . (RT back cover).[70]

How are we to understand a theology that centers in a dead God? In their own words, "How can man return to the Father when he died?" And what kind of salvation may one hope for, assuming there is any hope left in the world? Our radical theologians seek a new meaning of Incarnation and Resurrection as historical events in time. "Gods have always been in the process of dying," [71] they say, insisting that "it is in Christianity and Christianity alone that we find a radical or consistent doctrine of Incarnation. . . . Radical theology must finally understand the Incarnation itself as effecting the death of God" (RT xii).

Coming back to our original question (In which of the two worlds must God die?), we find that Hamilton kills him as the *immanent* Being in the mundane world, while Altizer murders him as the *transcendent* Being in the extra-mundane world. Consequently, and with radical consistency, each of these theologians is waiting for a return to God toward a different end: Hamilton toward the end of man's enjoyment of God, and Altizer toward the End of all ends, man's fusion with God. To put it in theological terms, the one is looking for salvation in a dead God's Resurrection in a scientific world, while the other anticipates God's self-negation through Resurrection in the Nothing.

The Arch-Enemy of Freedom

In Altizer's theology, the logic of individualism, which has its roots in the Age of Enlightenment, reaches a high point. Man is to

---

70. In another place Altizer emphasizes contemporaneity itself as the major issue, namely, as "the greater problem . . . of finding a genuinely contemporary meaning, a meaning which can be expressed in contemporary language, of that Reality which lies at the center of the Christian faith." Cf. Thomas J. J. Altizer, "Nirvana and the Kingdom of God," *New Theology no. 1.* Edited by Martin Marty and Dean G. Peerman (New York: Macmillan, 1967), p. 155. This article will be quoted below as Nirvana, with page numbers given in parentheses in my text.

71. This reminds us of Nietzsche's reference to an old Germanic saying "All gods must die." Cf. Friedrich Nietzsche, *Der Nachlass* I, 1.

be liberated not only from Church and State, but also from God himself, whom the radical theologians consider as the transcendent primordial oppressor, the arch-enemy of man's individual freedom. "Only by means of a realization of the death of God in human experience can faith be liberated from the authority and the power of the primordial God." [72] Altizer is quite correct in saying that "in the Western tradition the idea of God has always been philosophical," that is, the culminating idea of a metaphysical system (Nirvana 152). Such is also his own theology, only he tries to infuse it with revaluated metaphysical concepts, to form what he calls "a genuine doctrine of God." "We are forbidden," he says, "to make use of the traditional categories of the Christian faith, because they are both archaic and unbiblical" (Nirvana 153, 155). He rejects the Aristotelian Prime Mover in favor of a *coincidentia oppositorum* of Hegelian dialectics (or is it borrowed from Cusa?), and substitutes the Wholly-All-in-All for the Wholly Other, replacing transcendence with absolute immanence. His justification, however, is by reason not by faith, which is more dialectical than that of the other Western philosophers whose God he declares to be dead. His only complaint is that the others did not kill God with sufficient finality, which he now proposes to do by his own "genuine doctrine of God." In the Incarnation as well as in the Eschatological End he banishes the living God and seeks to establish a Kingdom of God in which God is totally, absolutely, and irrevocably dead. Thus his real problem, as he says, "is that of attempting to apprehend the Christian meaning of the Kingdom of God in a situation in which God is dead . . ." (Nirvana 155). At first he tries the way of "the radical immanence of the modern West," from which he derives his "radical theology," but when he reaches an impasse, he turns to the way of the Far East, "relating the Kingdom of God to Nirvana." His two roads cross in a new Eschatology of an apocalyptic nature, when Nirvana assumes immanence in dialectic fashion of the End of all ends. Let us follow him first as far as he goes along the Western road.

---

72. Thomas J. J. Altizer, *The Gospel of Christian Atheism* (Philadelphia: The Westminster Press, 1966), p. 112.

The Dialectic of Incarnation and Resurrection

Interpreting Nietzsche's slogan "God is dead," Paul Tillich writes:

> The concept of the "death of God" is a half-poetic, half-prophetic symbol; . . . it can only mean that God is dead as far as man's consciousness of him is concerned. The idea that God in himself is dead would be absurd. The idea is rather that in man the consciousness of an ultimate in the traditional sense has died. The result is . . . that somebody else must replace God as the bearer of the system of traditional values. This is man.[73]

Yet it is this absurd "idea that God himself is dead" that Altizer insists on in all seriousness. He means just that: "The Self-Annihilation of God,"

> an actual real event not perhaps an event occurring in a single moment of time in history, but notwithstanding this reservation, an event that has actually happened both in a cosmic and in a historical sense. . . . An authentic language speaking about the death of God must inevitably be speaking about the death of God himself.[74]

Altizer's metaphysical-theological problem is to reconcile a non-spatio-temporal God with man's existence in space and time, or as he designates the two states, the sacred with the profane. If anything is to be sacrificed in this situation, he maintains, it must be the sacred or God for the sake of the profane or man. Thus he makes God, whom he calls the primordial Beginning of a transcendent Reality, decompose himself into spatial elements "in a cosmic and in a historical sense," and merge gradually into the spatio-temporal existence of the human self (RT 140ff.). In this dialectic process, the primordial Beginning or the sacred negates its own sacredness, that is its unfallen form, so that it may "become incarnate in the reality of the profane" or in the fallen condition of

---

73. Paul Tillich, *Perspectives on 19th and 20th Century Protestant Theology* (New York: Harper & Row Publishers, 1967), p. 201.
74. Thomas J. J. Altizer, *The Gospel of Christian Atheism,* pp. 102-103.

man and affect its redemption at every moment of its existence. Incarnation is conceived here not as a one-time historical event, but as a perpetual ongoing process taking place in actual space and time. In Altizer's own words,

> The Fall is an actual and real event; the world and human existence are judged to be actually and truly estranged from their original divine ground, and consequently the process of redemption must occur in the arena of concrete time and space (RT 147-148).

In the same dialectical process and simultaneously with God's Incarnation, man as the profane negates his profaneness and becomes sacred, or his flesh becomes spirit, not, however, the Spirit of the Beginning or God (who is now decomposed and dead), but as a new sacredness, a realization of the "ever more fully dawning power of the reality of the profane." In its ultimate form it is neither spirit nor flesh but a union of the two, which Altizer designates as the Kingdom of God. This then is the meaning of the death of God in the new, radical theology: "The primordial God of the Beginning must die to make possible the union of the Spirit with flesh" (RT 154-155).[75]

Such is Altizer's vision of "total redemption" in "the possibility of an End that transcends the Beginning." It moves in a circle of negations, from transcendence to immanence to a new transcendence, first by murdering the transcendent God and then after having him dissolved into the spatio-temporal existence of man, by transforming man himself into the Kingdom of God which transcends the God of the Beginning—a kingdom of God without a God.[76] Since this new Kingdom has a spatio-temporal existence,

---

75. If in this spatio-temporal setting we take "flesh" to represent space, and "spirit" time, Altizer's conception of the new Incarnation is analogous to the modern physicist's concept of space-time as a new independent reality which is neither space nor time in the naive, traditional sense. Cf. H. Minkowski, "Space and Time," in *The Principle of Relativity*, by A. Einstein and others (New York: Dover Publications [1923]), pp. 191f.

76. This aspect of Altizer's soterics is very much akin to that of Marcion, the second century church reformer, who sought to liberate man from the oppressive power of God who created the cosmos, or

the profane fallenness rather than the sacred incarnation is the real power which transcends itself toward "total redemption." Man surpasses his God when the latter becomes decomposed into spatio-temporal elements; and even though these elements may ultimately be raised to a new sublimation, as Altizer intimates, they are still dominated by the profane rather than the sacred (RT 151). As Altizer now tries to reconcile his Kingdom of God with cosmic spatio-temporal reality, he finds that in the Western mode of thought, in which he seeks to resolve his problem of godless Reality, his dialectic of self-transcendence lacks cosmic finality. He then lifts his eyes to the Far East whence he hopes to receive some comforting help.

Existence of Nothingness

Not satisfied with his own doctrine of immanence, and rejecting the traditional teaching of transcendence, Altizer moves his new Kingdom from the Western planes to the Eastern heights of Nirvana. "It is impossible," he says, "for Western man to dissociate the idea of God from the idea of *kosmos,* the idea of a rational order which is embedded in the world. God and *kosmos* are polar expressions of one root idea: the rationality of the universe, or, rather, the very idea of the *uni*verse itself" (Nirvana 152). In our time, he avers, the cosmos has turned into *chaos* and neither man nor the Christian God can put it together again. He therefore turns to the Buddhist teaching of reality as "naked existence" without a cosmos. This, he says, is also the original meaning of Jesus' message of radical eschatology, namely, an End of the Cosmos and "the coming of the Kingdom of God, whose coming would annihilate the world." Then time will assume a higher metaphysical form, without a historic past or future and even without a present. Like Buddhist Nirvana, it will be a world which is not-world, in which there is no immanence or transcend-

---

the God of the Beginning, by leaving him and his world to self-destruction and by having man transplanted into a new Kingdom. This note is meant only to point to the anti-cosmic character of redemption which both theologians hold in common. Otherwise, their teachings are greatly divergent in many basic concepts, which, however, is not our purpose here to discuss.

ence, no this-side or beyond. Nevertheless, contrary to some Buddhist tenets, Altizer does not negate the present world, such as it is, even with its "anguish, death, and pain." Taking Mahayana Buddhism as the right way of the Bodhisattva, he advises man not to try to escape this world but bear it as his Cross in the knowledge that the one Reality is in the Kingdom of God—a not-world without distinction between spirit and flesh. This, in his view, is man's destiny, the price of "Christian contemporaneity" (Nirvana, pp. 154, 160, 163-164).

Altizer sees the new Kingdom of God actually breaking "into time in our midst," in our present-day life on earth. But if, as he implies, the advent of this Kingdom means that "the world as 'history,' 'nature,' and 'being' is brought to an end," what is happening to man's life with nature? Is it actually coming to an end? Altizer has no answer to this most embarrassing question of his excursion into Nirvana. What is actually breaking into our midst, he discovers, is the Nothing "as a reflection of ultimate Reality, . . . as the hither side of God," of the God who annihilates himself to become contemporaneous fallenness. "For the death of God," he reluctantly admits, "has been followed by the resurrection of the Nothing; the Nothing is now openly manifest in the deepest expressions of contemporary existence" (Nirvana, 167). Indeed, when a theologian pronounces the death of God as the condition of man's very existence, he must inevitably end up with the nothingness of that existence.

IV. End of An Era

14. LUDWIG WITTGENSTEIN: HOW LITTLE ACCOMPLISHED

> I am therefore of the opinion
> that in essence I have given the
> ultimate solution to the problems
> [of philosophy]. And if I am not
> mistaken, the value of this work
> consists also in this that it shows
> how little is accomplished when
> these problems are solved.
>
> WITTGENSTEIN,
> *Logisch-philosophische
> Abhandlung.* Vorwort.

Ludwig Wittgenstein, perhaps more than any other contemporary philosopher, represents the dénouement in the drama of the Enlightenment. He sets himself the same task at the end of this era that Descartes had undertaken at its dawn, namely, to save philosophy from scepticism. But whereas Descartes started with a heuristic method that may turn doubt into certainty, Wittgenstein ends with some "therapeutic" methods that can point only to "our failure to understand," and thus throws us back into rather hopeless doubt. As Norman Malcolm observed, "He was constantly depressed, I think, by the impossibility of arriving at understanding in philosophy." [1] For what the philosophers understand, Witt-

---

1. Norman Malcolm, *Ludwig Wittgenstein: A Memoir* (London: Oxford University Press, 1958), p. 32. It is noteworthy that, like Descartes, Wittgenstein regarded his own method as the most important achievement of his philosophical career. Cf. G. E. Moore, "Wittgenstein's Lectures in 1930-33," *Philosophical Papers* (New York:

genstein says, is just their entanglement in their own rules of language-games. Yet he considers these games as "part of an activity, a form of life," [2] and his own philosophy, it appears, has failed in this activity (PUi, 23, 53, 122).

Both in his early and later stages, that is, in the *Tractatus Logico-Philosophicus* and in the *Philosophical Investigations,* Wittgenstein is preoccupied with the problem of ascertaining the role of the mediator in the logical mode of thinking. His goal is not changed by the fact that in the former he tries to "explain" uses of language and in the latter only to "describe" them. This is a matter of applying different methods toward the same end, and that is to make clear how the mediator acts as a link in meaningful uses of language, which, he says, ought to be the philosopher's sole occupation. In his later work he declares an end to the business of "explanation"; it must be replaced by "description." By that he means to replace scientific observation and hypothetical theory with philosophical "insight" into the problems of language, which are nothing but problems of "misconstruction" of our language forms or problems of "grammatical witticism" (PUi, 109, 110, 111, 116).[2] He wants to take words, phrases, and propositions out of the realm of metaphysics and put them back into everyday usage. But when he sets out to examine and describe the forms of usage, he lapses into a scientific search for causes or mediators. His aim is to discover all possible intermediate members (*Zwischenglieder*) between the actual uses of a given word or phrase and to understand it as is. And here his philosophical problem turns scientific. He may not describe the intermediate links at random, but must choose them deliberately and even invent them (*finden und erfinden*), "overview" them, in order to see their interconnections

---

Collier Books, 1962), p. 316. "As regards his own work, he said it did not matter whether his results were true or not: what mattered was that 'a method had been found.' "

2. Ludwig Wittgenstein, *Philosophische Untersuchungen* 118, in his *Schriften I* (Frankfurt am Main: Suhrkamp Verlag, 1969). This volume of *Schriften* contains *Tractatus logico-philosophicus, Tagebücher,* and *Philosophische Untersuchungen* Teil I & II. This first will be quoted below as TR and section number, and the last as PUi and section number for Teil I, and PUii and section number for Teil II. Translations are my own.

(*Zusammenhänge*). Without rules and principles of selection and composition he might go on describing intermediates *ad infinitum* and never attain understanding, and that is his problem of mediation in the *Tractatus* as much as in the *Philosophical Investigations* (PUi, 122).[3] In neither of these works has he established a boundary to make the "between" real. In the early work he is in search of bounds inside a boundless logical circle, and in the later work he looks for intermediates between endlessly open ends. His difficulty in both stems from the fact that he fails to distinguish between "bound" and "limit"—a distinction which Kant regarded as fundamental to the philosopher's task of discovering the limitations of understanding.

The Philosopher's Role

Although Wittgenstein's aim in the *Tractatus* is basically the same as in the *Investigations,* the role assigned to the philosopher in each is different. In the former the philosopher is a theoretical investigator of the prime elements of logical space, out of which he builds a closed-in, self-sustained universal system. In the latter, he is a practical builder who arranges particular data and discovers or invents connectives between them, such that may hold them together in an open world. These two roles will help us understand the difference between what is generally accepted as the early and later Wittgenstein.[4] In line with this architectural

3. Cf. George Pitcher, *The Philosophy of Wittgenstein* (Englewood Cliffs, N. J.: Prentice-Hall, 1964), pp. 318-319. "Wittgenstein's methods are meant to help the philosopher to describe the uses of words, but not just any description will do."
4. Cf. David Pears, *Ludwig Wittgenstein* (New York: The Viking Press, 1970), pp. 95-96. "In spite of the differences between his early work and his later work, what he was trying to do was still the same kind of thing . . ." and that is "to plot the limit of language. . . ." Cf. Paul Feyerabend, "Wittgenstein's Philosophical Investigations," in *Wittgenstein: The Philosophical Investigations. A Collection of Critical Essays.* Edited by George Pitcher (New York: Anchor Books, 1966), p. 148. ". . . the *Investigations* (apart from their substitution of language-games for the one language of the *Tractatus*) are after all not as different from the *Tractatus* as they seem to be at first sight." Note: This Collection will be referred to below as *Critical Essays,* author, article and page number.

analogy, I will examine the nature of the space, the bricks, the mortar, and the scaffolding which our philosopher employs in establishing his new structure, first in the *Tractatus* and then in the *Philosophical Investigations*.

a. *The Tractatus: A Logical Edifice*

After Kant had shaken the foundations of the old metaphysic and set boundaries for a new world outlook within the confines of pure reason, his enterprise was likened to the Tower of Pisa: it leans but does not topple. For Kant did not mean to abolish metaphysics altogether, only to reshape it in conformity with his critical view of scientific truth. In the *Tractatus Logico-Philosophicus* Wittgenstein undertook the task of toppling the Tower, razing it to the ground, and erecting a different structure out of pure logic that would surpass Kant's limitations. He planned it without Kantian bounds of noumena or Ideas and envisioned a logical edifice that would set its own bounds and hold itself together from within through an intricate web of rafters, which, he hoped, could hold up against the strains and stresses of philosophical speculation for all time. In essence, he thought he had found the ultimate answer to the problems of philosophy, but admittedly his solution accomplished very little, as he could find no place for the philosopher in it.[5]

For Wittgenstein, as for Kant, the philosopher is a "critic" who analyzes the constituents of knowledge to their ultimate elements and ascertains how far they reach out into reality when they offer a scientific account of things in the world of everyday experience. That is, the critical philosopher is ready to admit that his knowledge is limited by the character of its own constituency, yet he wants to explore and utilize it to the very bounds of its limitations. If he finds that the bounds are not adequate to account for the whole of reality, he may venture beyond them into speculative ideas, as Kant did; or if he finds that his scientific foundations of the world are self-sufficient, he may just stop philosophizing, as Wittgenstein suggested when he reached the end of his *Tractatus*.

The basic material Wittgenstein uses in his *Tractatus* for the

---

5. Cf. *Tractatus*. Author's Preface, last paragraph.

construction of reality is language-space or logical space, which is infinitely divisible through logical analysis. His problem therefore is to set a limit to this kind of divisibility. He pondered this question in his *Notebooks* as follows: If we "assume that every spatial object consists of infinitely many points, then . . . I *cannot* arrive at the complete analysis in the old sense at all." But the question is, "Are spatial objects composed of simple parts" and can we analyze them to a point where they are no further analyzable? This is a question of the fundamental concept of analysis, as such, whether it involves simple components or must go on indefinitely, or whether there is a third possibility. That is, "the complexity of spatial objects is a logical complexity," and the problem of analyzing it is a logical problem. Now, while logic allows infinite divisibility, it demands, above all, that our knowledge be clear and definite; hence, we have to ascertain what is definite in a proposition or when its divisibility must end. Wittgenstein says that we arrive at this stage when a proposition reaches its fundamental sense, which lies in its simple element. Our main task then is to find the simple elements of language-space by setting limits at which propositions may not be broken up any further.[6]

Wittgenstein proposes to find these limits within his world structure of language-space as such. *"The limits of my language,"* he states, "mean the limits of my world. Logic pervades the world: the limits of the world are also its limits" (TR 5.6, 5.61). Accordingly, the things the world is made of must be represented or reflected in its constituent elements, which can be ascertained only through analysis of propositions. However, when our philosopher analyzes his propositions of language-space, he obtains a picture not of things but of relations or, as he puts it, "the possibility that things are related to one another in the same way as the elements of the picture" (TR 2.151). In other words, his objects of reality are "relations and properties," but not "what" is being related, because through further analysis the "what" always shows up as relation or, in his terminology, "object-relation"

---

6. Cf. Ludwig Wittgenstein, *Notebooks, 1914-1916.* Translated by G. E. M. Anscombe (Harper Torchbooks, 1969), pp. 62e-63e. This work will be quoted below as NB.

(*Sachverhalt*) expressed through "elementary propositions" (NB 61e and TR 5.101).[7]

What Wittgenstein regards as "facts" of reality are propositions as logical constructs of "elementary propositions" or relations, but not things; and the world mirrors only these elementary propositions which are reflected in the so-called propositions of fact. Basically, then, all we can say of his world is that it is neither one thing nor another.[8] We can speak of true or false possibilities in such a world but cannot say what is possible, for the propositions represent only object-relations, not objects as such. Insofar as objects may pop out of the object-relations, they are non-existents (like the "holes" in modern physical reality), because they are not expressible in language space; and what cannot be expressed in propositions, Wittgenstein tells us, cannot be spoken of. His whole schema is like a scaffolding of a world-structure which shows how it is held together, but not what is there. In his own words, "The propositions of logic describe the scaffolding of the world, or rather they represent it." Or "A proposition constructs a world with the help of a logical scaffolding, so that one can actually see from the proposition how everything stands in logic *if* it is true" (TR 6.124, 4.023). Having decomposed the world into indivisible "object-relations," which can mirror objects only

---

7. D. F. Pears and B. F. McGuinness in their translation of the *Tractatus* (London: Routledge & Kegan Paul, 1961) render the word *Sachverhalt* as "state of affairs," which I find difficult to apply in Wittgenstein's world schema. In physical theory, a state is a position of bodies and their velocities at some initial instant of time. Wittgenstein's "Sachverhalt" does not refer to a given position or time but to structural elements. He says the difference between *Tatsache* (fact) and *Sachverhalt* (object-relation) is that the latter "corresponds to an Elementarsatz if it is true," and the former "corresponds to the logical product of elementary props when this product is true." The difference seems to lie in the degree of complexity; but he did not elaborate on it. Cf. NB 129. For a more detailed discussion of this subject see Walter Schulz, *Wittgenstein: Die Negation der Philosophie* (Stuttgart: Neske, 1967), pp. 18ff. See further, Julius Hartnack, *Wittgenstein und die moderne Philosophie* (Stuttgart: W. Kohlhammer Verlag. Zweite Auflage, 1968), pp. 22f.

8. Wittgenstein derives his disjunctions and conjunctions of relatedness from the single connective of Sheffer's sign "p/q"—neither p nor q. Cf. Pitcher, *op. cit.,* pp. 63f.

as "nihils" of logical propositions, Wittgenstein cannot find in his language analysis the divine word that will recreate his world *ex nihilo*. Thus the winds of nihilism blow through his scaffolding, and the limits which he has tried to set for his language-space in the *Tractatus* do not actually limit, because they are whirling as quasi-existents in a logical space of endless possibles. This is the fate of logical analysis when left alone to establish its own limits. It abolishes not only metaphysics but all content of thought.

The actual world remains mystical for Wittgenstein, as it must for all those who try to construct it out of a logical space of one kind or another. One who wants to "see the world aright," Wittgenstein advises, "must transcend these propositions" (TR 6.54). But such a height is ineffable, like the divine mystery; it does not reveal itself in the world on earth, and, he says, we must pass it over in silence (TR 6.432, 7). The purpose of the *Tractatus,* as stated, is the setting of limits for the "expression of thoughts," by which is meant the limits of natural science (TR 4.11, 4.113). The philosophers of our era of Enlightenment have hailed scientific truths as the new verities that will bring salvation to man in all walks of life. Wittgenstein now admonishes them not to harbor such illusions (TR 6.371). "We feel that even when *all possible* scientific questions have been answered," he says resignedly, "the problems of life remain completely untouched." But in the same dictum he also pronounces an end to all philosophy, as he counsels: "Of course there are then no questions left, and this itself is the answer" (TR 6.52).

b. *Philosophical Investigations*

New Points in Language-Space

Not very long after the *Tractatus* was published, Wittgenstein realized that it did not give the correct language analysis in answer to the philosophical problem he had raised with regard to the limits of scientific thought. He therefore proposed to correct it in his second major work, *Philosophical Investigations*. But the problem of setting limits, which he propounded in the first work, remained equally poignant and equally troublesome in the second, except that instead of trying to find its solution in "the world of a limited whole," he now decided to locate it in the endless constituents of a world of language which is open at both ends. For that he needed a different method, one that does not analyze language as a structure of logical space, but as a process in actual use, one that does not explain how language may be composed of possible indivisible elements, but describes it in terms of endless possibilities of usage.

In the *Tractatus* Wittgenstein finds that, as his science of language sets limits to scientific thought, it also limits language itself. That is, he is confronted with the problem of scientific explanation of reality in which the measuring rod disturbs the reality to be measured. He then tries to show that the disturbing factor does not lie in logical thinking but in the philosopher's misunderstanding of the essence of language. Yet after clearing up these misunderstandings, he is left with a theory of language that all but eliminates the actual world. For his criteria in the *Tractatus*—the facts, objects, and object-relations—do not just disturb reality but replace it with language elements. In the *Philosophical Investigations,* therefore, he seeks to weed out all disturbing factors by setting up non-theoretical criteria and thus reach the reality of language in its purity. In the *Tractatus,* he concludes, his difficulties do not stem just from wrong methods of formulating his theories but rather from the fact that he theorizes at all. Now he wants to investigate reality in a practical way by observing and describing it as he may find it, without hypotheses or preconceived postulates. At the same time he realizes that for a descriptive presentation, too, he must have objective facts which he must locate in his language-space. As before, the crucial question is about the philosopher who handles the facts. Is he a discoverer, an inventor, or just an enumerator and arranger? In both works Wittgenstein warns the philosopher to beware of the pitfalls of his trade. In the *Tractatus* he advises him to eliminate philosophy because its language disturbs scientific theory, and in the *Investigations* he admonishes him to get rid of philosophical problems because their theorizing disturbs real language. In both, the philosopher's task is to put an end to philosophy.[9]

---

9. Cf. Paul Feyerabend, *op. cit.,* p. 147, n. 20. " 'Language dis-

Piero Sraffa's so-called disgusting movement of the hand, which reputedly marked Wittgenstein's turning-point toward his later philosophy, is significant not for the kind of gesture made, but for the fact that our philosopher could find no room for it in his language-space. This incident, which was the culmination of long discussions between the two friends, revealed to the latter the emptiness of his logical structure, its lack of concrete linguistic expression. He then decided that the philosopher's role was not to fashion logical systems, but to describe the actual objects of human discourse. Consequently, he had to abandon not only his former method, but also the facts and objects which he had painstakingly chiseled out of logical space, and to start reshaping his language-space into new forms.[10]

Actually, all Wittgenstein had to do was to pull down the logical scaffolding of the *Tractatus* and the whole structure would have collapsed. Without the elementary propositions, which make up the scaffolding, there is nothing that can mirror the world, and without the pictures of object-relations there is nothing that can express "agreement and disagreement with the world" or the possibility of situations. This also cuts down the "proposition with sense," which is nothing but "agreement and disagreement with the world" and which constitutes the cornerstone of the entire edifice. As it now lay in ruins, the logical world of language-space became meaningless and devoid of understanding. Overviewing these ruins, Wittgenstein surmised that the fault of his earlier undertaking was perhaps in his theory of "understanding and meaning," as it proved to be inadequate for everyday language. Instead of object-relations he now sought word-relations, which do not fall under fixed rules but are determined by fluid circumstances of everyday speech. Yet, even in this fluidity there must be factors that describe the correctness of usage, and there must be

---

guises the thought' is the position of the *Tractatus* (4.002). One could say that according to the *Investigations,* the (philosophical) thought disguises language."

10. Cf. Malcolm, *op. cit.,* pp. 15, 69. Cf. PU, Vorwort, with reference to Sraffa's influence on Wittgenstein's thoughts over many years. "To this stimulus [of Mr. Sraffa's criticism] I owe the most important ideas of this work."

criteria for ascertaining them. Even without fixed rules, there must be order in word-relations. We shall understand best the nature of this new order and how it was obtained, if we first examine what Wittgenstein abandoned of the old method and what he gained by the new one.

Methods

In the *Philosophical Investigations* Wittgenstein changes the method of explanation to a new method of description, because the new object of his investigation does not lend itself to the former method. His new object is language-games which have nothing in common with each other; that is, there is no general principle or single identifiable rule that can explain their operations in essence. All one can do is describe each language-game in its particular occurrence under given circumstances. These language-games have now become the bricks out of which the new world of language-space is built, not, however, as the logical elements of this space but as actual word usages. The new method is not an analysis of concepts in the framework of a science of language, but of a multitude of usages without reference to any framework, that is, without a scaffold, without a theory. At the same time, Wittgenstein realizes that one cannot go on analyzing usages at random, *ad infinitum,* for then there would be nothing to hold even a single language-game together; he must find rules for playing his games. For this he adopted a technological method of convention and invention or "finding and founding" (*finden und erfinden*).

By analyzing numerous examples of everyday language in actual use, Wittgenstein hopes to find how each word plays a part in making up a particular language-game. Inasmuch as the possibilities of usage are unlimited, he proposes to found or invent imaginary language-games, so-called intermediary cases, which may entail new applications of familiar words in a limitless variety of nuances.[11] But with all that, he has not established a single rule

---

11. Cf. Ludwig Wittgenstein, *The Blue and Brown Books*. Preliminary Studies for the "Philosophical Investigations" (Harper Torchbooks, 1965), p. 28. "That is also why our method is not merely to

of a general character that may apply to a class or set of language-games. As he notes, "there are words of which one might say: They are used in a thousand different ways which gradually merge into one another. No wonder that we can't tabulate strict rules for their use" (BB 28). What, then, does he mean by the word "rule"? In his vocabulary, "rule" is not a law or even a concept, and cannot therefore assume a universal character. It is a descriptive word that denotes, but does not connote, the *role* which a given word or sentence plays in an actual language-game under given circumstances. The same word may play different roles under different conditions, and there is no telling from one case how the word may be applied in another case. Moreover, one cannot generalize from any number of particular cases. "Don't always believe," Wittgenstein warns, "that you can pick your words from facts which, in turn, you may picture in words according to rules! For you would have to apply the rule in a particular case without guidance" (PUi, 292). A rule of how a word is used is described, not formulated, and the description is not a word-picture of a given thing, only how a word is applied in a given case. "What we call *'descriptions,'*" he says, "are instruments of particular applications" (PUi, 291). Several descriptions of language-game may resemble each other in a variety of "overlapping similarities" like members of one family, but there is no single trait or set of traits that may express the essence of each member, for none of the traits can be reduced to an essence.

While a rule, in Wittgenstein's language, is not a universal law, it does not mean that it is a one-time use of a given word or sentence that cannot be repeated. "It cannot be that a person can follow a rule only once." A rule, a communication, or an order can be followed numerous times. They are habits, practices, institutions. "To understand a sentence means to understand a language. To understand a language means to master a technique" (PUi, 199). Rules of language-games are thus obtained through actual playing, through communication or carrying out an order.

---

enumerate actual usages of words, but rather deliberately to invent new ones, some of them because of their absurd appearance." This book will be quoted below as BB. Cf. PUi, 122, 312, 510.

One knows a language-game by learning how to use it. The learning is not through theoretical explanation but through actual playing, for language-games are unexplainable; all we can say about them is that they are played (PUi, 66).

This new method of delimiting language-space cannot, as some maintain, be identified with empiricism or pragmatism, because these two are also theories involving a systematic structure of concepts and principles, even though derived empirically or pragmatically. The *Investigations* forego all theorizing, conceptualizing, and universalizing.[12] "Making scientific hypotheses and theories" is also nothing but a language-game, though of a different kind than that of everyday use. Neither can it be said that Wittgenstein plays his games as does the artist who creates a poem or a novel through the play of imagination, although the former often uses his words in this manner. Rather, his basic new approach to language is that of the technician as opposed to the

---

12. Cf. Renford Bambrough, "Universals and Family Resemblances," *Critical Essays,* pp. 191-199. Bambrough's attempt to show that Wittgenstein's "family resemblances" conceal a "theory of universals" does not hold. Bambrough maintains, e.g., that when "Wittgenstein says that games have nothing in common except that they are games," he establishes a real, not just a nominal, concept "game" which can be objectively applied to all games, though they have nothing else in common (p. 199). This is a sophistication (of "nothing-except") that Wittgenstein himself would decry as picture-making. Bambrough substitutes the word "game" for the phrase "have in common," intimating that "game" in itself is a certain picture, quality, or essence which is "common" to all games—a "grammatical witticism" of singling out the word game from its plural games, as if the singular form were some essence of the plural form. He further cites Ayer's remark, " 'It is correct, though not at all enlightening, to say that what games have in common is their being games.' " Bambrough agrees with it in the main but strongly denies "that it is unenlightening," even though he admits it is only "trivially and platitudinously true." But we might add in Wittgenstein's name that it is not just trivial but plain useless, and what is of no use is not a language-game. On the other hand, it is correct to say that Wittgenstein is not a nominalist, as suggested by Bambrough. The name "language-game" has no nominal meaning for him but is rather a sign for play-operation. This brings him into the fold of the modern physico-mathematical technologists for whom the "operator" is the only reality that matters. Cf. Henry Margenau, *The Nature of Physical Reality* (New York: McGraw-Hill Book Company, 1950), ch. 17, on Operators, pp. 331-337.

scientist-theoretician. His application is an art in the general sense of *techné: skill,* instrument, artisanship, that is, in a technological sense. "Think of words as instruments characterized by their use," he says, "and then think of the use of a hammer, the use of a chisel, the use of a square, of a glue pot, and of the glue" (BB 67-68).

Here in one sentence Wittgenstein has piled up the mortar and the tools he plans to use in bringing together the language-games which are his new points in language-space. "Also," he adds parenthetically (p. 67), "all that we say here can be understood only if one understands that a great variety of games is played with the sentences of our language . . ."—actually an unlimited variety. Yet his task here, as in the *Tractatus,* is to set limits to this variety, but not theoretically as heretofore, but technically. How can this be accomplished? The question has two aspects, an inner and an outer, to wit: (1) How are limits established within the confines of each language-game so that it does not degenerate into an endless analysis of word uses? (2) How are bounds drawn around language-games as a whole so that each game is not proliferated into an endless variety? In operational terms, the first question is, when can we be sure that a given game is complete with its rules or roles in actual play? The second question is, how can we know that a given game, even within its set limits, is adequate to express our needs in a given life-situation without having to pile up other related or unrelated games of the same or different families? These questions are, in the final analysis, fundamental to Wittgenstein's language-space, as to any other space, for they raise the issue of setting "inner limits" and "outer bounds" without which a space cannot function. In the *Philosophical Investigations* this issue becomes a matter of finding criteria, on the one hand, and of delimiting understanding and sensations, on the other.

Situational Criteria

The finding or inventing of criteria, as the case may be, is the key problem in Wittgenstein's attempt to set limits to his language-space. We must bear in mind, as stated, that he undertakes to find the limits and bounds through language techniques and not through scientific theory, and certainly not through speculative theory of metaphysics, as, for example, Kant did. That is, Wittgenstein's criteria are not to be found in some principle or hypothesis, but in usage or instrumentality of application. As Malcolm noted, "Perhaps the best way to elucidate it is to bring out its connection with *teaching* and *learning* the use of words." [13] Be this as it may, our concern here is to ascertain whether his technique, or for that matter any technology, is capable of setting its own limits and bounds.

Wittgenstein recognizes that, if we allow ourselves to be weighed down by the burden of having to adduce all possible situations without end before accepting any criterion, we fall prey to endless doubt, which leads nowhere. Hence he lays down a maxim, "Doubting has an end," meaning certainty permits no doubt. When pressed, "But are you not just closing your eyes to doubt, when you are *certain?*" he replies, "They are closed" (PUii, V, IX p. 537). What he is actually closing his eyes to is the fact that he establishes "normalcy" as his ultimate criterion without telling us what he means by it except to describe what he regards to be normal situations, namely, such that fit, are usual or commonly acceptable. If someone thinks a particular case of this kind abnormal, the burden of proof is on him.[14]

This "situational criterion," as we may call it, applies at best to a particular usage, which may also be applicable in exactly the same situation on different occasions. Intermediate situations may be discovered or invented in a given case to delimit the usage to a point of certainty. But such a point does not appear in the situation of itself; we simply make it "a point" and stop analyzing or

---

13. Cf. Norman Malcolm, "Wittgenstein's Philosophical Investigations," *Critical Essays,* p. 83. "This notion of 'criterion' [is] a most difficult region in Wittgenstein's philosophy." I would say, it is the most unsettled and inconclusive.

14. Cf. C. F. Chiara and J. A. Fodor, "Operationalism and Ordinary Language. A Critique of Wittgenstein," *Critical Essays,* p. 397. "In summary, we can roughly and schematically characterize Wittgenstein's notion of criterion in the following way: X is a criterion of Y in situations of type S if the very meaning or definition of 'y' . . . justify the claim that one can recognize, see, detect, or determine the applicability of 'Y' on the basis of X in *normal* situations of type S." That is, the definition of 'Y' must fit the *normal* situation of S.

looking for further intermediate steps. This is how the inner limit is established in language-space. Its outer bound is to make certain that a given language-game is sufficient to express our relation in a given situation. Two concepts which establish relations may satisfy this demand, namely, understanding and sensations. Before we examine their function in Wittgenstein's scheme, we have to clear up a distinction between limits and bounds which is highly pertinent to his problem of certainty in general. A limit puts a stop to inner analysis or outer extension; a bound or boundary embraces an expanse as a whole and separates it from everything that is non-extension. Both deal with spatial relations and are thus applicable also to language-space.

Limits

The concept of space, whether in geometry, language, or any other space-set, is that of a continuum which is limitless at both ends, that is, endlessly divisible within and endlessly extendable without. One can always divide a given spatial unit into smaller units or add to its extension other extensions *ad infinitum*. Setting a limit in space is a negation of continuity—to stop dividing or adding at any interval considered appropriate. The main feature of this limit is that the stopping-point or negation has no extension, yet lies within the space which it negates. That is, there is spatial extension on either side of this limit, and the point (no extension) may be shifted back and forth, like a point on a line, without stepping out of the spatial expanse. Thus, the limit has the same endless possibilities as space itself. It is obvious that space, as extension, cannot set its own limits, which is a negation of extension (dialectics will not do here). While the nature of a space-continuum makes the limits possible, even necessary, their setting is an act of negation by an outside agent.

Wittgenstein's limits are of the same nature, as his player of a given language-game is the only one who can put a stop to the discovery or invention of intermediate situations and deny the game further analysis. Such denial leaves each game open to endless possibilities. The analysis may be stopped but there is always the possibility of continuing it, and this raises a doubt as to the particular justification for stopping it. As long as there is no certainty why a given limit may be set (and there can be none when limits may be shifted without guidelines), doubt will prevail. It should be noted that this doubt is not of a methodological nature, as it is, for example, for Descartes. The latter employs a heuristic method of doubt turning itself into certainty. The doubt that Wittgenstein engenders does not eliminate itself by playing a language-game; on the contrary, it perpetuates itself. He has turned this paradox into a disease, as he calls it, and that is why he seeks "therapeutic" methods to cure it. Barring any theoretical frame of reference, and excluding a metaphysic of language-space, his technology of language-games fails to take definite steps to end its proliferation within and without. This, in general, is the basic problem of all modern technologists, and Wittgenstein is perhaps its greatest investigator in that he lays bare its hopelessness even as he tries to cure it. For, as stated earlier, he does not endeavor to resolve it but rather to show that it is not at all a problem. As we shall see later, he regards this type of resolution to be the philosopher's sole function.

Bounds

A bound or boundary lies outside the domain which it binds and differs from it in nature. A boundary of language-space is thus not within this space but envelops and separates it from everything that is not-space. What lies outside is not the same as on the inside. The latter is familiar space and the former is something not-spatial and non-comparable with the inside, and may never be known to us in spatial form. We can only know the bounds which hold the inside together but not really what lies beyond them. Unlike the spatial limit, which has a negative character, a bound is a positive entity, concept, or principle, separable from the space which it binds and having an existence of its own, be it real or illusory, but necessarily so. Whereas the limit is only a stopping-point within the continuum and can be shifted back and forth, allowing the continuum full sway, the bound binds it as a whole and prevents its extension. The former is like a sign-post in a wide expanse, the latter like a fence around it. And if the expanse thus being confined within its boundaries ever breaks out of them, it becomes the task of the philosopher to re-examine the bound, mend it or modify it, or perhaps lay new foundations for an entirely different world-structure. This, in the main, has been the history of metaphysical speculation in Western culture since the days of Plato and Aristotle.

In modern times the philosopher-scientists have tried to do away with metaphysics altogether, but this has not solved their problem of finding boundaries to the spatio-temporal universe which they have constructed out of what they consider to be physical reality. They have sought to establish bounds inside this universe, but these have turned out to be nothing but spatial limits, that is, theoretical non-extended points formed out of the same non-spatial elements as the physical theories themselves. Wittgenstein made a similar attempt in the language-space of his *Tractatus*. When he later realized its inadequacy, he changed his theoretical method to a technological one. Since he excludes metaphysical ideas, the only bounds he could possibly discover by his new method are understanding and sensations, which might be taken to have real non-spatial existence and thus serve as boundaries for his language-space. We shall now follow his excursion in these two domains.

Understanding

The issue here is whether there are mental processes of understanding and meaning that lie behind the language-games and are not of the same nature as the latter. To understand and to mean would thus be a non-spatial faculty of the mind capable of setting bounds to language-space. As Wittgenstein poses the issue:

> It means that there are *certain definite* mental processes bound up with the working of language, processes through which alone language can function. I mean the processes of understanding and meaning. The signs of our language seem dead without these mental processes; and it might seem that the only function of the signs is to include such processes, and that these are the things we ought really to be interested in (BB 3).

156

Having stated this possible function of understanding and meaning, Wittgenstein proceeds to demolish it as a misleading metaphor, "a muddle felt as a problem" (BB 6). He points out that we use the word "thinking" as a "mental activity" performed by an agent that thinks apart from the signs of the language-games. But, he says, there is no agent performing this activity outside the language signs, for "thinking is essentially the activity of operating with signs," whether these are made in the form of writing, speaking, or picturing. Here the agent is the hand, the mouth, or the imagination, and it is only when we separate the word thinking from the words speaking, writing, or imagining, that we look for a special agent called "mind," by analogy or metaphorically alongside the agent "hand." He acknowledges that this type of investigation is the proper field of the theoretical sciences of psychology, but, not being concerned now with theory-building, he dismisses it from his language-space.

In Wittgenstein's new spatio-temporal structure, the understanding is not a faculty of the mind that may grasp objects in or outside of it. It does not produce them by acting on perceptions and does not in any way point at them. In a word, the understanding does not deal with objects, and it therefore cannot explain language-games, or posit criteria for setting limits to intermediate cases or for establishing bounds against the endless extension of language-space as a whole. From these considerations it follows that there is no "explanation" of how a language-game must be played, only a "description" of how it is actually being played in a given situation. Even when we look at a family of language-games we cannot explain any of its members by the resemblances it may have with other members, for there are no fixed resemblances common to all of them, only sundry ones which we may find in some but not in others; we "see similarities crop up and disappear" (PUi, 66, 67). According to Wittgenstein, the best the understanding can do is what any part of language-space does, and that is to extend or describe case after case after case, or interpolate intermediate cases, in endless procession.[15]

---

15. Even a cursory look at the language-games that are being played nowadays in the agencies of industry, trade, education, and social and

Sensations

Perhaps sensations, not being spatial by nature, can serve as bounds in language-space. Wittgenstein warns that such a notion would be confusing the language of inner sensibility with that of outer observation. A word designating a particular sensation, such as "pain," does not have the same signification as a word designating an outer thing, such as "tree." Sensation words—"pain," "ache," "tickle," and the like—do not point to specific objects which are experienced by a person or which may be identified as the same objects experienced by other persons. The word "toothache," for example, does not identify an actual thing inside the person who says "I have a toothache." Its actual use denotes outer manifestations of whatever may go on inside the person, but does not point to an object inside him. It describes circumstances of behavior but does not denote the inner condition giving rise to the behavior, which may be due to a real sensation, a simulated one, or no sensation at all. Therefore, there is no outside, objective reality that may set a bound to its usage. Wittgenstein's clearest statement on this subject reads as follows:

> How do words *relate* themselves to sensations?—It seems there is no problem here; for do we not speak daily of sensations and name them? But how is the connection between the name and that which is named established? The question is the same as this one: how does a man learn the meaning of the names of sensations? For example, of the word "pain." This is one possibility: words are connected with the primitive, natural expression of sensation and substituted for it. A child has injured himself, he screams; and now the adults talk to him and supply him with outcries and later with sentences. They teach the child a new pain behavior. "Are you saying then that the word 'pain' actually designates scream-

---

governmental institutions will give us cause for deep concern about the disarray in our present orientation in reality. The welter of forms, questionnaires, tables, charts, and other bits of information we have to fill out at every step of our daily lives have turned our existence into a nightmare. And there is no end in sight to this proliferation. This is what happens when human understanding is converted into boundless description.

ing?" On the contrary, the word-expression of the pain replaces the screaming and does not describe it (PUi, 244).[16]

Wittgenstein admits that pain is a private sensation which is important to the person who may have it, but he argues that the *word* "pain" does not name or describe it; that is, this word does not point to a particular thing which it purports to denote. It means that "pain" is a sensation-word which is not derived from the experienced sensation of pain but from the language-game played with this word in certain situations. But how does it ever happen that one starts playing this kind of game? What criterion does one have for designating anything ("something" or "nothing") by this word?[17] Being unable to supply a criterion for sensation-words, Wittgenstein resorts to common sense: we can ascribe the word "pain" to beings that are capable of this kind of behavior. "Only of that which behaves like a human being can one say it has pain" (PUi, 283). Or, since we cannot imagine a stone having pain, we cannot speak of its pain-behavior (*ibid.*).

This kind of tautological reasoning stems from Wittgenstein's disregard of causal relations in sense-experience. That is, he does not have to explain (give the causes of) sensations, only describe them, and since he cannot reach their inner state, he can only use a word that denotes an external behavior, which may or may not correspond to the actual experience or, for that matter, to no experience of this kind. But if we look into the causal relations of sensations, we find that, indeed, the word "pain" does not have a "thing" behind it, but rather a tactile sensation caused by

16. But what if the child screams, but has no pain, yet is told to replace the scream with the word "pain?" He could never associate real pain with this word-expression.

17. Wittgenstein's parable of "The beetle in the box" (PUi, 293) is gratuitous. Since the "something" or "nothing" in one's box is not observable by others (as the "pain" in one's body is not felt by others), no one would think of calling it "beetle" unless he had prior experience with a beetle, not just beetle-behavior, in actual interhuman communication. For when he says "I have a beetle in my box," he wants the others to know that he has "something," and he would not call it "beetle," if it were not a word of their common previous inter-communicative experience with an actual beetle. Even if he simulates, he has to simulate "something" not "nothing."

something which disturbs the nervous system and to which the body, as-a-whole, reacts. The word "pain" points to that something, even though we may not specify it due to our lack of specific knowledge of what caused the disturbance. (In all causal explanations there is an element which is unknown, as there is always the possibility of finding additional intermediates between the stimulus and the response.) In this respect there is no difference between private and public objects or between inner and outer sensations.

In the statement "I have a toothache," the object of my sensation is not "toothache" (the grammatical form notwithstanding, which seems to be Wittgenstein's concern), but "something" in the tooth which causes the disturbance in the tactile center of sense-perception. Similarly, in the statement "My eyes hurt from the sun," the object of my sensation is not the "sunstroke" in my eyes, but "something" in the sun which impinges on the center of my visual perception. The same argument can be extended to other sense-perceptions; tactile, taste, etc., in which inner as well as outer objects impinging on the sense-organs may or may not be identified, depending on our knowledge of causal relations. (This is especially true of taste: how can we decide whether a lemonade is sour or sweet, pleasant or unpleasant?) The truth of the matter is that the words "pain" and "hurt" could never arise in human language unless something is experienced (and all our experience is inner) which may be designated by these names. Once the experience is there, its naming comes through an act of communication between human beings. For language, in general, is generated through interhuman relationships in which every one participates with all his faculties, sensation, imagination, cognition, and the rest. In living language there is no separation of sensation-words from intellection-words. Indeed, all sensation-words have conceptual pointers which make them communicable.[18] What gives

18. Cf. Sören Kierkegaard, *Fear and Trembling.* Trans. by Walter Lowrie (Doubleday Anchor Books, 1954), p. 70. "So soon as I talk I express the universal, and if I do not do so, no one can understand me." For an interesting observation on toothache see Jose Ortega y Gasset, *Unas lecciones de Metafísica* (Madrid: Alianza Editorial, 1970), pp. 65-66. "Pero saber, tener conciencia, es un modo especial, y ya más o menos intelectual, del darse cuenta. . . . Cuando me duelan

them meaning is the personal experience, which is concrete and identifiable through the very act of communication. How this is made possible cannot be resolved by an analysis of language-games, as these games are themselves predicated on the possibility of interhuman communication. It may be a problem for ontology or philosophical anthropology, of which Wittgenstein would be very suspicious, as he is of all philosophical problems.

The Philosopher's Illusions

"A philosophical problem," says Wittgenstein, "has the form: 'I don't know my way about'" (PUi, 123). That is, when a philosopher thinks he sees a problem, he only shows that he has lost his bearings; he is like a fly that doesn't know how to get out of the "fly-bottle" (Wittgenstein's well-known parable), and the reason he does not know how to get out is that he has failed to understand the nature of the trap. Therefore, one's "goal in philosophy" should be "to show the fly the way out of the fly-bottle" (PUi, 309). This does not mean that Wittgenstein knows of a hidden apperture of escape which no one else has been able to discover. Rather, he proposes to show that the "fly-bottle," that is the problem, is only an illusion which the philosopher has created for himself through his involvement in language analogies and similar entanglements, which he has no business meddling with. The more the philosopher tries to explain them, the more he entangles himself in the mesh of his own problems; for his business is not to explain language, but to describe it. Therefore, Wittgenstein advises that

> Philosophy should in no way invade the actual use of language; in the end it can only describe it (PUi, 124). For the clarity we aim at is surely a *complete* one. But this only means that the philosophical problems should disappear *completely* (133).

---

las muelas, el que me duelan no es un saber: saber no es dolor, pero sin duda el hecho dolor implica un ingrediente que es existir para mí el dolor, darme cuenta de él en el sentido de tener que contar con él." That is, to be conscious of pain implies also an intellectual account of something that gives pain and makes itself known in the sense that it has to be reckoned with.

How does Wittgenstein see these problems? He says, "In order to see more clearly, . . . we must keep an eye on the particular events," because each case poses different questions under different situations (PUi, 51). The problem, then, arises when the investigator tries to describe events in universal terms and falls into a trap of his own making. No doubt Wittgenstein's "fly-bottle" is nothing but the scientific method of the philosopher-scientist, who in truth cannot help but use universal concepts along with his particular findings. Wittgenstein offers to teach him how to spring the trap. He mistrusts science and has little use for the philosophy of science (cf. BB, p. 18). However, without them he has nothing to suggest that may set limits to his language-games or, indeed, to "real language." Instead, he proposes to make his language-games a self-operating enterprise. Like all technological schemes, it is self-defeating.

After showing the philosopher how to break the fly-bottle, Wittgenstein advises him to shake off his philosophical aspiration altogether and take his place as custodian or "overseer" in the technological plants of the language-games.[19] This overviewing activity may go on yet for a long time, considering the many illusions that prevail in modern thought. But there may come a time —and this is Wittgenstein's consolation—when this job will be completed and its function eliminated. This will be philosophy's great discovery: its self-liquidation. The language-plants will then run smoothly, like perfect technical establishments, presumably setting their own goals and limits, but, we must say regretfully,

---

19. Cf. the following examples of the philosopher's functions mentioned in the *Philosophical Investigations* (numbers in parentheses refer to sections). "The philosopher's work consists of a compilation of recollections for a definite purpose" (127). "The problems are solved not by adducing new experience, but through an arrangement of what has been familiar ever since. Philosophy is a struggle against a bewitching of our understanding through the medium of our language" (127). "When the philosophers use a word—'knowledge,' 'being,' 'object,' 'I,' 'proposition,' 'name'—and think they have grasped the essence of the thing, one ought to ask himself: Is this word actually ever so used in the language of its habitat?" (116). "The results of philosophy are the discovery of some plain nonsense and bumps which the understanding got by running into the limits of language" (119).

they will still be operating without direction or guidelines—without bounds.

Wittgenstein's Legacy

More than the cure, Wittgenstein's *Philosophical Investigations* reveals the symptoms of the intellectual ailments of our time. Since the advent of the scientific age, the philosopher has struggled to preserve his rightful place as an independent worker in the field of knowledge, or at least as a co-worker with the scientist. But as the latter advanced his claim to being the sole possessor of the right method of attaining truth, the philosopher was put on the defensive and, by now, has been all but discredited in the eyes of all so-called right-thinking persons. Wittgenstein, like others in his time and before, notably, Nietzsche, Husserl, and Buber, correctly looks at this state of affairs with alarm. He accepts the scientist's negation of metaphysical speculation, but finds science itself a poor substitute for the certainty which that speculation was able to offer, at least to its adherents. Science, he notes, has not succeeded in filling the gap created by its negation of metaphysics, and the philosopher-scientist, too, has not been able to make good his claim. For the philosopher who operates with scientific methods, precisely because he proposes to solve philosophical problems by these methods, creates for himself not just illusions but a veritable delusion (BB, 17-18). Yet Wittgenstein does not repudiate science, as such, so long as it stays within its proper field; he only rejects the philosopher who usurps its methods. But why is he unable to find another, more productive function for the philosopher in the new scheme of things? The answer lies in his transition from the *Tractatus* to his *Philosophical Investigations*. In both he contends against the philosopher, but whereas in the former work he treats him with some consideration, in the latter he shows little use for him, even regards him as a hindrance.

In the *Tractatus* Wittgenstein himself acts in the capacity of a philosopher-scientist, in the spirit of the Age of Enlightenment, insofar as he tries to transform the entire field of human knowledge into a self-contained science of language-space. The philosophical problem there is a problem of designing the correct

163

theory of language-space, and if the philosopher will learn to ward off the language confusions generated by improper theories, he will be converted into a pure scientist and give up his philosophical trade voluntarily. However, when Wittgenstein realized the incongruity of his endeavor, he turned his back on science and embraced the method of technology. This is his chief aim in the *Philosophical Investigations:* to become the prophet of modern technology, perhaps analogous to Kant's position as the philosopher of Newtonian physics. Instead of devising a new scientific theory of language-space, which he attempted in the *Tractatus,* he now searches for workable techniques in playing language-games, and in his pursuit of this goal he discovers that the philosopher, being out of joint with technology, can offer no help. As a problem-raiser, the philosopher only causes confusion and becomes inimical to the "normal" workings of the language-games; it is therefore best for him to eliminate himself from the scene.

In our despair with the crisis in science today, and as we tire of groping for new signposts in the stream of reality, we may welcome Wittgenstein's techniques of language-games, which are in many respects illuminating and refreshing. Indeed, Wittgenstein has supplied us with many buoys in uncharted deep waters. But when he raises anchor and takes us out on the high seas, he leaves us adrift, without compass or other device to find our "way about." He blames philosophy for this condition, but he has done no better, and we begin to yearn once more for some philosopher's guiding hand. Given a new orientation, the philosopher, as a sensitive problem-finder, may yet pull us out of the technological deluge which rages incessantly all around us.

V. Toward a New Orientation

> Tiresias:
> "A fearful thing is knowledge,
> when to know
> Helpeth no end."
>
> SOPHOCLES, *Oedipus*
> *King of Thebes*

15. THREE TYPES OF PAST ORIENTATION

Recapitulation of the Problem of Freedom

When the scientist of the Age of Enlightenment turned his attention to man as a subject of investigation, his chief interest was to discover in man a faculty that would serve as an instrument of gauging his environment in order to make it a safe place where he could function in absolute freedom. The question "What is man?," when it was first raised in that age, meant "What is man as the measure of all things?" Like all standards of measurement, he had to be fashioned or reshaped in the image of a scientific existent, that is, decomposed and calibrated into quantitative elements and then recomposed into a tool of gauging other quantities of the same calibration. This is how modern man asserts his freedom in relation to his social conditions: he has become an entity of his own creation.

A second aspect of the problem of freedom is that man wants to become also his own redeemer. He therefore tries to set himself up as the gauge of God's role in human life. But having realized that the living God cannot be encompassed within the confines of human calibrations, some theologians have declared Him dead, so that they could stretch their measuring tape over

165

him and thus devise means of extricating themselves from His dominion. A third aspect of freedom manifests itself in man's encounter with physical nature. In order to control it, man has developed technological tools, or machines, to such a high degree of automated efficiency that they have assumed an independent existence of their own and now threaten to rob him of the very freedom which he had hoped to attain through their use.

In the past, whenever man faced those problems in his relationship with his fellow men, God, and physical nature, he was able to formulate a world-view in which he could find himself as the master of his destiny, either alone or with the aid of the Supreme Being. In Western civilization we may distinguish three major types of such an orientation, which may be designated, respectively, as that of the philosopher-king, the philosopher-saint, and the philosopher-scientist. Before we consider new directions for the present age, we shall review briefly the salient features of these three orientations of the past.

a. *The Philosopher-King*

Following the Greek Age of Enlightenment in the fourth century B.C., there ensued a crisis in the socio-political, religious, and cultural life of the people, similar to the one we are witnessing today in the Western world. The crisis was particularly acute in the affairs of state, the problems of right and might, freedom in nature and control under law, the well-being of the individual and the good of the community, and above all, the meaning of life. Then, as now, the young generation was bewildered by the conflicts between teaching and practice, thought and action, scepticism and traditional values, and a relentless drive for individual freedom which undermined respect for authority and shattered family and communal ties. The resolution of the crisis was then, as now, a matter of educating and guiding the young toward a new orientation in reality, toward finding the real goal of man's existence in the world. This task was undertaken by Plato in several of his dialogues, notably in his *Republic*. It is noteworthy that this dialogue addresses itself directly to youth and that Socrates' interlocutors are two young men, Glaucus and Adeimantus, who take an aggressive part in the discussion. The subject is the nature of justice and how and by whom it may be realized in everyday affairs of the state.

The advancement of the natural sciences by the Greek philosophers of the previous century did not lead man to a true knowledge of his social conditions and of the means of coping with its problems. Attention was now directed to another kind of nature, namely, the ideas of good and just, and to the kind of men who may possess the necessary virtues for cultivating them in the life of the individual and of organized society. For the state, Plato reasons, can be only as good and as just as are the men who govern it. On the other hand, the men who are to govern the state will be as good and as just as is the state which produces, educates, and influences them. This poses an almost insurmountable dilemma. There must be an ideal state to cultivate ideal men, and there must be ideal men who will establish the ideal state. Under then existing conditions, neither was in evidence. Moreover, even though some young people showed a high quality of character, they were being corrupted by wealth and power, which no one seemed strong enough to resist. Thus Plato arrives at his famous paradox of the philosopher-king:

> Unless either philosophers become kings in their countries or those who are now called kings and rulers come to be sufficiently inspired with a genuine desire for wisdom; unless, that is to say, political power and philosophy meet together, . . . there can be no rest from troubles . . . for states, nor yet, as I believe, for all mankind; . . . I know what a paradox it would be, because it is hard to see that there is no other way of happiness either for the state or for the individual.[1]

While philosopher-kings could be effective only in an ideal state of their own creation, it was not altogether impossible, Plato thinks, that, even before such a state was established, at least "a single one could be saved" from corruption, and that this "one would be enough to effect all this reform that now seems so in-

---

1. *Republic*, V, 473d. Cf. *The Republic of Plato*. Translated with Introduction and Notes by Francis MacDonald Cornford (New York: Oxford University Press, 1965).

credible, if he had subjects disposed to obey." [2] He could accomplish this reform by giving a select number of youths of the right moral qualities a new orientation in what is real and what apparent, what enduring and what ephemeral, and, most important, he would put them through a regimen of intellectual and physical training, extended over many years from childhood to young manhood, in order to render them impervious to falseness and injustice. These youths, both men and women, upon reaching maturity, would become the rulers and guardians of the state, insuring the well-being of every class in the community.

We need not dwell here on the kind of training and the manner of domestic life which Plato prescribes for the initiates or the philosopher-kings and their auxiliaries. Our interest is rather in the kind of reality he confronts them with and how he expects them to make themselves and their ideas acceptable to the populace. For as Plato is fully aware, the people are not only sceptical of what philosophers teach, but also look askance at their ability to govern. He therefore distinguishes between a true philosopher and one who makes an empty show of philosophizing. The former is a man who knows the Ideas of good and justice, absorbs them as integral elements of his very being, and tries his utmost to apply them in their purity in everyday life. Plato recognizes the distance which separates the philosophers from the rest of the people in outlook on reality and in manner of living, but he hopes that this could be bridged by a gradual change in human character through an educational program to be instituted for the entire population, and in particular for the future philosopher-kings. In essence, this was the purpose of his famous Academy in Athens: "So the philosopher, in constant companionship with the divine order of the world [of Ideas], will reproduce that order in his soul and, so far as man may, become godlike." He will also "not lack the skill to produce such counterparts of temperance, justice, and all the virtues that can exist in the ordinary man." [3] As the people come to recognize the true nature and goal of the philosopher-king, they will believe in his teaching that happiness may be found only in a state which is patterned after the divine order.

---

2. *Ibid.*, VI, 502a-b.
3. *Ibid.*, 500a-e.

Plato's vision of the philosopher-king is seminal for the conception of both the philosopher-saint and the philosopher-scientist, as all of them contain the principle of an ideal human character and of a capacity for practical leadership. The effectiveness of such a ruler depends not so much on knowledge of absolute good (though for Plato this is a prerequisite) as on his moral integrity and willingness, or, as we say today, his credibility, to govern in truth and justice. If this credibility wanes or is seriously undermined by political and economic tensions and by the breakdown of character, the people must look for a new type of ruler in whom they may put their trust.

b. *The Philosopher-Saint*

The deterioration of the Graeco-Roman social order and of the belief in man's ability to govern himself in truth gave rise to a new world-outlook which centered entirely in the realm of the divine. According to this new orientation, man can be saved only by divine intervention; a true and just order may be attained only in the heavenly city; the human king must not be just godlike, as taught before, but God Himself in human appearance. Plato's paradox of the philosopher-king cannot be resolved, because man, being fundamentally sinful, cannot transform himself of his own accord into a new character in order to establish the ideal world-order; for until such an order has come into being there is no social force available to produce the desired new character. The transformation must therefore come directly from God. The "single one . . . to effect all this reform that now seems so incredible," whom Plato had hoped to produce through his Academy, must now be sent to the world by the divine Ruler of the world Himself. Moreover, this "single one" must be of the same nature (*homoousion*) and possess the same powers as the one who sends him, in order to be able to transform the human soul. This is the message of the Gospel of John (RSV 3.16-17).

> For God so loved the world that he gave his only Son, that whoever believes in him should not perish but have eternal life. For God sent the Son into the world, not to condemn the world, but that the world might be saved through him.

169

The condition for salvation, according to this Gospel, is almost identical with that of Plato's philosopher-king who could effect the transformation "if he had subjects disposed to obey," that is, believe in him. In both the emphasis is on the people's faith in the efficacy of their sovereign. Plato calls on man to believe that the paradox of a philosopher-king, or the appearance of the "single one," is not impossible of solution; Christianity calls on man to believe that the paradox has been resolved, because the "single one" has already appeared. Yet the philosopher's problem, that is, his preoccupation with "heavenly beings" and his distant view of earthly life, remains the same for Christianity as for Plato.

In the Christian orientation, the perfect order is the Kingdom of Heaven in which Jesus Christ is King. Those who believe in Christ may enter his Kingdom. In the days of the New Testament, all baptized and converted Christians without distinction were considered saints, meaning that they were separated from this world, freed by Christ from the guilt of sin, and consecrated unto the service of God. Later, when masses of people converted, the appellation of saint was reserved for bishops and departed heroes, notably martyrs. After Christian persecutions had ceased, the saints were select men and women among the departed of the higher clergy and among those who led a monastic life.[4] A saint, then, is one who has been sanctified by divine Grace through baptism and granted special powers to intercede in the heavenly regions on behalf of men on earth. If such a person is also endowed with the power to grasp the divine truth of salvation intellectually, he may be designated a philosopher-saint.[5] His role as teacher and guide of the community of believers is similar in cer-

---

4. Cf. Philip Schaff, *History of the Christian Church* (Grand Rapids, Mich.: Wm. B. Eerdmans Publishing Co., Fifth Edition Revised, 1971). Vol. III, pp. 428ff. Dionysius the Areopagite conceived of man's relation to God on the basis of a hierarchy of saints, divided into two branches, one heavenly and the other earthly, each divided into several degrees of closeness to the divine Ruler, and each higher degree being the mediator of salvation to the one below it (*ibid.*, p. 431).
5. Cf. Etienne Gilson, *The Elements of Christian Philosophy* (New York: A Mentor-Omega Book, 1963). "The Teacher of Christian Faith," pp. 12f.

tain respects to that of Plato's philosopher-king, but more particularly to that of the king's auxiliaries or helpers who, as "earthborn" mediators, come into contact with the people more directly than does the king, and who carry out the latter's orders.[6] The two most prominent and revered men of this type in Christendom are Saint Augustine and Saint Thomas Aquinas.

SAINT AUGUSTINE's philosophy centers in two human capacities, belief and reason. "For if thou doest not believe," he says, "thou wilt never apprehend, since thou wilt remain less capable. Let faith then purify thee, that understanding may fill thee." [7] Nevertheless, he acknowledges the primacy of rational insight into accepted doctrine insofar as the former confirms the latter, even though it cannot penetrate its mystery, which ultimately remains ineffable through reason.[8] For him philosophy occupies a prime position in his apologia against those who question the Christian faith on rational grounds. Thus, for example, on "what is meant by the true beatitude," he says, ". . . I shall appeal not only to divine Revelation but to such natural reasoning as will appeal to those who do not share our faith." [9] Similarly, even though he makes faith appear completely rational with regard to the Trinity, he exclaims: "Which of us comprehendeth the Almighty Trinity? . . . Rare is the soul, which while it speaks of It, knows what it

---

6. Cf. Plato, *Republic*, Book III, 415d-417b. Cf. Gilbert Murray, *Five Stages in Greek Religion* (New York: Doubleday Anchor Books, 1955), p. 147, on the adoration of some of the Greek philosophers, such as Aristotle building an altar to Plato. "It is the same emotion—a noble and just emotion on the whole—which led the philosophical schools to treat their founders as 'heroes,' and which has peopled most of Europe and Asia with memories of worship of saints."

7. *Selected Writings of Saint Augustine*. Edited and with an Introduction by Roger Hazelton (New York: Meridian Books, 1962), p. 230.

8. Cf. Wilhelm Windelband, *A History of Philosophy* (Harper Torchbooks, 1958), I, p. 282. Augustine "teaches also that the appropriation of divine truth is effected not so much by insight, as through *faith* or belief. . . . Full rational insight is indeed first in dignity, but faith in revelation is first in time."

9. Saint Augustine, *The City of God*. An abridged Version from the Translation by Gerald G. Walsh, *et. al.* (New York: Image Books, 1958), Book XIX, ch. 1, p. 427.

speaks of." [10] Philosophy's role in Christian belief is fully expressed in Augustine's doctrines of free will and predestination. "As Christian and philosopher," he writes, "we profess both—foreknowledge, as a part of our faith; free choice, as a condition of responsible living. It is hard to live right if one's faith in God is wrong." Moreover, to gain "a fortitude that finds strength in faith . . . we need, as even the wisdom of this world assures us, that true philosophy which, as Cicero says, is given by the gods to very few. . . ." Such a philosophy "can be given by no less a divinity than the One than whom, as even the polytheists admit, there is no greater." [11]

We thus see in Augustine himself the prototype of the philosopher-saint, the rational believer who teaches, guides, and by personal example influences the people through faith and reason to accept the truth of the heavenly kingdom which is governed by Christ the King. He describes very much his own role when he writes in his *Confessions,* "Now then let Thy [Christ's] ministers work upon the earth . . . by preaching and speaking by miracles, and Sacraments, and mystic words; . . . and let them be a pattern unto the Faithful, by living before them, and stirring them up to imitation." [12] However, the truth that Augustine teaches is of the heavenly domain, in essence separated from the earthly realms which are riddled with sin, corruption, and lust for power, and are predestined for eternal damnation. Even among the believers only a small unknown number is saved by the grace of God. Augustine's philosopher-saint looks toward the perfect, ideal state of heavenly existence, which is attainable only by a select few in afterlife. [13]

---

10. *The Confessions of Saint Augustine.* Translated by Edward B. B. Pusey (New York: A Cardinal Edition, 1952), Book XIII, p. 274. Cf. Karl Jaspers, *Die grossen Philosophen* (München: R. Piper & Co., 1959), Erster Band, pp. 346ff. "Augustine's conception of the Trinity made it possible that faith became rational and confirmed through philosophy, . . . that faith and philosophy became the same" (p. 350).

11. *The City of God,* Book X, p. 110, Book XXII, pp. 522-523.

12. *The Confessions,* Book XIII, p. 286.

13. Cf. *The City of God,* Book XXII, p. 522, on the role of the saint in guiding man toward eternal life. Saint Augustine writes: "It is true that, even in this life on earth, through the intercession of the saints we have many holy comforts and great remedies. Nevertheless,

Although this belief may be confirmed and strengthened by reason, philosophy, as such, is not accorded here an independent function even with regard to a knowledge of the ideal state. It was Thomas Aquinas who established philosophy as a science in its own right both in heavenly and earthly things.

SAINT THOMAS AQUINAS draws a distinction between the philosopher-believer, or as we call him the philosopher-saint, and the philosopher-nonbeliever. This is not a matter of two separate realms of reality or of a double truth, but rather of two types of philosophizing men, each aiming at a different goal and therefore having a different object of knowledge in view. What both have in common is a philosophizing method of constructing a self-contained science, one a sacred doctrine or the knowledge of God, and the other a rational knowledge of the universe. Although the second may also lead to a knowledge of God's existence, it does not offer true theology. On the other hand, the science which has God as its object also deals with everything God has created and is therefore all-embracing and superior to the science which deals only with the creatures. But this is not its chief claim to supioriority.

Aquinas' concern with philosophy, as is the concern of every philosophizing man, is its purpose in human life. As a Christian philosopher, his prime interest is man's salvation according to Christian doctrine, which is divine truth obtainable only through divine revelation, to be accepted as a matter of faith. This truth constitutes a set of first principles underlying the sacred science, and this science, accordingly, cannot reach a knowledge of God through reason without faith, because no science can function without first principles. Even in certain areas where reason may function independently of faith, such as in proving God's existence, it is still insufficient for man's salvation, which is the goal of the sacred science. As Aquinas explains, apart from the fact that very few people have the capacity of rational knowledge, reason at best is imperfect and full of error; only faith in revealed truth has absolute certainty, so that the knowledge of God's existence

---

such favors are not always given to those who ask—lest such favors be mistaken for the real purpose of religion, which is felicity in that other life in which all our ills will be no more."

may be truly ascertained only through faith.[14] It means that by natural reason alone the philosopher can demonstrate that God exists, but whether He exists as the Christian God of salvation, which, according to Aquinas, is the essence of His existence, is a matter of divine revelation and thus of faith.[15] Therefore, the difference between sacred and natural science is in their respective objects of knowledge, the first being the God of salvation, and the second merely of God's existence.

One could conclude from Aquinas' argument about the revelation of reason to faith that man's salvation lies in his faith in revealed truth, supported by natural reason, if one needs such support, and the person best suitable to aid man toward this goal is the believing philosopher or the philosopher-saint. However, in considering man's final purpose Aquinas finds both reason and faith insufficient for his ultimate beatitude. For the kind of knowledge of God our philosopher-saint envisions is that of "seeing" the divine Being in His concrete existence and in the fullness of His essence, and not just through a knowledge of abstract essences, as taught, for example, by the Platonists.[16] "Man's ultimate happiness," he writes, "consists solely in the contemplation of God," in which "the intellect sees [God's essence] through the divine essence itself; so that in that vision the divine essence is both the object and the medium of vision." [17] Intellectual vision, however, is not obtained through rational demonstration, speculative reason, or faith; for even "in knowledge by faith, the operation of the intellect is found to be most imperfect as regards the contribution of the intellect. . . . There is therefore some knowledge of God that is higher than the knowledge of faith. . . . [18] This

---

14. Cf. *Summa Theologica*, Question 2, Article 2, Reply to Obj. 1.
15. Cf. Etienne Gilson, *The Elements of Christian Philosophy*, p. 27. "Even when the natural reason can establish a certain truth about God, it never grasps it in its fullness as applying to the God of the Christian faith."
16. Cf. *Introduction to Saint Thomas Aquinas*. Edited with an Introduction by Anton Pegis (New York: The Modern Library, 1948). Editor's Introduction, pp. xviiiff., on Aquinas' rejection of Plato's method of abstraction.
17. *Summa Contra Gentiles*. Third Book, chs. 37, 51, in Pegis, *op. cit.*, pp. 454, 468.
18. *Ibid.*, p. 459.

highest knowledge man is unable to acquire in his earthly life and therefore "it is impossible for man's happiness to be in this life." [19] Man can "see" God in His essence, which is the ultimate goal of salvation, only through the kind of intellectual knowledge which can unite with the divine essence, but "which the human mind possesses after this life ... [when] the saints *shall be as the angels, who always see God in heaven (Matt.* 18.10)." [20] Thus, while reason and faith help man in this life on earth to strive toward his final goal, his true happiness is oriented toward the world beyond, where both reason and faith are surpassed by a still higher knowledge inaccessible to him in this life. The philosopher-saint strives for something which is unattainable in man's earthly existence.

c. *The Philosopher-Scientist*

Although Aquinas subordinated reason to faith, the impetus he gave to philosophical inquiry as an independent method of obtaining certain limited truths extended through the Renaissance and the Age of Enlightenment into a new means of salvation through reason itself, which reached a high point in Kant's "Critiques."

IMMANUEL KANT divests the problem of man's goal from the religious issue of faith and establishes a double world outlook, one as a metaphysic of nature and the other as a metaphysic of morals, the first dealing with theoretical knowledge and the second with practical reason. There is no bridge between these two worlds, and the only thing they have in common is a scientific method of investigating the capacities of human reason, one for its theoretical and the other for its practical achievements. The salvation which Kant offers man is freedom under the moral law derived through a science of practical (that is, non-theoretical) reason, which assures it universality and necessity, or certainty. The laws that govern the science of nature are obtained through theoretical reason, and their certainty lies with the categories of the understanding alone. Beyond these categories, the philosopher-scientist may not

---

19. *Ibid.,* p. 463.
20. *Ibid.,* p. 467. Cf. p. 470.

175

venture, because he would land in the field of speculation or "transcendental illusion."

This dual outlook leaves man with insurmountable barriers in his earthly life. In his natural state, which is governed by his sensible experience in time and space, he cannot be free; only in his moral state of "supersensible existence," which lies beyond his spatio-temporal experience, can he be considered a free being. In the final analysis, for Kant as for Plato, man's ultimate goal toward freedom is to step out of his sensible existence into a world of ideas or into a realm of moral heights where only saints may dwell. (Kant considers sainthood to be the highest character of human personality.) Since the philosopher-scientist deals only with spatio-temporal contingencies and is therefore himself unable to reach the higher spheres of moral certainty, what can be his role in the affairs of human life on earth? Kant assigns him the function of advisor to kings and other rulers of state. "Science," he says, ". . . is the narrow gate which leads toward the doctrine of wisdom . . . a science whose preserver must always be philosophy." [21] If the kings and rulers of human affairs will heed the teachings of the philosopher-scientist, they will be able to lead the people toward their maximum good. This, in fact, has been the scientist's role in social-political matters to this day. He himself lives in a dual world of natural science and morals, unable to build a bridge between them or to see them together *sub specie aeternitatis.* Beyond the sensible world his scientific certainty turns into moral uncertainty, his methodological doubt into moral scepticism. It was Nietzsche who first saw the depth of this human predicament as a problem of scientific nihilism, and he tried to overcome it through a revaluation of the philosopher's purpose in human existence.

FRIEDRICH NIETZSCHE attempts to remove man from the Kantian dual world of phenomena and noumena and place him entirely in an intelligible world of "perspective interpretation," that is, one world interpreted from different perspectives. The Kantian type of philosopher-scientist, he maintains, is unable to give a true account of either of the two worlds; therefore, instead

---

21. *Kritik der praktischen Vernunft.* Beschluss, 292.

of philosophers of truth, we must cultivate true philosophers, who will themselves become the standards of what is true and good. This type of man comes very close to being a philosopher-god, a very rare specimen, designated by Nietzsche as the Supreme Man, who forms "the future caste of rulers," "the Lords of the Earth," that is, those who have one set of morals for the purpose of promoting their self-perpetuation and another set for the rest of mankind, the vast majority, who are to serve that purpose.

Nietzsche may have demolished Kant's dual system of nature and morals, but he replaced it with a dual standard of morality. Instead of dividing the world into two unbridgeable realms in which man may live simultaneously, as Kant did, he divided mankind into two opposite entities, striving against each other in eternal recurrence. Thus Western philosophy has come around full circle, from Plato's philosopher-king who gazes at the realm of pure Ideas, to the Christian philosopher-saint who hopes to attain the highest state of knowledge in afterlife, through Kant's philosopher-scientist who separates the truth of nature from moral freedom, back to Plato's divine man in the form of Nietzsche's philosopher-god, who becomes himself the highest goal of human existence.

LUDWIG WITTGENSTEIN proposes to solve the philosophical problem of modern man by eliminating the problem together with the philosopher who poses it. In truth, however, he only wants to eliminate the philosopher-scientist and replace him with the technologist. He is impatient with theorizing and wants to get down to the "practical" business of building a spatio-temporal world out of language-games within a framework of language-space. The philosopher may still serve a purpose in supervising or "overseeing" the language structures, watching out against theoretical incursions and other problematic disturbances, which are, in Wittgenstein's view, nothing but illusions. When the new edifice will have been completed, that is, when all problems of a scientific, theoretical character will be "completely" eliminated, the philosopher himself will do his best to remove himself from the scene. Thus Wittgenstein visualizes a self-regulating technology which needs no outside forces to set its limits, and in which certainty prevails in spite of doubt. By repudiating the philosopher-scientist and espousing the technological method of exploring man's spatio-temporal existence, he has splintered the world into entities which know no bounds and which leave man floating in a language-space without guidelines. And yet his great contribution to our thinking today may lie in his very emphasis on the technologist's role in giving modern man a viable perspective of his surroundings. I will explore this perspective in its broad features, not, however, from Wittgenstein's viewpoint, but as I see in it the possibility of shaping a new orientation in reality.

16. THE PHILOSOPHER-TECHNOLOGIST: A RENEWAL OF FUNDAMENTALS

In view of the steady advancement of the technological process, modern man cannot possibly think of reversing it, even if he were able to do so. Rather, he must learn to consider its benefits in proper perspective and to gain mastery over its potential. He has to learn to set bounds to technology which, by its very nature, it cannot set for itself.

By technology is meant here not just the electric media of communication or the highpowered instruments of production and distribution of material goods, but also all forms of social, political, even cultural and religious organized life, which are being administered by a variety of mental as well as physical contrivances. It includes not only the machinery of industrial and commercial establishments, but also the techniques used in government, education, information services, in the administration of justice, in the organization of religious institutions, and all other social forms, extending to individual interrelations. Now the philosopher who tries to embrace these techniques within the purview of his knowledge of reality finds himself in conflict with the technologist who tries to give them an independent existence. These conflicting views may find their reconcilation in the philosopher-technologist, who will develop a new orientation in the fundamentals of human existence, namely, those relating to purpose, truth, certainty and trust, universality and necessity, finitude and infinity, and ultimately in relation to the Absolute.

a. *Purpose*

Meaning of human existence can be established only in a world-outlook which is purposive. Since the beginning of Western civilization, man's purpose has been to promote his own well-being, individually and socially. Expressed in philosophical and technological terms, this has meant the control of the spatio-temporal exigencies of nature and the liberation from external determination. In modern times, especially, it has assumed the form of a struggle for life and death between man and nature, in which the former has seemingly gained the upper hand through his technological devices. But it has already become apparent that in this so-called "conquest of nature" man has scored but a "Pyrrhic victory": the real loser is man who, through his technological proliferation, has alienated himself from nature as well as from his fellow man. He can gain a real victory if he will recognize nature's purpose in its own right, and view himself and nature as occupying two central positions, like two foci, in one universal orbit.

In the early stages of Enlightenment, Kant placed the human condition in juxtaposition to the rest of the world in the following dictum: "In all creation everything one may want or may have in one's power can indeed be used *only as a means;* only man, and with him every rational creature, is an end in himself" (*Kritik der praktischen Vernunft,* 155-156). As we enter a new era, we may revise our view of the world and extend Kant's maxim to read: Act in such a way that you treat *humanity* and *nature* in your own person, in others, and in the world around you, not just as a means, but always at the same time as an end.

b. *Truth*

The kind of truth which has served man as a guide to his thoughts and actions through the Era of Enlightenment is what the scientist discovers or attempts to discover in objective reality. It is a truth hidden in the things, only to be uncovered through rational insight and brought to light in the form of a theory about observable facts. Once it makes its appearance, it becomes self-evident and inevitable as a natural law and may therefore be pur-

179

sued for its own sake. Furthermore, science assumes that even though its truth may be hampered by human error, it can never be false in itself. Accordingly, many scientists do not hesitate to experiment in areas which may be detrimental to mankind, as, for example, in certain aspects of nuclear physics and genetics, on the contention that they are in pursuit of objective truth.

Now this kind of truth may not be claimed by the technologist or the philosopher. For neither one discovers or uncovers his truth but rather establishes it through the pursuit of human ends. Fundamentally, science is logical, while philosophy and technology are teleological. The latter seek their truths not in their activities, as such, but in purposes of goals toward which their activities are directed. Their truths come into existence through their human interaction with nature as two entities intertwined in one destiny: neither side can attain its goal by trying to overpower the other. To say, therefore, that the technologist may generate techniques and devise instruments just because "it can be done," without regard to the ends which they may serve, is to advocate a self-defeating enterprise. Similarly, for a philosopher to engage in philosophizing for its own sake, just because he has the intellectual capacity for it, is a dreadful mental exercise.

c. *Universality and Necessity*

Another aspect of the scientific enterprise is that it tries to establish its laws as universal and necessary. If by necessity is meant that what is established as a law of nature cannot be or be conceived otherwise, it may in principle apply to science but not to technology, for the latter is in the realm of the possible and its results may always be conceived and produced otherwise. The only way of applying universality and necessity to technology is in relation to the purposes of man and nature, which it is to serve. In the same manner, philosophy may arrive at universal and necessary principles in relation to its world-outlook as a whole, embracing mankind and nature in their totality. Detached from these ends, the philosopher's speculations are neither necessary nor universal, and may be altogether aimless.

d. *Certainty and Trust*

In each of the past orientations, Western man was particularly preoccupied with the problem of certainty. He was always troubled by doubts about correct thinking, absolute knowledge, or the lack of predictability in his human condition. He tried to overcome his doubts through rational proof of absolute truth or through the belief that such truth had been revealed to him from a divine source. In our own time, the quest for certainty expresses itself in a yearning for security—individual, national, and international. To be sure, man will not cease being concerned with these problems as long as he feels insecure or uncertain about his relation to things on earth or beyond. The degree of certainty he has obtained through scientific inquiry does not stand him in good stead when he tries to apply it to the field of technology. On the contrary, the more complex and extensive his instruments become, the less certain becomes his reliance on them. With the increase in complexity there is a decrease in predictability and control, for the slightest malfunction of a single part of a very intricate piece of machinery will put the whole apparatus out of commission, and may affect an untold number of beings who depend on it for the promotion or protection of their lives. The threat of universal annihilation lurks in all of the modern technological devices, not just in the atomic bomb, and this threat is on the increase with their unbridled accumulation. This is the tragic paradox of man's search for certainty through science and technology.

Modern man cannot hope to resolve this paradox simply by positing an ideational certainty against his technological uncertainty. It would mean again placing himself in a system of two worlds with an unbridgeable gap between them. Instead, the philosopher-technologist has to seek a new orientation not through certainty but through trust, not by trying to uncover a truth that lies beyond a shadow of doubt, but by establishing what is true through a life of trust with his fellow men and in particular with nature. Indeed, trust rather than certainty is the most positive factor in man's relation to nature and generally to what is beyond the human condition.

e. *The Infinite and the Absolute*

The danger of technology lies not only in its tendency to hew its own path independently of the philosopher, but also, and especially, in its drive to extend itself as an infinite and absolute power in the face of man's finite, relative existence. This is an illusion which the philosopher-technologist may dispel if he places himself in one and the same spatio-temporal world that is common to both technology and philosophy. Technology aims to attain the infinite through a sharpening of its spatio-temporal contrivances. Every one of its devices is constructed out of spatial units designed to multiply themselves with breathtaking speed in a fraction of time. As the spatial units are further reduced in size (as in the constantly refined electronic devices), the speed increases in proportion, approaching the infinitesimally divisible space units. This creates the notion that man can overcome the limits of space and time through technological advancement and may reach a point of instant communication, instant production, instant living. Thus the illusion arises that man can gain absolute freedom from the determinations of space and time in his personal and social existence, or, as the advocates of pure technology promise, that through the new electronic media of communication he can attain the "Pentecostal condition of universal understanding and unity."

This condition stems from man's failure to realize that, as a being-as-a-whole, he does not live in actual space and time, but on the contrary, space and time assume actual existence in his life with nature in their mutual interaction. Both man and nature are finite and relative with regard to each other's existence and to being as such. Therefore, when the technologist tries to *decompose* the spatio-temporal elements of human life into infinitesimal bits of information (productive and communicative), he actually decomposes man and nature; and when he presumes to *re*compose those elements into life-giving processes, he can only succeed in producing a dehumanized and denaturalized contrivance, unable to sustain life in reality.

The technological illusion of attaining the infinite and the absolute is being fanned by man's drive to become an infinite, absolute

182

being himself, or to merge with such a being. It is the illusion of a "becoming God," human or superhuman, which some philosophers have promulgated as man's eschatological hope and built up on the notion that what is conceptually regarded as finite and relative may be turned dialectically into an infinite and absolute. If there is an Absolute, man can neither conceive him in terms of his own finite, relative being, nor demonstrate his existence through rational proof; man can only relate himself to him as a matter of trust. Whatever name may be given to the Absolute, it can have meaning only as a divine Being, that is, as the One who is totally unlike and surpasses all other kinds of being known to us in nature. Neither may the Absolute be viewed as a concept, a principle, or a process, for then he is turned into a God-idea, that is, a function of our speculative thinking or a mere abstraction. In relation to the Absolute, man may not strive to overcome his finiteness but to reconcile himself with the infinite by recognizing his own limitations or what is generally considered to be his creaturely existence. Through this relationship man may find his own and nature's purpose in the universal scheme of things.

17. PAIDEIA

In the preceding chapter I have indicated some basic ideas which need rethinking and reshaping toward a new orientation in reality, new not in the sense that it was never thought of before, but in renewing the fundamental realities of man's life with nature and with the Absolute in the light of our technological age. This ought to be the aim of our young generation of philosophers and technologists, as well as of the young thinking men and women in all walks of life, but especially of those who occupy leading positions in our schools, from the elementary levels through the colleges and universities, where the future of mankind is being determined. Our educational establishments are the most complex technological instruments that shape our lives, surpassing all our industrial-commercial combines. Properly oriented, the young generation will then be able to devise new techniques for the promotion of human values, but only if their education is directed toward this end. For learning is a way of life, not just a preparation for "making a living." Even now, education is becoming increasingly a life-giving process, that is, a way of relating to reality with a purpose, viewing man and nature as ends in themselves. And if the Absolute has a bearing on this outlook, it means our recognition of a divine purpose in the universal scheme of things. Our life in this world is not a mere game of intellectual contemplation or technological proliferation. If there is hope for human redemption, man will be redeemed if he also helps to redeem nature.

APPENDIX

IS NIETZSCHE A METAPHYSICIAN?

Two historical figures of universal proportion loomed large on Nietzsche's philosophical horizon: Jesus and Kant. They impressed him by their force of thought and nobility of character. But Nietzsche could not forgive the one for having become the foundation of what he (Nietzsche) considered to be a decadent morality, and the other (an "underhanded Christian," as he called him) for having raised that morality to the pinnacle of metaphysical necessity.[1] We can comprehend Nietzsche's philosophy best in the light of his fencing with the Kantian idea of a pure moral domain. Here we can see his sparks flying as he bends his efforts toward a revaluation of that idea, his ultimate repudiation of the ethical principle, as such, and of man's responsibility under God. Yet, as he sounded the battle-cry against the "great Kritiker . . . from Königsberg," he himself donned the armor of modern thought, which he borrowed from his adversary. It is instructive merely to compare the moral vocabulary of the two philosophers:

---

1. Nietzsche spoke at least once of the "philosophical workers according to the noble example of Kant . . ." (*BG&E,* 211). Of "the Hebrew Jesus" he said: "He died too early: he himself would have retracted his teaching, had he reached my age. He was noble enough for retraction" (*Zarathustra* I, On Free Death). Cf. Walter Kaufmann, *Nietzsche,* p. 342. Cf. Karl Jaspers, *Nietzsche,* p. 140. Nietzsche attacked Christian morality but, "an astounding fact—he stopped at Jesus: here everything is genuine, without falsehood, the reality of life's practice." But of Kant he also spoke as "eines hinterlistigen Christen zu guter letzt" (in the final analysis, an underhanded Christian). Cf. *Twilight,* " 'Reason' in Philosophy," 6. Cf. *Will to Power,* 101. "Kant: . . . a fanatic moralist à la Rousseau; with an underground Christian character of values; . . ."

Kant's good will and bad will, supersensible existence, respect and despising, self-perfection, strength and hindrance, noble and ignoble; and Nietzsche's revalued concepts of good and bad, respect and despising, noble and despicable, strength and weakness, self-sublimation, and the like. What is most striking in this comparison is that Nietzsche did not revaluate morals but rather the metaphysic of morals.

Anyone who says anything about Nietzsche's metaphysic is bound to run into the controversy going on among Nietzsche scholars about source and system. Where in his writings does one find a metaphysical system? Are those sources authentic, and if so, are they organized and sufficiently developed to be rightfully regarded as a metaphysic? One of the main issues centers on the reliability of the collection of notes published under the title *The Will to Power,* from which one may cull most of the philosopher's metaphysical concepts. It appears that no one questions their authenticity, only their value as a system. Walter Kaufmann points out that those notes were jotted down by Nietzsche at different times in the course of his later philosophical development (1883-1888) and must be taken only as raw material, "full of sketches, drafts, abandoned attempts, and unfinished dreams." [2] Karl-Heinz Volkmann-Schluck, on the other hand, holds that "the collected piece under the title 'Wille zur Macht' show Nietzsche at work on conceptual analysis which does not fall behind in rigor the system-building works of his predecessors."[3] A more balanced view, which I find acceptable, is offered by Karl Jaspers, who regards *The Will to Power* and the entire *Nachlass,* of which it is a part, as representative of the philosopher's thinking as are any of his other writings. "Nietzsche's work," says Jaspers, "is really not centralized anywhere; there is no main work." [4] And Jaspers himself quotes from the *Der Wille zur Macht* as freely as he does from the completed works.

---

2. Nietzsche, *The Will to Power.* Edited by Walter Kaufmann. Editor's Introduction, pp. xv-xvi, and Appendix, p. 557.

3. Karl-Heinz Volkmann-Schluck, *Leben und Denken. Interpretationen zur Philosophie Nietzsches* (Frankfurt am Main: Vittorio Klostermann, 1968), p. 64.

4. Karl Jaspers, *Nietzsche,* p. 12.

Granted then that the sources are reliable, can they be construed as a metaphysical system? We see Nietzsche fighting against metaphysics throughout his writings and now we want to saddle him with one of his own. The real issue is whether his concept of "the will to power" may be regarded as a metaphysical principle underlying his entire philosophy of man and the universe. It may have come to him as an afterthought, as Kaufmann suggests (*Nietzsche,* p. 420), but all metaphysical speculations come as an afterthought. Kant, for example, never intended to write his *Prolegomena* except as an afterthought to his *Critique of Pure Reason.*[5] Similarly, Aristotle's *Metaphysics* came only after he had established his system of physics.[6] And so is every metaphysical structure posited as a basis for a given science of physics, whether the *physis* is of things, man, life, or the universe.

Now Nietzsche set out to revaluate all values about the nature of man through the science of physio-psychology, and not just man but with him the entire universe and all the sciences that aim to interpret it. For all that, he was not a scientist but rather a philosopher, and since he raised philosophy above the sciences (that in itself is a metaphysical assertion—witness Aristotle), he was constrained to pose and answer philosophical questions as to what he was revaluating and where he found it. He did not expect an answer from science (empirical or otherwise) and he therefore had to venture beyond (*meta*) it. The metaphysical issue is thus not being imposed on him; it grows out of his particular approach to the problem of man or, as he puts it, the problematic of human morality (*BG&E,* 23, 204, *Genealogy* III, 23). How does he face this problem?

Nietzsche places man at the center of the world and urges him to "become what he is." This implies a world potentiality that calls for actualization. Since he rejects Darwin's concept of evolution from a lower to a higher species, that is, a potency coming

---

5. Cf. Immanuel Kant, *Prolegomena zu einer jeden künftigen Metaphysik* (Philosophische Bibliothek, 1965), Vorrede, 261, and Anhang, 372. For that Critique (of Pure Reason), he says, must stand on its own before one can even think of letting metaphysics come up.

6. Cf. Werner Jaeger, *Aristotle* (London: Oxford Paperback, 1960), pp. 378-79.

from below the human species, he must account for the world potential either as already existing in man, in which case there is no becoming in the sense of elevation (because Nietzsche rejects progress from lower to higher man), or as existing outside of man, as a universal power that seeks self-realization through him. Our philosopher posits it not as a hypothesis but as a first principle of universal dimension. That is, it is not a hypothesis to explain the universe, but an active principle of "interpretation" interpreting itself, much like Aristotle's metaphysical prime thought thinking itself.

One may still ask, if Nietzsche has no system at all, by what right do we ascribe a metaphysical system to him? Are we not imputing something alien to his thoughts by our very act of systematizing them? That depends not on what we read into his writings by implication, but on what we read out of them by selection, for systematization means just that: selecting all basic elements that constitute a comprehensive unity. If by system is meant a unity held together through connectives of cause and effect, then Nietzsche does not have such a system, as he does not operate with those connectives, not as criteria of truth anyway. By the same token his metaphysic does not fall back on the logical principle of "no infinite regress" which requires a prime, unmoved mover (Aristotle) or on an unconditioned *Grenzbegriff* (Kant). But he does deal with a unity which is held together by a certain system of relations, though not of relata (no "things"). If he left it at that, it would just form a natural science of man in terms of physio-psychological coordinates, such as we find today in some aspects of the theory of relativity in physics. But he goes beyond that and brings all of his coordinates into "perspective" with one overriding immanent-transcendent principle, namely, "the will to power." This reveals his systematic thinking, even though it is not carried out entirely in schematic form (obviously due to his protracted illness and untimely death). Indeed, he did not shun schemata. "Rational thought," he writes, "is interpreting according to a *schema,* which we cannot reject" (WP, 522). What he did reject is language as a schema, which he regarded as too confining for his dynamic mode of expression. And even that he could not escape entirely, for he recognized that "we cease to think when we don't want to do it within the confines of language . . ." (*ibid.*).

We thus find in Nietzsche's works a coherent, directional world-view which he calls a free "incomplete system." "It requires a totally different strength and mobility," he observes, "to hold fast with free, unbound perspectives in an incomplete system, rather than in a dogmatic world" (*Nachlass* II, 220). His is not one of those "great 'systems' " built by "schematic heads," but a dynamic unity of *becoming,* and its metaphysical problem is to ascertain the ultimate *dynamis* from which it derives its *being.* As he tells us in the opening statement of his "Recapitulation" of the section on "Science" (WP, 617): "To impress the character of being on the becoming—that is the highest will to power." When he breaks down his predecessors' metaphysics of being and becoming to a nihilism, he does it only provisionally, to get rid of what he considered to be the error of a "true world" and the falsity of "fact" of the phenomenal world, both of which reduce themselves to a naught, a *nihil.* He then reaches a moment when he is ready to bring the essence of becoming out of action itself. He calls this moment "the interim period of nihilism: before there is strength to reverse the values and to deify and confirm the becoming, illusory world as the only one" (*ibid.,* 585A). It is a very short period, like "Noon; an instant of the shortest shadow; end of the longest error; humanity's high point; *incipit Zarathustra"* (*Twilight,* "How the 'True World' Finally Became a Legend," 6). The era of Zarathustra set in. Having thus prepared the ground for a new dynamic metaphysic, Nietzsche goes forth in search of "new philosophers . . . to revaluate 'eternal values' . . . (*BG&E,* 203). But on his way he has to devise new guidelines for their orientation in a world of sheer becoming, sheer doing. In that world "there is no 'being' behind the doing, acting, becoming; 'the doer' is only a fiction added to the doing—the doing is everything" (*Genealogy* I, 13). And since the "doer" is only an innovation, he cannot be man as such. Rather he is the universal "will to power" realizing itself in man and at the same time transcending him: not exactly a Being, yet a Unifier of Doing.

189

Eternal Recurrence

Some scholars suggest that if Nietzsche has a metaphysic it should be charged to his theory of "Eternal Recurrence," rather than to his "Will to Power." However, if we examine the nature of this theory, we shall find that it does not shape up in a metaphysical structure but rather in a "scientific hypothesis" about the physical operation of the universe. Its structural units are space, time, and energy, conceived in the modern "scientific spirit" and set in a world plenum (no void inside) which is in perpetual motion, like a floating island in a sea of "nothingness." Its basic elements are the "simplest forms" (atoms) surging back and forth, coming together in manifolds and breaking up again into their simplest states, as "a becoming that knows no saturation, no weariness, no exhaustion . . ." (WP 1067).[7] Nietzsche proposes to prove that this perpetual becoming cannot be thought of otherwise than as an "eternal recurrence" of the same plenum with all that is contained therein. His "scientific hypothesis," as he calls it, is based on three premises: (1) Infinite time and finite space, (2) Eternity of motion, and (3) Conservation of energy. Briefly, his argument runs as follows.

Since there is a limited quantity of energy active in a finite space in infinite time, the world, if it were going in a linear direction toward a definite goal, would have reached its goal a long time ago and would now be at a standstill, as a being but no longer a becoming. But the world, as we observe it, is in a state of becoming. Therefore, we must conclude first, that it is not capable of assuming a state of being, and second, that it moves in a circle, always coming back to its original elementary forms and moving again toward its complex states, eternally repeating its cycles and recreating itself in identical shapes. We may picture this process as each cycle exhausting all possible combinations of the limited

---

7. Without going into specific comparisons, it should be noted that Nietzsche's physical universe resembles in many respects the atomistic world of the Epicureans. Epicurus' world of atoms is, like Nietzsche's world of "simplest forms," a turbulent totality, operating "without the agency of gods." Cf. G. H. Clark, *Selections from Hellenistic Philosophy* (New York: Appleton-Century-Crofts, 1940). "Lucretius: On the Nature of Things," Book I, pp. 8-13.

amount of energy available in the world and, therefore, every cycle must, of necessity, repeat the identical shapes from eternity unto eternity (WP 1062). An interesting corollary of this argument is an allusion to Einstein's field theory. "The shape of space," Nietzsche writes, "must be the cause of eternal motion and ultimately of all 'incompleteness' " (WP 1064).[8] Whatever its destiny in human affairs, Nietzsche's hypothesis of "Eternal Recurrence" may at best serve as a physical home for his metaphysical "Will to Power." That is, perhaps, what he meant by ascribing "incompleteness" to eternal motion, which is the fate of all physical theories, and which may be completed only by a metaphysical principle.

---

8. Cf. above, Part II, Chapter 5. "A Limited World without Bounds," esp. notes 66 and 67.

Index

d'Abro, A, on gravitational field, 43
Absolute, immanence, 135; and man, 183; and technology, 182-183; trousers, 82; vision of, 82; and world orientation, 182-184
Age of Enlightenment, and Descartes, 140; English, 6; and freedom, 2; French, 104n; Greek, 166; and history, 3; individualism, 3; Kant on, 1; and man, 165; man's maturity, 1, 10; and Newton's physics, 13; and physical theory, 36n
alienation, of man, 72; of senses, 72
Altizer, Thomas J. J., see radical theology
American Physical Society, 15
antimatter, physical concept of, 43
aphorism, dynamics of, 71; Nietzsche, 97
Aristotle, on tragic character, 102n; conflict between science and metaphysics, 4; *Metaphysics,* 187; metaphysical speculation, 156; on the middle, 16; prime (unmoved) mover, 102n
Ashby, Eric, technology and the academics, 5n
Augustine, Saint, see philosopher-saint
automation, see McLuhan

Bambrough, Renford, on Wittgenstein's family resemblances, 151n
behavioral engineering, see Skinner
Berelson, Bernard, on behavioral sciences, 59

between, see mediation
biochemical manipulation of the brain, 59
bounds (boundaries), human, 95ff.; of knowledge, 143; logical circle, 142; of new horizons, ix; and reality, 143; setting of, 155-156
Bohr, Niels, discussion with Einstein, 35n
Bridgman, P. W., on statistical mechanics, 79n
Brillouin, Leon, on information, 79n; negative entropy, 78n, 79n
Buber, Martin, knowledge of God, 11; on Nietzsche and Sartre, 113n; open field, 3; and science, 163
Bukharin, N., Communist method of production, 58

Camus, Albert, and absurdity, 126n
Cassirer, Ernst, on concept of field, 45n; on Kant's concept of freedom, 3; on mathematical science, 34n; on mediation, 45n
Categorical imperative, see Kant
causality, dynamics of, 71; instant speed, 73; perceivable, 73; pure, 71, 73; and sensations, 159-160; simulated, 78-80
certainty, and security, 5; in science, philosophy, technology, 180-181
Cézanne, on his self-portrait, 82
Chiara, C. F., on Wittgenstein's criteria, 153n
class antagonisms, see Marx
classless society, see Marx; Skinner
collage, see McLuhan

Communication, electronic, 69; and forces of production, 50; machine, 68; media of, see McLuhan; new medium of, 73

Communism, and dialectic materialism, see Marx

content, and electric information, 78; mathematical, 78; of message, 75; and pure cause, 79

continuum, space and time, 38; space-time, 36; world, 35n

coordinates, physical measurements, 37; scaffold of, 42; space-time, 37; space-like and time-like elements, 37

Copernican revolution, 22

crisis, in ancient Greek life, 166; of faith, 10, 115; and freedom, 46; Jung on, 86n; in orientation, ix; of science, 10, 46, 115, 164; in self-knowledge, 3

Darwin, Charles, evolution, 187

death of God idea, "all gods must die," 110, 134n; and man, 136, 165; and Kingdom of God, 135; Marcion, 137n; radical theology, 130; slogan of, 136; and supreme man, 95; see Nietzsche; Sartre; radical theology

Deity, Newton on, 20

Descartes, René, and Age of Enlightenment, 140; certainty, 5; doubt, 120, 140, 155; freedom, 10; man's existence, 114; meaning of reason, 2; method, 140n

determinism, and electric machine, 71-76; and freedom, 63, 74; and science, 64; see Skinner

dialectics, of incarnation and resurrection, 136-138; science of motion, 49

dialectic materialism, see Marx

Dingle, H., on certainty, 35n

distance, see Newton; Einstein

division of labor, see Marx

doubt, Descartes on, 120, 140, 155; and language, 153; and man, 120; and science, 3-4

drugs, discredit sensory world, 92; —Movement, 94; LSD, 87n; mescaline, 81, 82; peyote, 81n, 82n; self-realization, 89; self-transcendence, 81-82; spiritual state, 89; see psychedelic; Huxley; Masters; Houston

Einstein, Albert, and bounds, 45; continuum, 35n; cosmological problem, 46n; distance, 39; "Einstein Interval," 40-41; electromagnetic field, 43-44; elementary experience, 34; field theory, 191; force, problem of, 32; gravitation-energy, 43; gravitational ether, 43;—field, 19n, 39, 42n, 43, 44; illusion and reality, 33ff.; limited world, 45f.; mathematical, physics, 32, 33;—thinking, 33; matter, 43, 45; mediator, 39; metamathematics, 5, 32ff.; motion, single principle of, 42n; Niels Bohr, discussion with, 35n; not-distance, 42; Parmenides' equivalence, 42; pure thought, 33; real and imaginary, 41; reality, 32, 34; relativity, general theory of, 39; method of, 35; problem of being, 35; princple of theory of, 17; Riemannian geometry, 40; scaffold of coordination, 42; scientific principle, 33; self-contained system, 42f.; sense-perception, 34; space-like, universe, 37, 38;—factor, 41; space-time, 38, 40, 45; spherical or elliptical world, 45; time-like factor, 41; unified field (unitary field), 4, 32, 44, 46

Engels, Friedrich, and Karl Marx, *Deutsche Ideologie,* 50n

entropy, and information theory, 79-80

ethics, ought, 30; science of, 22, 24f.; see morality

Faust, Faustian tragedy, 80; and negation, 80

Feyerabend, Paul, on Wittgenstein's early and later works, 142

Fischer, Kuno, work on Kant, 24
Fodor, J. A., on Wittgenstein's criteria, 153n
Franz, Marie-Louise von, on self-realization, 85
freedom, in Communist society, 53; and determinism, 63, 74; and force, 63; from church and state, 10; individual, 22, 166; and man, 165; and morality, 29; negative, 53, 63; paradox of, 67; problem of, 165; and science, 46, 63; and state, 63; vs. technology, 61-64
Frederick the Great, of Prussia, 101n
Freud, Sigmund, and man's maturity, 2

Galileo, method, 23; scientic revolution, 8
genetics, experimentation, 180
geometry, construct, 36; Euclidean, 36; limits of, 45; of physical events, 38; Riemannian, 36, 45; see Einstein
God, of the Beginning, 137; belief in, 106; and cosmos, 138; in everyday life, 11; existence of, 25; and freedom, 10; Kingdom of, 135, 137; knowledge of, 10; liberation from, 134; and metaphysics, 14; primordial, 135, 137; sacrifice of, 11-12; and salvation, 133; "self-annihilation" of, 136, 139; spatio-temporal existence of, 137; as substitute, 94
God-idea (God concept), abstraction, 183; confrontation with, 94; and cosmos, 138; and nothingness, 12; philosophical, 135; radical theology, 130
God-is-dead, see death of God
Goethe, *Faust*, 80
Gospel of John, on salvation, 169
gravitation, cause of, 19, 39; mediator, 20; metaphysical existence of, 17f.; since Newton, 32
gravitational energy,—ether,—field, see Einstein
Gutenberg galaxy, see McLuhan

Hamilton, William, see radical theology
Hartmann, Nicolai, on art, 102-103; on typology, 98n
Hegel, antithesis, 80; dialectic, 135
Hesiod, and chaos, 80
Hessen, B., and machine-wreckers, 57n
Hilbert, David, metamathematics, 33n
hole in being, and antimatter, 124n; and reality, 123-124, 145; see Sartre
Houston, Jean, see psychedelic self-realization
Hoyle, Fred, on essence of matter, 15
Hume, David, causality, 35, 73
Husserl, Edmund, and science, 163
humanum, man as such, 13, 49; and metaphysics, 13; objective conditions of, 57; plant of, 112; principium, 50, 51n, 56
Huxley, Aldous, and Eastern mysticism, 83; self-transcendence through drugs, 81-83

individualism, and drugs, 82; and Enlightenment, 3; escape, 81; free association, 60; freedom, 135, 166; individuation process, 85, 92; logic of, 23, 26, 134; and not-self, 82; paradox of, 31; passion for, 85
inertia, and being, 18; and motion, 17; see Newton
infinite, man striving for, ix; and technology, 181-182
Innes, Harold, style of writing, 71
Is-ness, and pure being, 81
instant information, instant speed, see McLuhan

Jammer, Max, on Newton's metaphysics, 16n
Jaspers, Karl, on Augustine's faith and reason, 172n; on Nietzsche's ambiguity; on *The Will to Power*, 186
Jesus, eschatology, 138; ethics of

195

free, 129; creator of his world, 9f; and death of God, 136, 165; dialectic of, 80; dyad of self and value, 128; and electric media, 70; end in himself, 179; enslavement of 57, 58; experiencing information, 79; fall of, 136-137; as *fatum,* 112; freedom of, 165; individual, 49; integrated, 84; liberation from God, 134-135; and machine, 47, 53, 54, 56, 68; metaphysics, 14; and mode of production, 50; and nature, 179; and his nothingness, 128; problematic of, 13, 52; as producer, 47; reduction to elements, 83; "of *res-sentiment,*" 101; self-realizazation, 81-82, 83, 84; *sui generis,* 51; and technology, 58, 83; to be a god, 95; a transplant of wants, 67; typological, 70; "What is Man?" 49, 114, 165; and world, 84; and world-view, 166

Marcion, and death of God, 137n

Margenau, Henry, on causality, 17n; on "operators," 62, 151n

Marx, Karl, class, anatgonisms, 54, conflicts, 55; interests; classless society, 58; communication, 50; Communism, 55; dialectic materialism, 55; dialectics, 9, 49, 54; division of labor, 50, 51-53; factory system, 54; forces of production, 52; freedom, 51, 53; guild craftsmen, 54; individual, 48; machine, 47, 53, 54, 56;—breaking, 57; man, 47, 49; material antithesis, 80; materialism, dynamic, 48; mechanical, 48; merchant capitalists, 54; nature, 179; political, struggle, 56; — power, 56; presuppositions, 49; production, means of, 52; mode of, 48, 49, 50, 58; relations of, 48, 52; proletariat, 54, 55; society, bourgeois, 55; capitalist, 53; classless, 54, 56; social, power, 52;—relations, 49, 52-53, 54, 55, 58;—revolution, 55;—scientist, 49; will, 52n

Masters, R.E.L., see psychedelic self-realization

McLuhan, Marshall, allatonceness, 76; amputation, 70;—of senses, 69, 72; aphorism, 70; automation, 74, 77; cause, pure, 73, 79; simulated, 78-80; causal dynamics, 71;—connection, 73; collage, 71n; content, 78; determinism, 72, 74; disorder, 79; electric, communication, 69; see media; entropy, 79-80; environment, 74, 75; folk singing, 74; freedom, 74; Gutenberg, galaxy, 69;—technology, 72; Hume's scepticism, 73; information, experience of, 79; instant, 74; pure, 78-80; machine, 68, 78; automated, 74; electric, 71-76, 78; mechanical, 72, 73; man, 72, 73; autonomy of 72, 75; media, electric, 70, 73, 75, 76, 78, 80; message of, 70; message, 75; Narcissus, 75; negation, 79-80; negentropy, 79; nervous system, 70, 74; operation, 77; oral society, 71; order, 79-80; philosophical speculation, 71; reciprocal reduction, 75; relations, 73; scientific experimentation, 71; self, 70;—extension, 73; senses, 73; sense-extension, 69; sense-ratios, 69; simultaneous happening, 76; society, 69; somnambulism, 72; space, 76, 77; vanishing —, 76-78; style of writing, 71; synesthesia, 74; tactile sense, 72; technological reversal, 72; technology, 70; television, 74, 75; time, 76; touch, sense of, 8; typographical man, 70; village, 74, 75, global, 76; unity, organic, 77, 78, organized, 77

mediation, action at a distance, 39; causal, 73; communication, 68ff; electric, 70, 76, 78; environmental 74, 75; gravitational field, 39, 44 gravity, 20; in logical mode, 141; machine, 68; the middle, 17; and motion, 32; and

Psychedelic self-realization, drugs, 83, 86, 92, 93; drug-state, 84, 87, 92; eidetic images, 90; God, encounter with, 91, 93-94; to become —, 93; the guide, 89f., 91, 93, 94; inhibitions, 87; integral level, 89, 91; Jung's psychology, 84-85; LSD, 57n; Lucifer, 93; man, 84; other, no actual, 91-92; Plato's "divided line," 89; psyche, in the, 85, four levels of, 88; psychedelic, meaning of, 86, 89; psychic state, 84; psychology, 86; reaction to things, 92; reality, fundamental, 91, vision of, 88; recollective-analytic level, 88, 91; religious experience, 91, 92, 93; Self, encounter with, 91-92, integration of, 92f., subliminal, 85, unconscious, 86; sensory level, 88, 91; the session, 89f.; the setting, 90-91; spiritual state, 89; the subject, 90f.; symbol, 86, 87, 92; symbolic level, 88, 91; technological devices, 83, 86; transformation, 92, 93; unconscious, 84, 85;—Self, 86

pure thought, and reality, 33

purpose, in philosophy and technology, 179

Question, philosophical, 22; what to ask, 21

Radical theology, American theology, 133; Bodhisattva, 139; Buddhism, 138; Christian faith, 134n, 135; contemporaneity, 139; cosmos, 138; eschatology, 135; ethics, Christological, 132; freedom, 130, 134f.; God, death of, 131, 132, primordial, 135; God-idea, 130, 135; incarnation, 134, 135, 136-138; individualism, 134; immanence, 138; Jesus, 132; 138; Kingdom of God, 135, 137, 138, 139; man, essence of, 130, fall of, 136-137; new faith, 133; new theology, 134; Nirvana, 138, 139; nothingness 138, 139;

primordial Being, 136; reality of the profane, 137; religious a priori, 131; resurrection, 133, 134, 136-139; sacred and profane, 136, 138; sacrifice, divine, 133; salvation, dual, 131, 133; science, 133; space and time, 136, 137, 138; technology, 133; time, 138; two worlds, 130; world, this, 132

Rapoport, Anatol, on information experience, 79-80

reality, bounds of, 143; of distance, 39f.; godless, 138; measurable, 34; and mediation, 35; order-in-itself, 34; physical theory of, 34; and physics, 42; as possibility, 121; question of, 34

reason, and Age of Enlightenment, 1; paralogism of, 66; practical, 26; theoretical, 24

relativity, theory of, see Einstein

responsibility, ethical, 129; in God, 102; individualistic, 129; release from, 82; and technology, 68

Riemann, Bernhard, concept of measurement, 42; on distance, 40; on geometry, 40; n-dimensional space, 36; space-point and time-point, 41

Romans (7:17), on sin, 66n

Rousseau, Jean-Jacques, on general will, 31; and Kant, 30; man's individuality, 81; social contract, 31

Russel, Bertrand, on subject of mathematics, 78

Salvation, dual, 131ff.; in Gospel of St. John, 169-170; new Gospel of, 65; through ethics, 133; through the "single one," 169-170

Sartre, Jean-Paul, Adam Kadmon, 120; atheism, metaphysical, 116; bad faith, 121-122; becoming, 117, 118, 121; being, in-itself, 118, 119-121, its failure, 123, hole in —, 123; bounds, 125; Christ, 126; consciousness, 125;

creation *ex nihilo,* 115, 116, 118; crisis, of faith, of science, 115; death of God, 11, 113f.; destructive philosophy, 115, 121; doubt, 120; emptiness, 121; ethics, 130; for-itself, origin of, 123; freedom, 10, 127, absolute, 113-116, Cartesian idea of, 113, 114, 129; Gnostic overtones, 114n; God, existence of, 113, is killed, 113, and man's existence, 116; passion to be —, 126, and freedom, 130; God-idea, 114, 116; hyphen, use of, 119; immanence, 125-126, absolute, 125; incarnation, 126; lack, 125, 126-127; man, an absolute event, 118, is alone, 128f., the being who questions, 121, cannot be God, 116, is condemned to be free, 129, 130, as dyad, 128, existence of, 114, fall of, 123, for-itself, 118, 120, and value, 127; Marcion, 114n; metaphysical, ground, 128f.;—atheism, 116, 129; middle term, 125; morality, 126-128; negation, 118; negating —, 120; negative theology, 116; nihilation, 125;—nihilating, 117; nothingness, 116, 119-122; as hole in being, 123, 125, 126, 127; otherness, 118; ontology, 116-117, phenomenological, 117n; possibility, 120, 122, 129, 130; preposition, use of, 119; questiontion, 81-82, 83, 84; *sui generis,* 119-120, 126f., upsurge of, 123-124, 127, incomplete, 129; self-consciousness, 117; separation, act of, 119-121, and annihilation, and unity, 119; space, 118, pure, 117; transcendence, 125-126; absolute—in absolute immanence, 125; Trinity, 126, 127, Christian —, 126; value, 127-128

scepticism, and self-knowledge, 4, 5

Schoeck, Helmut, on Nietzsche's ideology, 98n

science, in ancient Greece, 167; behavioral, 63; and determinism, 62; and doubt, 3-4; of ethics, 24f.; and faith, 133; logical method of, 22; mediation, 16ff.; and metaphysics, 13ff.; natural— and man's self-knowledge, 14; and reason, 24; space and time, 9; and technology, 5f.; and truth, 179-180; unified —, 16, 83, 109

self, encounter with, 91-92; as mediator, 86; not-self, 82; true nature of, 84; unconscious, 84

self-transcendence, 81-82

senses, alienated, 72; amputation of, 69, 72; and electric medium, 73; extension of, 69; sight, 69; touch, 8, 72, 74; vision, 7f.

Skinner, B.F., behavioral engineering, 62, 63, 64, 68,—science, 62n; classless society, 60; determinism, 63, 64, natural, operational, scientific, 62; division of labor, 61; freedom, 61, 63, no —, 62; hate, 65-66; Jesus, 64-65; love your enemy, 64-66; law, view of, 65; machine, 68; man, 67,—scientist, 65; Manager, 62; Marxian principles, 60; paralogism of word "enemy," 66, of freedom, 67; planned society, 61; Planners, 67, scientist —, 62; positive reinforcement, 65, 66, 67; positive science, 61; power, 66; private property, 61; responsibility, 68; salvation, 64; scientific reductionism, 67n; Skinner, man of good will, 59; social engine, 62, 67; social laboratory, 60-61; state, no control, 61, 65; technology, 68, of behavior, 59, — vs. freedom, 61-64; utopia, 60, 61, 64

soul, immortality of, 26

space, and control of world, 9; language —, see Wittgenstein; logical —, 142; and man's limitations, 9; and matter, 43; Minkowski's, 36; pure, 117; reality of, 40; Riemannian, 36, 40; super —, 41; vanishing of, 76-78

space-like, 37, 41; see Einstein
space-time, 41; continuum, 36, 40, 45; discrete manifold, 40; distance unit, 41; Minkowski's view of, 37; mathematical, 38; reality of, 37; and physical events, 38; see Einstein
Safra, Piero, influence on Wittgenstein, 148
Sullivan, Walter, on revolution against the physicists, 15
symbol, and dreams, 84; meaning of, 84; and sign, 84n; and unconscious, 84

Taube, Mortimer, on electronic and mechanical machines, 78n
technology, of behavior, 59ff.; control of, 8; and enslavement, 58; and escape, 82; faith in, 133; and Gutenberg type, 72; and language-games, see Wittgenstein; and limits, 9; of love your enemy, 64; and machine, 8; and Marx, 58; meaning of, 8; and media of extension, 70; its promise, 47ff.; psychedelic, 83; and responsibility, 68; to revolutionize the world, 15; and science, 5f.; teleological character of, 180; and truth, 180; versus freedom, 61-64
teleology, and philosophy, 180; and technology, 180
television, see McLuhan
Tertullian, on Praxeas, 115
Tillich, Paul, on God is dead, 136; on *Übermensch*, 96n
time, and control of world, 9; and man's limitations, 9; measurement of, 37; naive sense of, 37; relation to space, 37; and space-time, 41
time-like, 41
time-point, 41
trousers, see Huxley
trust, in philosophy, in technology, 180-181
truth, in science, philosophy, technology, 179-180

typographical man, see McLuhan

Unconscious, and conscious, 85; and dreams, 86; as guiding spirit, 84; subliminal, 85; and symbols, 84, 86; transcendental power of, 85; see psychedelic self-realization
unified science, see science
universality, in science, philosophy, technology, 180
unlimited, method of finding, 36
utopia, scientific shaped, 60

Vermeer, about his still-life paintings, 82
Volkmann-Schluck, Karl-Heinz, on *The Will to Power,* 186
Voltaire, man is a metaphysical animal, 5
Vorländer, Karl, on Kant' ethics, 22; on second formulation of the categorical imperative, 29n

Wahl, Jean, on Sartre's neontology, 116
Walden Two, see Skinner
Weyl, Hermann, on Einstein, 39n, 44
Whitrow, G. J., on time, 41n; on Riemannian geometry, 42n
will, general, 31; good and bad, 30; as *is* and *ought,* 29f.; lower and higher, 30; paralogism of free —, 31; universal lawmaker, 31; see Nietzsche
Windelband, Wilhelm, on Augustine's view of reason and faith, 171n; on Enlightenment, 2
Wittgenstein, Ludwig, and Age of Enlightenment, 140, 163; the beetle in the box, 159n; bounds, 142, 143, 152, 153, 154, 155-156, 157, 158; causality, 159-160; criteria, 147, 152-154, 157, 159; description, 141, 147, 149, 150, 161; doubt, 153, 155; early and later works, 142n; elementary propositions, 145, 148; empiricism, 151; explanation, 141,

147, 149, 159; "expression of thought," 146; facts, 145, 147; family resemblances, 151n; fly-bottle, 162; illusion, 177; invention, 149; language, forms, 141, limits of, 142n, 144, signs, 157, learning of, 153; language-games, 149, bounds of, 154, description of, 155, families of, 150, 152, 157; limits of, 152, in modern institutions, 157n, and sensation, 159f., technology of 155, no theorizing, 151, and thinking, 157, and tools, 152, and understanding, 156-157, and usage, 151; language-space, 144, 146, 147, 148, 149, 150, 152, limits and bounds of, 155, 156, theory of, 164; limits, 152, 153, 154-155, 157; logic, pure, 143; meaning, 156-157; mediator, 141, 142; metaphysics, 143, 155, 156, 163; metaphysical speculation, 163; mind, 157; nominalist, 151n; normal situation, 153; object-relations, 144-145, 148; pain, 158, 159n, 160; philosopher, role of, 142, 143, 147, 148, 155, 162n, 163, his illusions, 161-163; philosopher-scientist, 162, 163; *Philosophical Investigations,* 147-162; philosophy, problem of, 140, 141, 143, 161, end of, 146, 147, 162; pragmatism, 151; role, 150; rule, 150; scaffold, 145, 148, 149; science, 163, 164, natural —, 146; scientific, method, 162; observation, 141; sensations, 157-161, and causal relations, 159-160, criteria of, 159, experience of, 160, private —, 159, words of, 158, 160; simple elements, 144; space, logical, 142, 144, 146, 147, 148, 149; teaching, 153; technique, 150, 151, 152; technological method, 149; technologist, 177-178; technology, 151n, 152, 153, 155, 156, 162, 164; theorizing, 151; therapeutic method, 140, 155; thinking, 157; toothache, 158, 160; *Tractatus,* 143-146; understanding, 156-157; world, actual, 146, open, 142; world-relations, 148-149

Wittgenstein's legacy, 163-164

world, annihilation of, 138; closed system, 45; elliptical, 45; intelligible, 25, 29, 30; and man, 84; and metaphysics, 14; non-spatial, 81; noumenal, 28; phenomenal, 28; psychedelic, 86-89; sensible, 30; and sense-perception, 34; spherical, 45; this —, 132; two worlds, 25, 30, 130, 181; without bounds, 45f.; without God, 138